Dublin Nazi No. 1

First published in 2007 by
Liberties Press
Guinness Enterprise Centre | Taylor's Lane | Dublin 8 | Ireland
LibertiesPress.com | info@libertiespress.com
Editorial: +353 (1) 402 0805 | sean@libertiespress.com
Sales and marketing: +353 (1) 415 1224 | peter@libertiespress.com

Trade enquiries to CMD Distribution
55A Spruce Avenue | Stillorgan Industrial Park | Blackrock | County Dublin
Tel: +353 (1) 294 2560
Fax: +353 (1) 294 2564

Copyright © Gerry Mullins, 2007

ISBN (hardback): 978–1–905483–19–8
ISBN (paperback): 978–1–905483–20–4

2 4 6 8 10 9 7 5 3 1

A CIP record for this title is available from the British Library

Cover design by Dermot Hall
Index by Sharon Corcoran
Set in Garamond

Printed by CPD | Ebbw Vale | Wales

This book is sold subject to the condition that it shall not, by way of trade or otherwise, be lent, resold, hired out or otherwise circulated, without the publisher's prior consent, in any form other than that in which it is published and without a similar condition including this condition being imposed on the subsequent publisher.

No part of this publication may be reproduced or transmitted in any form or by any means, electronic or mechanical, including photocopying, recording or storage in any information or retrieval system, without the prior permission of the publisher in writing.

DUBLIN NAZI NO. 1

THE LIFE OF ADOLF MAHR

GERRY MULLINS

To the spirit of Albert Bender

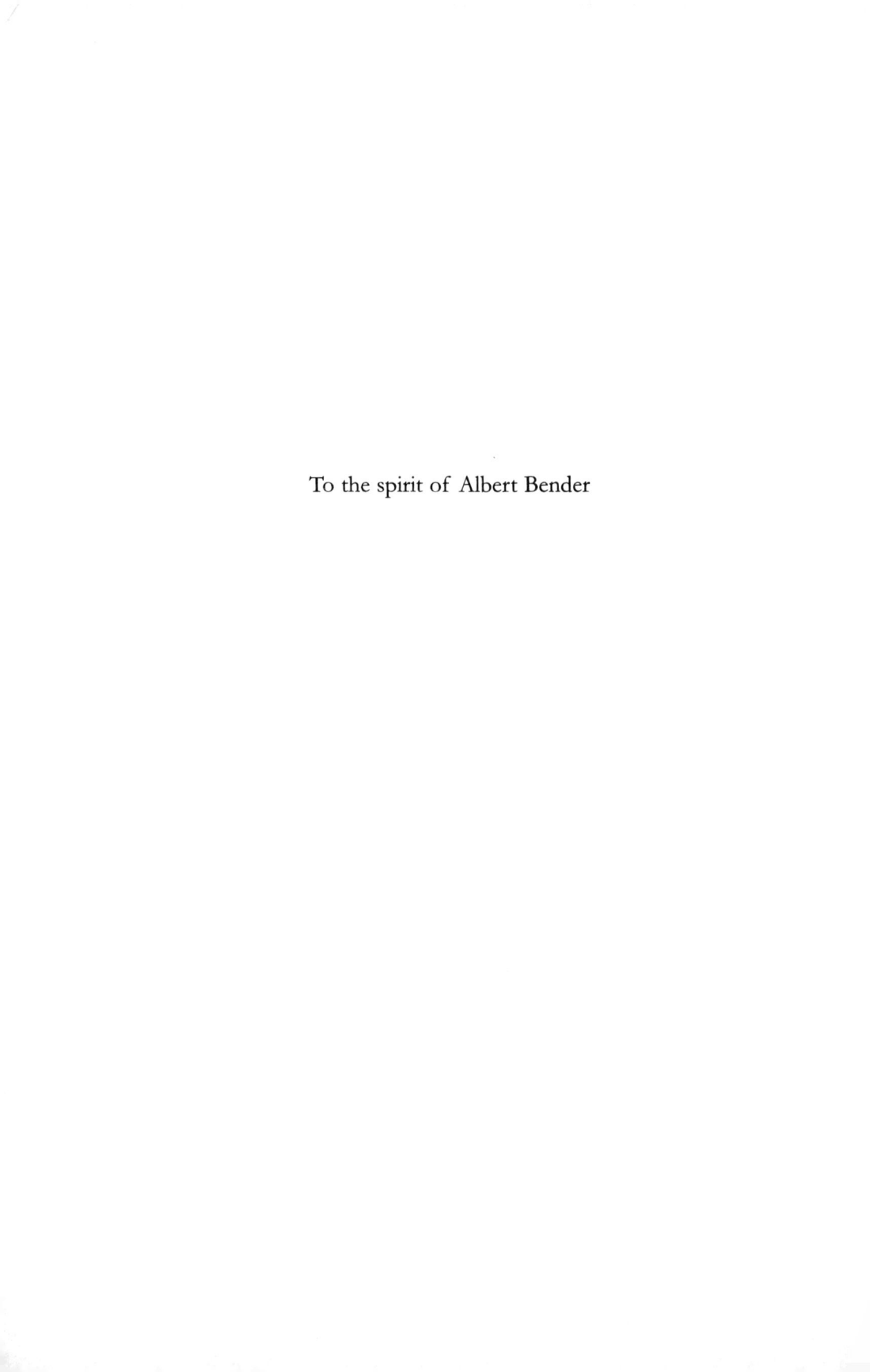

Contents

	Acknowledgements	7
	Mahr Family Tree	8
	Map of Germany	9
	Foreword by Cathal O'Shannon	11
	Prologue	13
1	Family Life: The Mahrs in Dublin	17
2	Official Life: At the National Museum, 1927–34	30
3	Nazi Life, 1933–37	47
4	Impending War, 1937–39	68
5	New Life in Germany, 1939–43	105
6	The Tide of War Turns, 1943–45	133
7	Hilde's Journey, 1945	152
8	The Dust Settles, 1946–47	171
	Epilogue: Picking up the Pieces, 1947 onwards	209
	Bibliography	225
	Notes	229
	Index	245

Acknowledgements

This project began life as a study of Albert Bender while I was working at the *Irish Herald* in San Francisco, and it evolved to become this book seven years later. Along the way, it took the form of a journalism project at DCU, where the advice of my supervisor Dr Colum Kenny was most insightful. The ever-obliging Seamus Hosey helped me convert it into two radio documentaries at RTÉ, produced by Lorelei Harris. An invitation from Skerries Historical Society to present a slide show on the Mahrs focused my mind upon writing a book on the subject.

Once the book idea was under way, Michael Collins helped organise the necessary foreign trips; Regina Standún, Deirdre Cronnelly and Laura Wipfler were generous with their translating talents; Jonathan Williams showed dedication that went far beyond his role as literary agent; and Maurice Mullins's proofreading of an early draft of the text was most helpful.

The project would not have been possible but for the infectious enthusiasm of Dr Pat Wallace; the shared files and knowledge of Dr David O'Donoghue; the trust and generosity of the Mahr family; and the love and support of Jennifer Spurling, who showed confidence in the book by marrying me during its gestation.

To the above, and the dozens of people who took my calls and answered my e-mails, I owe a debt of gratitude.

Gerry Mullins
Dublin, February 2007

Mahr Family Tree

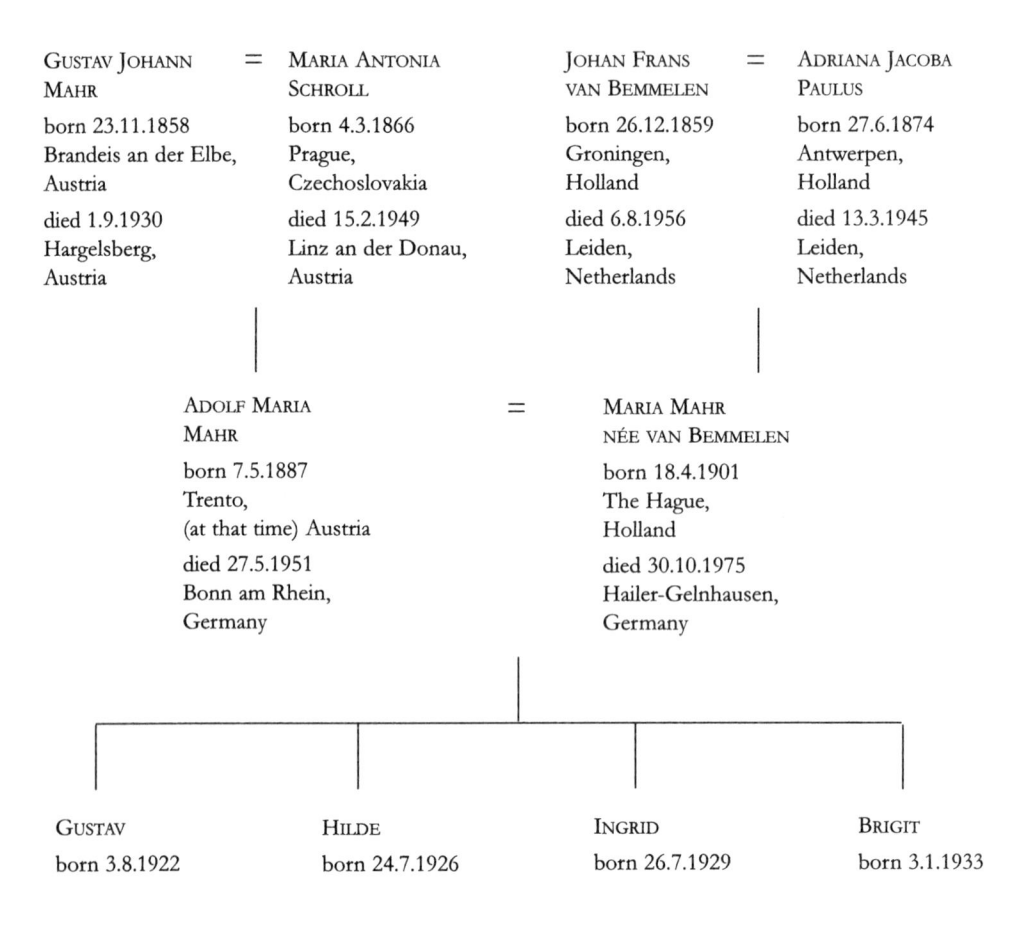

Gustav Johann Mahr	=	Maria Antonia Schroll		Johan Frans van Bemmelen	=	Adriana Jacoba Paulus
born 23.11.1858 Brandeis an der Elbe, Austria		born 4.3.1866 Prague, Czechoslovakia		born 26.12.1859 Groningen, Holland		born 27.6.1874 Antwerpen, Holland
died 1.9.1930 Hargelsberg, Austria		died 15.2.1949 Linz an der Donau, Austria		died 6.8.1956 Leiden, Netherlands		died 13.3.1945 Leiden, Netherlands

Adolf Maria Mahr = Maria Mahr née van Bemmelen

Adolf Maria Mahr — born 7.5.1887, Trento, (at that time) Austria; died 27.5.1951, Bonn am Rhein, Germany

Maria Mahr née van Bemmelen — born 18.4.1901, The Hague, Holland; died 30.10.1975, Hailer-Gelnhausen, Germany

Gustav	Hilde	Ingrid	Brigit
born 3.8.1922	born 24.7.1926	born 26.7.1929	born 3.1.1933

Map of Germany

Foreword

This is a book I have been waiting half my lifetime for. Although there have been many references in recent works to Adolf Mahr and other Germans who were in Ireland *before* the Second World War and who worked in German radio and the German foreign service during the war, there has been little that has really spelt out the lives and machinations of the Nazis in Ireland in the period of the mid-1930s to 1950. Here at last is such a book.

I know of the potency of the very words 'Nazi' and 'Ireland' because I was recently involved in some television documentaries on the Nazis who came to Ireland *after* the war. Perhaps a gap in those programmes was that we did not pay enough attention to the Nazis in Ireland in the pre-war period. And while I welcome Gerry Mullins's book, I would like to have read more of others than Adolf Mahr: people like Fritz Brase, and the rag tag and bobtail of some of those who were brought here by the Irish government to build the mighty Shannon Scheme.

Adolf Mahr was undoubtedly the leading Nazi in Ireland from the time he came here in the early 1930s to the National Museum. He was also undoubtedly a fervent anti-Semite. Either of these titles is enough to condemn him in the minds of people like myself, who lived in an Ireland that was not just anti-British and therefore anti-Allied but also significantly sympathetic to Germany. Irish governments, pre- and post-de Valera, sought out Germans to come to Ireland and the new Free State, rather than the former colonial ruling classes.

But Gerry Mullins does not just skim over the political and cultural life and times of Mahr: he analyses, often with great sympathy, Mahr's career, his motives, his sometimes tortured musings. This is a significant work of research, of intimate probings into the life of a rather complex man. Here was a virulent anti-Semite who did favours for individual Jews and was the friend and beneficiary of a wealthy Irish Jew living in America who significantly added to the collections of the National Museum, where Mahr was the first Keeper of Irish Antiquities and then Director.

The book adds little gems to our lore of Irish-Nazi history – the fact that Mahr was in touch with the ghastly Julius Streicher; that Field Marshal Keitel had a daughter at Trinity who helped lead the Irish branch of the Hitler Youth; that Bertie Smyllie, editor of the *Irish Times* when I was on the staff, attended the German Christmas parties organised by Mahr, when walls were draped not just with the Tricolour but with the Swastika as well.

I am not convinced, as the author is, that Mahr was not guilty of actions harmful to Ireland during his years here and during the war, when he was with the Irish radio section in Berlin and elsewhere, but the case is well argued.

As in all good books, heroes – or heroines – emerge. In this case it is one of Mahr's daughters, the feisty Hilde, who comes through a defeated Germany, a land in ruins, to safety.

An important contribution to the history of the period, too, is what happened to Adolf Mahr after the war. He was, as Mullins points out, a distinguished and able administrator when he was in the National Museum, and he was an archaeologist of great distinction. This did not guarantee his return to Ireland once the war was over. He had left Ireland in August 1939 to attend a seminar in Germany but got stuck there when the war began. His attempts to get his job back after 1945 ended in failure, in spite of a well-mounted campaign by friends and personal begging letters to Éamon de Valera, letters which went ignored, perhaps on the advice of Dan Bryan, the head of Irish Military Intelligence.

Was he hard done by? I don't think so, though the small pension he was granted would have done little to help him survive in a starving and defeated Germany. One of the great additions to this book is the fascinating collection of photographs that the author has gathered together. It is startling today to see groups of young Irish and German boys and girls lined up in places like Malahide and Balbriggan, stiffly at attention, with the Swastika above them, their arms outstretched in the Nazi salute, with Adolf Mahr at their head.

Cathal O'Shannon
January 2007

Prologue

History has known few more terrifying places than Berlin in April 1945. During that time the city was under such heavy attack from British bombers at night and American bombers by day that hospital officials were no longer able to keep count of the dead. There had been eighty-three air raids since the beginning of February,[1] and they ceased only when the Red Army made its assault on the city. Instead of air raids, the Russians fired shells from field guns, 1.8 million during the last two weeks of April alone.[2]

Hardly a building remained intact, so the once proud population of Berlin now lived in ruins, without electricity, sanitation or running water. Most had grown thin after months of severe food rations, and some were sick because they had drunk unclean water. There were not enough shelters to cater for the city's population of three million,[3] and those that were available were severely overcrowded. Condensation dripped from the concrete walls, and when generators failed, those inside were plunged into darkness. Toilets were sometimes sealed off because so many people had gone inside, locked the door and killed themselves.

The air in the bunkers quickly became fouled. Berliners learned to use candles to measure the diminishing levels of oxygen. When a candle placed on the floor went out, children were picked up and held at shoulder height. When one placed at chin level began to splutter, the whole bunker was evacuated regardless of the severity of the air-attack outside.[4]

By mid-April the Red Army was so close to the city that Hitler's companion Eva Braun wrote that she could 'already hear the gunfire from the front'.[5] Locals learned from returning soldiers and railway workers about the terrible retribution Russian forces were exacting upon German civilians. Fleeing refugee columns were machine-gunned, or run over by tanks. Men were taken for forced labour in Soviet gulags, from which few ever returned. Women of all ages were raped by Russian soldiers, often by groups. Already that year, close to two million German women had been raped by Red Army troops.[6] Most of the city's remaining population were women; any man fit enough to fire a gun had already been sent to the front.

Perhaps the cruellest twist was the German government's decree that any civilian leaving the city would be considered 'defeatist',[7] a crime that was punishable by death. Along the exit routes from Berlin, the Nazis displayed the corpses of those caught simply trying to leave their own city.[8]

The civilian population of Berlin could only wait for the arrival of the Soviet troops. Any attempt to escape was punishable by their own soldiers, and the inevitable surrender was punishable by the Soviets. It was simply a matter of waiting; waiting in the bunkers, waiting in the ruins, waiting in pain in the hopelessly inadequate hospitals, waiting in hunger and thirst, waiting in fear of what lay ahead. Waiting, and of course hoping that the Americans would reach Berlin before the Russians. Any prospect of a German victory had long passed.

Into this appalling scene, stepping over dead people and horses, and the rubble of Berlin's once-magnificent buildings, came Hilde Mahr, an eighteen-year-old from Dublin. Dismissed from a labour camp north-east of the city the day before, she had arrived in the German capital at 2.30 a.m. on 17 April, in the aftermath of yet another air raid. Standing in the blazing chaos of this strange place, she pondered her next move. She knew Ireland better than she knew Germany, the English language better than the German one; and recognised Berlin hardly at all.

Hilde was alone in Germany, as far as she was aware. Her father, the one-time head of the National Museum of Ireland, the former head of the Nazi Party in Ireland, and the former head of the German propaganda radio service to Ireland, may still have been in Germany, but she had no way of knowing if he was still alive. Her brother, who had been drafted into the German army, was now a prisoner of war. Her mother and younger sisters were, she hoped, in Austria. She didn't know if they were dead or alive, or alive but behind Russian lines. Whatever their situation, they represented her best hope of survival and she had no choice but to get out of Berlin and look for them. But how?

She had a logical – although naive – plan to leave Berlin by underground train. As she descended the stairs of a U-Bahn station, several people tried to pull her back, warning her about what she would see there.

She continued down regardless, but encountered a horrific scene. Tens of thousands of people took shelter from the bombs every day and night in the underground stations. There in the dark tunnels deep beneath street level, they thought themselves safe. But on this particular night the explosions were so destructive that an underground structure gave way, and allowed a canal or river to pour into the tunnels. Hundreds, or maybe thousands – nobody will ever know – drowned in the darkness below. Hilde quickly realised why people had tried to prevent her from going inside the station, for as she descended the stairs she could see stretched out before her a 'sea of bodies'.[9]

Returning to street level, she decided to simply walk south out of Berlin, but she stood little hope of getting by the *Feldgendarmerie* who patrolled the major exit routes, ready to execute defeatists. She set out instead for the Anhalter Bahnhof station, about 5 kilometres away. She reached there and found a battalion of soldiers boarding a train that was heading south. This was her only hope. Civilians were no longer permitted to travel by train, but because Hilde was wearing the uniform of the State Labour Service and held a permit that granted her leave from her unit, she stood a good chance of being allowed on board. She approached the battalion's sergeant, knowing that if he said 'yes', she could at least escape Berlin and take her chances from there on. If he said 'no' . . . the consequences were unthinkable. There was so much hanging on such a small word: 'yes' or 'no'.

*

A year later, in April 1946, a dishevelled man emerged from a British prison camp in northern Germany. It was Adolf Mahr, Hilde's father, one of the world's leading archaeologists, and the former 'Dublin Nazi No. 1'. He ached from starvation, maltreatment and sickness, and his clothes hung loosely on his emaciated body. It seems that he had been released because he was close to death, and the British preferred that the inevitable would happen outside their walls. Nobody had been notified to collect him from the camp so, despite being barely able to walk, he set off for the nearest village alone.

*

How had their lives come to this? How had a girl who had enjoyed an idyllic childhood in Ireland found herself alone at the climax of history's most murderous war? And how had the man who had enjoyed such high esteem in international academic circles contributed to his family's downfall? Had he betrayed his children by taking them to Germany on the eve of war, or had his love and guidance given them at least a chance of surviving the catastrophe?

How could such a thing happen? How could they survive? Could life ever be good again? These questions needed answers, but first Hilde Mahr had to speak with the sergeant.

1

FAMILY LIFE: THE MAHRS IN DUBLIN

Hilde Mahr was born in Klagenfurt, Austria, on 24 July 1926 and arrived in Ireland a year later with her parents. She was the daughter of Dr Adolf Mahr, a thirty-nine-year-old Austrian archaeologist at the Natural History and Prehistoric Museum in Vienna, and his Dutch wife Maria van Bemmelen, fourteen years his junior. Hilde's brother Gustav, four years older than Hilde, completed the group that landed from a German steamship in Cobh Harbour, County Cork, on 15 September 1927.

It was an exciting time for the Mahrs. Adolf had been appointed Keeper of Irish Antiquities at the National Museum of Ireland. Although he had a poor command of the English language and little experience of Irish archaeology, there was every reason to expect that he would do well in his new position. He had already learned Dutch, Italian, Serbo-Croat, Spanish, French and Latin, as well as his native German,[1] so English should not, he felt, present much of a problem. Furthermore, he had a strong record in archaeological work in Continental European institutions where he had reorganised provincial and local museums.[2] He had simultaneously held the posts of Curator and Deputy Director of the Anthropological-Ethnological Department at the Natural History and Prehistoric Museum in Vienna.[3] He was energetic and ambitious, and had a wide network of contacts in other institutions across Europe.

The fledgling Irish state had purposely chosen a man of German extraction for the position at the National Museum. Following independence in 1922, the professional class had mostly left Ireland for Britain, where salaries were higher and there was greater political stability. Facing a deficit of suitable management candidates at home, the Irish government was forced to recruit abroad. The recruitment of British managers would have been politically unwise, so instead the Irish government advertised in German newspapers for a Keeper of Irish Antiquities.

Dr Walther Bremer, formerly of Philipps University, Marburg, had filled the position in 1925, but he fell ill and died soon after his arrival in Dublin. The competition was rearranged. At this time Adolf Mahr was working at the prehistoric saltmine and graveyard of Hallstatt, high in the Austrian mountains. The mine, now a United Nations World Heritage Site, dates back to the late Bronze Age (1200 BC), although the major activity is of the early Iron Age (700–500 BC).[4] Salt is still mined there to this day.

Next to the mine is a large Iron Age graveyard where about 3,000 miners were buried, along with their wives and children, and their weapons. Because of the presence of salt in the ground, the corpses, clothing and mining tools were preserved, providing archaeologists with excellent opportunities to study the local Iron Age culture. In the winter of 1926, Mahr went down the mine to excavate it more thoroughly. He used gunpowder to make his way through the mountain, and collected and documented his finds.[5] It must have been a lonely time because the area was sparsely populated during the cold winter months. The roads were blocked by snow, and the traffic went back to the frozen lake, or on sleighs. He would have spent a lot of time in the only inn that was open in Hallstatt, and it was there, Gustav Mahr believes, that his father read in a Viennese newspaper the advertisement placed by the Irish government for a new Keeper of Irish Antiquities.

He wrote to ask the Irish civil service to postpone the submission deadline to allow him time to return to Vienna to collect his papers. Permission was granted and Mahr's application was the last of thirteen. In May 1927, the Civil Service Commission in Dublin wrote to Mahr, inviting him to come for interview in Dublin, and that he was 'the only candidate being summoned for interview in this first instance, and that you must bear your own expenses in coming for the interview'.[6] Mahr wrote to his wife's parents to explain that he did not have the money to attend the interview in Dublin, and they – as they often did – supported him.

Mahr's interview was successful and, against the advice of his friends and family, he accepted the position. He took English lessons from his Dutch father-in-law, and in November 1927 formally switched the focus of his career from Austrian-Celtic archaeology to Irish-Celtic archaeology.

It seemed that each new period in Mahr's life was destined to be complicated by unforeseen factors. Shortly before leaving for Dublin, he wrote to his wife's parents in Holland requesting a loan to fund his family's passage and settling-in costs. The Department of Education in Ireland would not fund Mahr's travel expenses, and this presented an immediate burden for the family. His sizable library needed to be shipped, bringing the cost of transporting his goods to £140, nearly a quarter of his salary for the following year. Now aged forty, Mahr first had to explain himself to his parents-in-law:

> I wanted to explain why we are asking for help again.... I'm sitting on my packed cases and boxes and we have to pay our tickets, and living in a hotel for four weeks because solicitors are not being quick ... £12 fee for the solicitors. Then I have to pay rent for the house half a year in advance, another £50. Also I have to pay taxes, electric installation in the house, floorboards for two rooms, a few chairs so we can sit at the table and eat.... You know I don't like to complain, but it is a very bitter start to my life here, and especially when one with good conscience can say 'it is not my fault'.[7]

Mahr surmised that it would take two years before the family recovered financially from the move, and have enough money to 'have a bit of fun besides work'. He promised his father-in-law that he would start selling any books he no longer required, and hoped to raise £100 in this way. But he needed the same sum again from Professor van Bemmelen, and he offered the rest of his library, valued at £400, as a guarantee.

Eventually the Mahrs moved into 37 Waterloo Place (now Upper Leeson Street), which was then, as now, a fashionable area within walking distance of Dublin's city centre. They defrayed costs by renting out two rooms to a young Dutchman, Henri Broekhoven, who, like Mahr, had been brought in to take a senior position in the fledgling Irish economy. Broekhoven was first commercial manager, and later managing director, of the Siemens-Schuckert company in Ireland,[8] which built the Shannon hydroelectric power plant, opened in 1929.

Despite the initial difficulties, the Mahrs lived in an elegant and spacious home, and enjoyed a relatively comfortable lifestyle. Adolf was a permanent and pensionable member of the civil service, at a time when most Irish people did not have a regular wage. His worked enabled him to travel all over Ireland and abroad, sometimes taking his children with him, at a time when most Irish people did not go on holidays.

Mahr was eager for his offspring to retain their Germanic identity and required them to speak German in the home. This rule became difficult to enforce once they went to school and their command of English surpassed that of their German. Hilde and Gustav liked to speak English in their rooms, but their conversations were often cut short with a loud '*Deutsch sprechen!*' (Speak German!) from their father at the bottom of the stairs.[9]

Maria Mahr played the piano in the house in the evenings, after the children had gone to bed. Sometimes an elderly friend, Mrs Burke, came to the house and the two would sit at the piano together and play Diabelli and Haydn sonatas that had been rearranged for 'four hands'. Maria was a lively and chatty person, in contrast to her husband, who was more serious and quiet. She had been born with a dislocated hip, a condition that made one of her legs slightly shorter than the other. Throughout her life, she adjusted her heels, which made her limp barely noticeable. Despite this impediment, she enjoyed playing tennis.[10]

Adolf Mahr had little interest in music, although he came from several generations of bandsmen. His father, two grandfathers and an uncle had been conductors in the army bands of the Austro-Hungarian Empire. One of his sisters had studied piano. He announced as a youngster that since all his family were musicians, he was going to do something different. He had little understanding of music, and never requested his wife to play particular pieces. One friend observed: 'her daily practise drove Adolf mad as he was tone-deaf'.

Adolf was what we would now call a workaholic. Hilde remembers him often at his desk until 2 AM reading or writing: 'He didn't get up until 8.30 or 9 AM, but then he would work right through the day and night.' He enjoyed an occasional pint of Guinness, but avoided society events. He had a soft spot for movies and often took the children to the Savoy cinema to see the latest Laurel and Hardy or Mickey Mouse release. Maria Mahr sometimes complained that he went out more with the children than he did with her.

The Mahr children were given Teutonic first names. When the Mahrs' first Irish-born child arrived in 1929, she was named Ingrid Erika Roswitha Mahr. Four years later, when their fourth and last child arrived, she was named Ulrika Brigitta Wilhelmina, although she would go by the name of Brigit. The morning after her arrival, Adolf brought Gustav, Hilde and Ingrid to the hospital to see their new sister. There was another woman in the same room who had given birth to a baby boy, and the eleven-year-old Gustav took his father aside and asked him: 'Can we take that boy? I have enough sisters!'

In 1927, Gustav started in Tullamaine, the prep school for the Methodist Wesley College, about two hundred metres from their home, where the Burlington Hotel now stands. Hilde enrolled there in 1932, but within a year developed tuberculosis, and had to miss much of that school year. She started in Tullamaine again at the age of seven. Ingrid soon joined her there, but by then the older two had progressed to Wesley, which at that time was on St Stephen's Green.

The students of Wesley College were predominantly of an Anglo-Irish background, and because there was no Jewish secondary school in Dublin at the time, Wesley also had a strong Jewish representation. (Israel's first prime minister, the Belfast-born Chaim Herzog, attended Wesley during the 1920s.)[11] So in a microcosm of the soon-to-be-divided Europe, Gustav Mahr, who would serve in the German army during World War II, sat alongside boys who would fight on the British side, as well as Jewish boys and girls. The tensions that divided adults of these backgrounds were also felt in the classroom. According to Gustav:

> The Jews kept very much to themselves. We Christians had our own circles, and the Jews had their own circles, even if we were in the same class. They went home, as I did, but they belonged to a different community. They never came in on a Saturday morning, as the rest had to. They went to their Hebrew School, and they didn't participate in the many activities, even in the school teams.[12]

The rivalries often led to fights:

> We threw bread at each other. You got sandwiches for your lunchtime break, and then you took a few bites, and the rest was hurled at somebody you didn't like. This went on all the time.... Of course there was anti-Jewish competition and sentiment in Wesley. I had a fight with the best Jew in my class; Mr Jaswan, was his name. I was the winner. I think it was the only battle I won. Jaswan was pretty well knocked about. He

was a bit smaller than I was . . . . But then I was bashed up by one of the boarders who came from Achill Island. I think his name was Hackett.

Gustav's German background was the most obvious point of attack, particularly by children who were employing prejudices left over from a war they were too young to remember. 'When the kids met me in the lane, they jeered at me, saying: "Who won the war?", "German Sausage!" and "Hun!" That was the way we were treated. And even at a Methodist school, that should be tolerant,' he says. 'It probably prompted me to become very aware of my affiliation and my denomination, and my roots.'

Every effort was made in Wesley to get the boys to play rugby and cricket, but Gustav had little interest in either sport. He managed to avoid cricket, but was forced to play rugby. Even that did not break down the barriers between him and his peers. When he failed to attend a school rugby game, as a player or a supporter, he came in for some rough treatment:

> You had to go through a very narrow corridor with high walls into school. And both sides were lined with boarders saying 'where were you yesterday?' And they bashed you all the way through until you got into the schoolyard.

Hilde has fewer memories of such strife, but was frustrated for other reasons. She was an energetic child – something that would stand to her in later years – and resented the fact that the boys were let out to play on the grounds during break, while the girls 'were always shut up somewhere in a dark gym':

> Wesley was a very sophisticated school, not a lively school with activities, and there were no sports for girls. The girls in the boarding school had access to the tennis courts and the hockey, but the day pupils had no sort of physical exercise. Once a year we had the summer festivities – a sports day with races – but nothing in between. That's why I liked to go to the Brownies.[13]

In the Mahrs' home, the children spoke a mixture of German (their father's language), Dutch (their mother's), English (their preferred tongue) and also a little Irish, which one of their housekeepers taught them. At school they learned French, Latin and Irish, a subject that has been problematic for generations of Irish students – not to mention first-generation immigrants who could get little help with it at home.

In Wesley, Padraig Cloone, from County Clare, had the unenviable task of teaching Irish to classrooms of Anglo-Irish, Jewish, and immigrant children. Gustav remembers him as 'a fierce guy with a big fist who used to smash his grammar into our heads'.

Hilde's experiences of learning Irish were no more pleasant. She did not learn the language at Tullamaine but, on changing over to Wesley College, was placed in a class made up of children who had learned Irish in their previous school, or at home. 'It was a strange and foreign language to me . . . the other children would mock me,' she says, but 'I was a very good pupil. I got lovely reports.'

The limited opportunities for making friends at Wesley did not worry the children's parents. Adolf Mahr, in particular, was keen that his children retain their German identity and preferred to see them making friends with other children of German extraction. There was a small German and Austrian community in Ireland at the time, numbering about 250, and they had formed the German Association, which organised social activities where children and adults could mix with others of a similar national background. The association was also a contact point for visiting Austrians and Germans.

During June and July 1928 the Austrian Expressionist painter Oskar Kokoschka came to paint in Ireland. In London that year, some of his paintings were priced at £1,350, an enormous sum at the time: as a result, the German colony saw him as an important visitor. Mahr was asked to look after his fellow countryman, and did so by bringing him on a tour of Dublin's art galleries and museums, and on a visit to the ancient burial site at Loughcrew, County Meath. The wives of both men came too, as did Gustav and Hilde, and Mahr's photographer friend Thomas Mason and his son. In 1937 Kokoschka fell foul of the German authorities. His expressive portrait style was judged decadent and unworthy of Nazi approval, and was removed from galleries in Germany. But the Mahrs did not wait that long to form such an opinion. They liked neither the man nor his art. 'They were much too conservative for Kokoschka's style,' says Hilde.[14]

During the 1930s, many German and Austrian families had come to Ireland in circumstances similar to the Mahrs', often brought in as managers in state organisations. They included Heinz Mecking of the Irish

Turf Development Board, Otto Reinhard, head of Forestry in the Department of Lands, and Colonel Fritz Brase of the Army No.1 Band. As we shall see later, these people had an important role to play in further developments of the German colony. For the Mahr children, they simply provided other German-Irish children to play with.

One of Gustav's best friends was Arthur Forster of Dun Laoghaire, who had one German parent and was raised as a Catholic. Gustav would cycle the twenty kilometres from his home to Forster's at weekends. A keen cyclist, he developed a competitive element to his journey; he would wait for the Dun Laoghaire tram to pass the Mahr home, and then race it all the way out along the route. The two youths often swam off the West Pier of Dun Laoghaire Harbour before Gustav began his return journey.

Gustav was frequently joined on long journeys by his friend Eric Ashman, and Eric's brother Mervyn. In those days of uncongested roads, the teenagers cycled from their homes into the Wicklow Mountains, through the Sally Gap, and back, a distance of more than 130 kilometres, in a day. They also crossed the city to Howth and Clontarf, and went down the coast to Killiney. They also swam at the famous Forty Foot in Sandycove. What James Joyce described in *Ulysses* as 'the snot-green scrotum-tightening sea', Gustav remembers as offering the chance for 'a wonderful dip'.

Gustav shared his father's interest in archaeology, and cycled out to the excavations in Drimnagh, which were run by Howard Kilbride-Jones of the National Museum, and by Joseph Raftery, later Director of the Museum. 'I caught the bug early,' Gustav says; 'it was very romantic to go out there aged fifteen and take part in the excavations'.

Both Gustav and Hilde cycled out to the seaside town of Malahide. They played tennis there, usually only with other members of the German-Irish community. The Mahrs were also friendly with the neighbouring children at Waterloo Place. Hilde was pally with a girl from two doors away, Terry Meagher, and Gustav befriended her brothers, Donald and Desmond. There, in the Mahrs' back garden, they could play, immune from the bullying at Wesley.

Hilde was closer to Gustav than to Ingrid, even though she was nearer in age to her sister. Ingrid was a chatty attention-seeker, while Hilde was more responsible and well-behaved. Hilde explains: 'Ingrid and I were different sorts. She was far more my mother's way, and I was more my dad's way. She was the little flirty girl, and I was the stricter elder sister . . . . I liked climbing up the mountains and every sort of physical activity'.

The siblings all agree that their father favoured Gustav. Hilde attributes this to the old Greek and Roman ideas of successful manhood: 'First you must educate yourself, then you must build a house, and then your wife must give birth to a son.' Gustav was the first-born, and a boy, and further ingratiated himself by sharing his father's interest in geography and archaeology. 'Every young lad of that age reveres their father and tries to emulate him, and get his approval. And I did too, of course,' he says. 'And he was very fond of me too. I know that.'

Hilde, however, enjoyed the status of eldest daughter: 'I adored my father, and I think he adored me too, and Gustav was very jealous. He was a nasty brother to me, which is quite natural. Until I arrived he was the prince of the family. And then comes a little princess. And that's difficult for a boy of four years. But we all knew that Gustav was the star of the family, and he was an excellent pupil. So if I had any troubles at school, I needn't ask Father; I just asked Gustav.'

Hilde found the few archaeological digs she went on very exciting, such as the one at Drimnagh: 'I went to one in a big graveyard and I was there with [Michael] Duignan, and Kilbride-Jones. There were a lot of skeletons, which had been exhumed. There was a drawing where all the grave findings were put. Kilbride-Jones taught me how to tell the difference between a male and a female skeleton. It is by the bump in the occipital ridge [protuberance over the brows present in a male], and females have wider hips,' she says.

For Adolf Mahr, stamps were valuable items through which children learned history and geography. Hilde says that, for him, they were as precious as a piece of jewellery, and he was appalled when people threw them away. The favouritism towards Gustav extended into stamp collecting and he was the sole peron who could be trusted with his father's cherished collection. Only Gustav was allowed to collect the stamps that came attached to his father's international mail. 'I only got the throwaways,' says Hilde, 'and my father spent very much time with him, collecting and arranging the stamp albums. I was only allowed to take the stamps off with water, and dry them.'

Adolf Mahr became friendly with the film-maker Robert Flaherty, who in 1933 made the landmark film *Man of Aran*. Both men had a great interest in the traditional Irish boats, the currach (used off the west coast) and the coracle (used on the Rivers Bann and Boyne). It is likely that Flaherty visited Mahr at the museum while researching his film, and invited him to the set on the Aran Islands. The prospect of seeing history being recorded on film must have thrilled Mahr, and once again Gustav was the lucky one brought along when Gustav spent a few days watching Flaherty at work. A famous scene in *Man of Aran* shows three men in a currach being tossed around by high waves while pursuing a basking shark that was larger than the boat itself. Nowadays the scene would have been shot using a mechanical shark, model boats and stuntmen, but Flaherty craved authenticity. He was later criticised for allowing the men to go out in such dangerous conditions, and admitted afterwards: 'I should have been shot for what I asked these superb people to do, all for the sake of a keg of porter and five pounds apiece.'[15]

Adolf and Gustav watched the filming from a little steamer that had been hired by the crew. It was, says Gustav, 'very tense'. The Mahrs stayed in a thatched cottage with a real turf fire that Flaherty rented near the village of Cill Ronan. Being of a similar age to the child star of the film, Mike Dillane, Gustav struck up a friendship with him immediately. The two built a little shelter and lit a fire in it, and played together in between Mike's filming duties. Both Adolf and Gustav Mahr attended the film premiere in Dublin in 1934, and the following year it won the Grand Prix at the Venice Film Festival.

Upon his return from the Aran Islands, Gustav learned that another trip awaited him before his return to school in the autumn. Adolf had been invited to Zurich to inspect a private collection of early Iron Age material from the former Austrian province of Carniola, then part of Yugoslavia. Gustav would travel with his father as far as Holland, where he would stay with his maternal grandparents. His father would then continue his journey to Switzerland, and once his business was completed, he would collect Gustav in Holland and the two would return to Dublin. The eleven-year-old was thrilled but, as Adolf described in a letter that summer, Gustav got appendicitis and was unable to travel:

> Poor chap, he was operated on on Monday, having fallen ill on Monday morning. He wept bitterly, not about the operation (which he took calmly as a necessary evil), but about the spoilt holidays. If there was a thing

which annoyed him still more, it was the withholding of food. "Now I'm like Gandhi", he said in caustic self-persiflage.[16]

Adolf compensated Gustav for the loss of his holiday by arranging for the boy to recuperate at Monksgrange, an estate at the foot of the Blackstairs Mountains in County Wexford. Although this must have seemed to Gustav to be scant compensation for missing a trip to Holland, the sojourn turned out to be Gustav's most cherished childhood memory, one that he frequently recalled in the decades to come.

Monksgrange was owned by the Richards-Orpen family, whom Adolf had befriended through a shared interest in archaeology. Edward Richards-Orpen had a German wife and was a member of the National Monuments Advisory Council. He had a deep knowledge of Wexford's history and antiquities, something he probably had inherited from his father, Goddard, who had exchanged a career in law for a pastime of historical research. The first two volumes of Goddard's landmark work *Ireland Under the Normans* were published in 1911, and he added two more volumes in 1920.[17] In short, the Richards-Orpens were Adolf Mahr's kind of people.

On leaving hospital, Gustav was placed on the train that took him from Dublin along the east coast to Enniscorthy, where he was met by one of the daughters of the house. From there, it was a short drive over rough roads to Monksgrange, a large house built in 1759, set on 253 acres, with stables, a furniture factory and a team of labourers.[18] For ten days Gustav recuperated while living the country life of the Anglo-Irish gentry. It was late August and the farm was a hive of activity. He learned carpentry in the farm's furniture factory, swam in the small lake on the estate, and worked in the fields. It was much more fun than visiting his grandparents in Holland, as Gustav explains:

> Mr Richards-Orpen grew strawberries, and I learned how to pick them, and plant them, and weed them properly. I spent many happy hours collecting them in the fields, and I accompanied him to Enniscorthy, in his old ramshackle car, loaded up with the take, and brought it to the market. That time provides some of my most vivid childhood memories.

There were two daughters in the family, Virginia and Puffet, both a little older than Gustav. He admits to having revered both girls, and to falling in love with the younger of the two, Puffet; but it wasn't to be. Puffet, who was also known as Charmian, later married into the Hill family. Charmian Hill achieved fame as the owner of Dawn Run, the only horse to have won the Cheltenham Champion Hurdle and the Cheltenham Gold Cup Steeplechase, as well as the full set of Irish, English and French hurdling championships.[19]

During the summers of 1934, 1935 and 1936, the Mahrs rented a big house at 4 St James Terrace in Malahide, about fifteen kilometres north of Dublin city. It belonged to the Reverend Wilhelm Tanne, a Lutheran minister who funded his holidays back to his native Germany each year by renting out the house. The Mahr children loved the seaside town because it had a long beach and was surrounded by countryside that was ideal for cycling. Hilde, in particular, loved to cycle and she roamed the town and countryside on her own, often – to her mother's consternation – for the entire day. Gustav learned how to sail and play tennis there, and spent much of his time on the strand with the fishermen.

In July 1935, the Mahr children were guests at Malahide Castle. When Maria Mahr's parents visited Dublin that summer, the castle's owner, Lord Talbot, invited them to the castle and to walk in its surrounding 250 acres of woodland (something of interest to Maria's father, a well-known professor of zoology at Leiden Groote University in Holland). Three generations of van Bemmelens arrived, and for an afternoon, the castle became a playground for the young Mahr children. Lord Talbot, an old man who had no children of his own, was understandably nervous for the safety of his delicate heirlooms!

During the summer of 1937, the four Mahr children holidayed in Skerries, a seaside town north of Malahide. Maria Mahr had to visit her parents in Holland, so their housekeeper, Grete Spiegelfeld, looked after the children. They stayed at a local hotel owned by a German, Mr Joebges. (The name is pronounced 'Yob-gis', but locals preferred a more direct pronunciation, 'Mr Joe, be Jaysus'.)[20]

The 1930s was generally a happy period for the Mahrs, especially when compared with what lay ahead. Although it was the time of the 'Economic War', the Mahrs were financially secure and settled in their new country. In a time of great poverty in Ireland, the Mahrs had a comfortable middle-class existence. Sixty years before most Irish families owned a video player, Gustav got a small projector that allowed the family to watch Charlie Chaplin films at home. They also had a gramophone, on which they played German seventy-eights, and later Irish records when they became more widely available.

Ingrid sums it up: 'That's why I'm so fond of Ireland. It was a time in our life when it was happy and good; we had a marvellous time. We had lovely parents. There was nothing to upset us. For us children, there was no politics.'

2

OFFICIAL LIFE: AT THE NATIONAL MUSEUM, 1927–34

> Mahr was a vigorous and energetic man who did not take too kindly to a bridle. He shamelessly overspent his purchasing account, and ordered new cases without clearing the matter with the Office of Public Works.
>
> *G. F. Mitchell, in a report to the Royal Irish Academy, 1985*[1]

> At present there is a commission busy that is reorganising the museum according to modern ideas. I have been asked to give them advice, and together with a Swedish expert, Dr Lithberg, we have been invited to help them. Practically it means that Lithberg and I make out the whole plan, and the commission more or less just 'rubber stamps' it.
>
> *Adolf Mahr, in a letter to the van Bemmelens, 1927*[2]

In his role as Keeper of Irish Antiquities, Adolf Mahr created and nurtured a network of landowners and collectors from all over Ireland who acted as his eyes and ears when items turned up in the soil or became available from private collections. Their ranks were mostly made up of Anglo-Irish men whom Mahr had met through the Royal Dublin Society or the Royal Society of Antiquaries of Ireland, but their number also included many priests and schoolmasters, because it was to them that farmers would bring stone battleaxes and other weapons they found of their land.[3] His network spread far beyond Ireland. The archaeologist Howard Kilbride-Jones, a close friend of Mahr's, point out that 'Adolf Mahr took pride in knowing everyone in the world of archaeology'.[4]

Of his numerous contacts in many countries, none could have been more unlikely than Albert Bender, an Irish Jew living in San Francisco, who had made his fortune in insurance. Bender, a collector and patron of the arts, exchanged 170 letters with Mahr between 1931 and 1939: the correspondence provides the greatest insight into Mahr's life in the period immediately prior to World War II.[5] There is a poignancy about the letters because, although Mahr was aware that Bender was Jewish, it is possible that Bender never found out that his correspondent was a high-ranking Nazi.

Albert Bender was born in Dublin in 1866, the son of Rabbi Dr Philipp Bender and his Catholic wife, Augusta Bremer. His father held the post of Minister to the Jewish Community in Dublin for twenty-one years, and taught Jewish, Protestant and Catholic children at a school in Lower Mount Street. It was said of him that 'in a city where sectarian spirit ran so high, he had the high privilege of overcoming the suspicion with which the Jew was regarded, and was the means of disseminating the seeds of knowledge and promoting harmony and goodwill amongst the children or representatives of the three great creeds'.[6] At the age of sixteen, Albert left for San Francisco and began his working life in the office of his mother's brother, William Bremer, a shipping and insurance broker. By 1895, the uncle and nephew had set up an insurance brokerage partnership called Bremer and Bender, and seven years later Bender went out on his own to form Albert M. Bender Insurance, an insurance and oil-brokerage company at 311 California Street.[7] By 1914, his business was a success: he insured the Levi Strauss company, and also chaired the insurance committee of the 1915 World's Fair in San Francisco. By that stage, his home on Post Street had become a famous meeting place for all sorts of colourful characters.

Bender never married, and instead poured an estimated 90 percent of his income into San Francisco's charitable, educational and creative institutions.[8] While other wealthy individuals collected works by dead artists, Bender insisted that the best way to further the arts was to support living artists. In San Francisco he was often described as 'the patron saint of the city's artists'.[9] Bender financed beginners by buying their works, and then helped them gain recognition by donating his purchases to museums. As a result, virtually every painter, photographer and sculptor in California passed through the doors of his office on California Street, hoping for assistance. Bender was California's greatest patron of the arts in the 1920s and 1930s. Each December from 1936 through to 1940, the San

Francisco Museum of Art, as it then was, devoted all its exhibition space to donations which had been received from Bender during the previous twelve months. The opening of each year's exhibition was said to be the social event of the season in Los Angeles.[10]

Conscious of his Irish heritage, Bender decided that 17 March was his birthday (even though it wasn't) and each year he threw a huge birthday party for himself. He joked to friends: 'In our youth, St Patrick and I were cronies in Dublin, and we agreed to share birthdays.'

'Mickey' Bender (as his friends called him) didn't drink, but he maintained a well-stocked liquor cabinet for his guests. He never drove, but always had a good Buick car, in which friends chauffeured him.[11] The great photographers Ansel Adams and Dorothea Lange owed their early successes to his patronage. By the early 1930s, Bender had established art and precious-book collections in many institutions in San Francisco. He wanted to make donations to the city where he was born, and discussed his plans with a visiting friend, Dr Walter Starkie, an academic at Trinity College Dublin and a member of the board of the Abbey Theatre. On Starkie's advice, Bender sent a cache of antiquarian books to Trinity College. It was housed in the main library of the college, and was subsequently expanded by Bender. The collection was named for Albert Bender's father, Philipp Bender.

Bender seems to have received insufficient reaction or appreciation from the college, so he asked Starkie to suggest an alternative institution in Dublin for a set of twenty-two Tibetan paintings on leather which he would like to donate. Starkie spoke to the director of the National Gallery of Ireland, who told him that that institution would not be suitable for it. 'As the director told me, it is devoted to countries such as Italy, France, Holland, Spain, England.' The director suggested instead that he send the paintings to the National Museum of Ireland, and both Starkie and the Minister for Education, Tom Derrig, who had also been consulted, agreed.[12] Starkie told Bender that he would contact Dr Mahr about the paintings as soon as he had returned from vacation. It is interesting to note that, although Tibetan paintings should not have been part of Mahr's brief as Keeper of Irish Antiquities, it seems that as early as 1930 he was regarded as having the safest pair of hands at the museum.

Bender wrote to Adolf Mahr for the first time in December 1931 to say that he would like to send a gift to the museum 'in the name of my dear mother Augusta Bender'. He told Mahr that he had hesitated to send them 'because they might not prove to be a gift which the authorities of art in Dublin would consider suitable. I spoke to Æ [the poet and artist George Russell] about them when he was here, and also to Dr Starkie, both of whom expressed themselves as approving the ideas and urged me to send them.'[13]

Bender, no stranger to gentle manipulation, added: 'Today I entertained at my house one of the ex-directors of the Louvre, who was so interested in the pictures that he asked me to present them to that institution. I explained to him that I felt they should first be offered to my native city.' Mahr immediately asked the museum's photographer, Thomas Mason, to photograph the paintings so that experts in London could identify them. He then selected a place for their display at the National Museum.

Dorothea Lange described Bender as a plain little man, a professional Irishman who walked about town with presents in his pockets:[14] 'Anywhere you met him he would fish into his pockets as though he'd been looking for you all day and he'd give you some quite beautiful thing.'[15] This tradition was maintained in his mail, and in March 1932 he sent the Mahr children in Dublin a present of candied fruits. Adolf Mahr replied to say: 'My children said they had never tasted such beautiful fruits, and my boy, who is a great geographer, told me all he knew about golden California. Being only nine, he knew more then I expected, and your kindness therefore made also [*sic*] a father proud.'[16]

In the spring of 1932, Bender sent several other donations of Asian art to the National Museum, including a bronze head mounted on wood, three Japanese tapestries and three Chinese embroideries. The two men exchanged letters regularly, and by May Mahr felt that the relationship was strong enough for him to adopt a more familiar tone, and to explain some of the difficulties he was experiencing with his museum. Apparently even the workaholic was reaching his limits:

> I wanted to write to you sooner in the matter but our only typist got ill and I have to write all my letters myself at a time at which I hardly know how to get all the other work done. We have to make all the preparations for the Eucharistic Congress and for the First International Congress of Prehistory (meets in London but comes over for a visit). I had to

excavate two burials recently, write a paper about them, have to write another for the Congress, prepare my paper which I have to deliver, and at the same time I have to bring out our hundred-and-thirty-plate album [book] of Early Christian Art in time for the Eucharistic Congress! You will understand that I never go to bed before 1 o'clock in the night as the work for the album has to be done very carefully. I open myself to the criticism of all European scholars if I commit serious mistakes and the trouble is that nearly all the good modern literature about the history of Christian Art is absent in Ireland. Our predecessors must have slept a lot![17]

Mahr was referring to the thirty-first International Eucharistic Congress, which took place in Dublin in June 1932, to coincide with what was believed to be the 1,500th anniversary of St Patrick's mission to Ireland. More than a million and a half people attended masses in the Phoenix Park over five days.[18] The Irish government commissioned Adolf Mahr to prepare a book about early Christian art in Ireland for the event.

Bender did not comment on Mahr's difficulties, but instead expressed delight at receiving a copy of Mahr's book, *Christian Art in Ancient Ireland*. 'I take great delight in anything scholarly or artistic that comes out of Ireland,' he wrote, 'especially early Ireland, showing a high place of culture long before other nations had entered the ranks of civilisation.'[19] Bender also sent a collection of thirty-one works of Japanese artists from the eighteenth century, and expressed the hope again that he would build up an 'interesting and attractive collection' in the memory of his mother 'that will be worthy of her and of my native city'.[20]

By August 1932, Mahr's mood had improved immensely. He was most at home with scholars and at professional gatherings, and he got the opportunity to enjoy both at the first International Congress of Prehistoric and Protohistoric Sciences in London. It seemed to him that the deep rifts that had divided the world during the Great War were finally healing, and in a long letter to Bender he expressed optimism and idealism about the future, but also his concerns about Ireland and her national museum. He proudly told Bender:

The 'savants' have finally come together again, after many years of alienation, and let us hope that their mutual understanding is only a forerunner of a still wider mutual understanding of civilised people. It so happened that Germany lost the war, that Britain nearly lost it, that France won it and that America pays [for] it. We anthropologists look upon it with nearly complete detachment as we know that the present national and racial boundaries are a thing of very late origin and that the boundaries which separated mankind in the Stone Age are probably more important that the make-shifts of our present politicians. There is a growing sense amongst anthropologists . . . to lose all interest in what is today miscalled 'politics' and I should say that the world would be better off if also the politicians took less interest in politics.[21]

After the congress, Mahr brought twelve 'of the best European men' to Ireland to examine some of his recent Stone Age acquisitions. 'It was the first time that selected men of our profession came over as a body,' he told Bender. 'They were overwhelmed by the beauty, value and importance of our material, its bearing on Europe, and they were astonished to see how very little work has been done hitherto. They said that the improvised trip to Ireland was the best of the whole congress. The result is that my two new assistants have been invited to go to the Continent, to receive training in excavation techniques. A third apprentice is being sent from Belfast. The Dutch Archaeological Institute will excavate next year in Northern Ireland . . . .'[22]

Mahr is sometimes referred to as 'the founding father of Irish archaeology', and his last point above illustrates why. Part of his legacy is that he produced a new generation of archaeologists who were trained in the most modern digging techniques, often while on travelling studentships that he had arranged with his friends in Continental Europe. One can only imagine the thrill of a young student who was sent abroad for training for a period of up to fifteen months at a time when overseas travel was a rare privilege for most Irish people.

Mahr's purpose in sending the new recruits abroad was twofold: to expose them to the best modern museum practises and excavation techniques, and to use them to catalogue holdings of Irish material in foreign museums.[23] In a letter to one of his recruits, Michael Heaney, in 1932, he said: 'I want you as well as Mr O'Riordan [*sic*] to share two purposes at the same time; to do your own work and to learn . . . . And to card-index the

Irish stuff in the individual institutions so that sooner or later we will have at least something to guide us in the question of how the Irish stuff is scattered.'[24]

Mahr had a penchant for card-indexing, something he passed on to his apprentices. In the late 1930s Howard Kilbride-Jones recalls seeing at the museum for the first time an index that Mahr had assembled, 'with details of every find ever made in Ireland. It was a splendid idea and it saved hours of thumbing through publications. A special case had been constructed to contain the index.'[25]

Privilege though it was for the individual concerned to go on a paid study tour, a studentship was not a holiday. Mahr set a rigorous schedule, and an examination of O'Riordain's letters to his boss in 1932/33 shows him meeting Mahr's Continental colleagues, training or digging with them, and sending reports back to Dublin. In the autumn of 1932, for example, O'Riordain went to England, where he made card-indexes of Irish material at local museums in Bristol, Salisbury, Farnham in Surrey, London, and Sidcup in Kent. In October, he went to Groningen in the Netherlands, took part in an excavation at Exinge, and examined museum collections at Assen, Groningen and Leiden. In November, he travelled to Germany, where he studied museums in Berlin, before attending lectures in Kiel and visiting an excavation at Hedeby. He returned to Cork for Christmas, but in January was back in Hamburg, before moving on to France and Switzerland.[26] The trips were partially funded by the Royal Irish Academy and the Irish government, and costs were generally kept low by the kindness of their hosts – usually as a favour to Mahr.[27]

O'Riordain was in France and Germany in 1933 – the year Hitler came to power in Germany – and Mahr warned him to be careful in his discussions in view of the unfolding political developments. When meeting Professor Lantier of the Musée des Antiquités Nationales at St Germain-en-Laye, Mahr – who had already joined the Nazi Party – told O'Riordain: 'Do not speak of political developments in Germany' because 'there is no use in your being mixed up with inter-continental quarrels'.[28]

The next generation of museum directors and professors all sprang from this group of apprentices. They included Michael Duignan (the first 'real' professor of archaeology in Galway, according to the National Museum's current director Pat Wallace),[29] Joseph Raftery (later Director of the National Museum) and Seán P. O'Riordain, who became professor at Cork and Dublin (UCD). Raftery, in particular, was Mahr's protégé. Hailing from County Laois and a recent graduate of UCD, he was sent by Mahr to study for a doctorate in Germany. Upon his return, Raftery worked at the museum. One night in 1938, Mahr invited Raftery to dinner at his favourite haunt, the Red Bank Restaurant on D'Olier Street. Another of the invitees was a young Montessori teacher, Charlotte (Lotti) Lang of Heidelberg, whose mother had asked Mahr to look after her during her tour of Ireland. A romance between Raftery and Lang developed, and they married the following year. Their son Barry is currently Professor of Archaeology at UCD. He jokes that the result of this union, more than anything else, was Mahr's great contribution to Irish archaeology.[30]

Despite Mahr's generosity towards the young archaeologists, his manner made him unpopular with many of the staff at the museum. Joseph Murray, who was still in his teens when he worked as a messenger at the museum, recalls Mahr as being 'aloof', 'dour' and having a 'cold personality'. He says, 'Mahr should have had an interest in all the staff, not just the chosen few', and continues:

> He arrived in the main door every morning. With his busted arm he would hold his briefcase tight and walk across the hall to his office. He didn't look left or right and didn't talk to anyone he didn't need to talk to. Nobody liked him. He had an assistant who was treated as a servant, who did personal errands for Mahr, and this caused tension because we already had a lack of staff . . . . Mahr talked to me when he needed something done, but I wasn't to talk to him. He would not look at me, even though I was in his office several times per day.[31]

It should also be noted that Mahr is not universally recognised as 'the father of Irish archaeology'. The late archaeologist and writer Frank Mitchell says that George Coffey, who was appointed as superintendent of Irish Antiquities in 1890,[32] deserved the title.[33] Michael Ryan, current Director of the Chester Beatty Library and former Keeper of Irish Antiquities, says the title belongs to either Coffey, George Petrie or Sir William Wilde (father of the poet Oscar Wilde), who died in 1876.[34] Ned Kelly, the current Keeper of Irish Antiquities at the National Museum, is not comfortable about awarding Mahr such a title either: 'He certainly made a major contribution, but he was simply implementing the Lithberg plan. Mahr was a great implementer, but it was Nils Lithberg's plan.'[35]

The National Museum had opened in 1890 to house the collections of the Royal Irish Academy, the Museum of Irish Industry, the Natural History Museum and the Dublin Museum of Science and Art. It was, according to Mahr, 'nothing more than a mere provincial annexe to the archaeology of Britain.'[36]

The museum reflected a British world-view, and the importance of Irish archaeology and Irish antiquities were downplayed. Items such as field guns that had been captured by the British army from the Sikhs in 1846, and the Lord Chancellor's Coach, which had been built in London and imported into Ireland in 1790, took pride of place in the museum's rotunda.[37] Such artefacts would have been of little interest or relevance to Ireland's majority Catholic and nationalist population. Soon after the establishment of the Irish Free State in 1922, the museum's outlook became increasingly Irish and Celtic. The academic Dr Elizabeth Crooke described the museum in its early days as 'an opportunity for London to exercise its influence, while later it was a place for those in Ireland to implement their own authority and to affirm an Irish national identity'.[38]

In December 1927, shortly after Mahr's arrival in Ireland, a committee headed by Professor Lithberg produced a report on the purposes and needs of the museum. The government accepted the Lithberg Report's recommendation that the main aims of the National Museum of Ireland should be to 'accumulate, preserve, study and display such objects as may serve to increase and diffuse the knowledge of Irish civilisation, or the natural history of Ireland and of the relations of Ireland in these respects with other countries'.[39] This marked a significant departure from the role previously assumed by the museum, and Mahr, as Keeper of Irish Antiquities, was charged with implementing many of the report's recommendations. He reorganised the displays, brought the antiquities collection into the central hall, and took the gold and other special treasures out of their strongroom and incorporated them into the general systematic collection.[40]

At the time of Mahr's arrival, the museum was not involved in archaeological excavation; indeed, the current director, Pat Wallace, says: 'There was no worthwhile work done in the museum during the thirty years before Mahr arrived.'[41] Even those involved in excavation often did more harm than good. 'They used to dig with shovels, and worse,' says Wallace. 'A certain professor in UCD used dynamite to investigate the passage graves in County Sligo.' Mahr set out to change this and rescue Ireland from what Wallace describes as 'Indiana Jones-style boom-and-blast archaeology', and introduce careful scientific excavation methods in its stead.

In 1931, a major archaeological excavation project in Ireland was mooted by Harvard University as part of a wider programme conducted by the Harvard Division of Anthropology. Mahr welcomed the American archaeologists, knowing that they would bring to Ireland for the first time methods of scientific excavation – the practices used on archaeological digs today, where not only the objects recovered are important, but also their position, surrounding artefacts, depth in the soil, type of soil, and other such details. The Harvard team applied to the Ancient Monuments Council of Ireland for a licence to excavate, but it was refused. Mahr was furious, and, as he admits to Bender, he 'broke the law' and gave them a site to dig:

> As I knew that the Americans would not abuse my confidence and were very capable diggers, I got so annoyed about the stupidity of my Council that I simply broke the law (of which I am supposed to be the main watchdog). I gave them the best crannóg to excavate of which I knew. Incredibly as it may sound it was the first crannóg which was ever scientifically excavated in Ireland.[42]

Mahr's 'best crannóg' was in Ballinderry, County Westmeath, a major Viking-age enclave in the middle of Ireland. The dig at Ballinderry was successful, and the Harvard group, which had a policy of handing over to the National Museum objects found on digs, presented Mahr with several important items, including a bronze church lamp, a tenth-century wooden game board, a longbow, and a ninth-century iron Viking sword, one of the finest such examples from the Viking period. All these items are still on display at the National Museum. One can only imagine Mahr's excitement with the sword in particular. It has an elaborate, pattern-welded blade, inlaid with the name of the swordmaker, Ulfbehrt. Swords by the same maker were exported from the Rhineland and have been found as far east as Russia.[43]

Wallace believes that Mahr sidestepped the law rather than broke it, but he can understand Mahr's frustration with his own Council:

> There was no scientific excavation done before the Harvard Mission came to Ireland. [Mahr] was trying to do something new, something big, of world importance. Of course the narrow little outlook of some of the members of the Council couldn't make the leap to jump with him, the great man that he was, to allow the Americans to do the excavations in Ireland . . . . A lot of the younger people, like O'Riordain, Duignan and Raftery, were trained on those excavations, so the first generation of diggers – native-born diggers – were produced from that expedition.[44]

The Harvard team investigated seventeen sites between 1932 and 1936.[45] Every archaeological dig in Ireland since then has followed similar scientific practices, and this has prevented the destruction of hundreds of sites and artefacts. The Harvard excavations also marked a turning point in how the general population viewed archaeology, because of the press coverage and public interest the digs that were generated. The excavations attracted the interest and support of Éamon de Valera, who became leader of the Free State in 1932. He could see in archaeology a tool for his nation-building plans. Irish nationalism was built upon the idea that the Irish were descended from a Celtic people, and that there was a Golden Age when they had enjoyed intellectual, social, political and ethnic integration, before it was corrupted by the arrival of the Normans, and then the English. This could be put right only by a return to the values of the Golden Age.[46] Archaeological sites and artefacts became the material evidence to support Irish nationalism.[47] The success of the Harvard team validated de Valera's view of Ireland, which in turn reflected well on Mahr.

As a result of Mahr's petitions, the Unemployment Relief schemes of 1934 included a provision to fund 'excavations for archaeological purposes'. Twenty-six excavations were carried out with the aid of this funding, and hundreds of previously unemployed workers were taken on, particularly in Counties Clare and Sligo. This gave rise to fifty supervisory positions for professional archaeologists.[48] A similar measure was adopted in Northern Ireland the following year.

Much as he enjoyed the success of the Harvard Mission, Mahr knew that improving standards at his museum would be far more difficult. To add to his concerns, Albert Bender was still sending valuable Asian artefacts from California, in the hope of forming a permanent collection in his mother's name. Mahr felt that his patronage was well intentioned, but extraneous to the museum's requirements. He took the difficult decision to discourage further donations from Bender. In a long letter in August 1932, he warned Bender: 'the honest truth is that my museum is not worth such valuable gifts and such sacrifices on your part. We are not (or not yet) good enough an institution to be favoured with such magnificent gifts. I am sorry I can't fly to Frisco in a hurry and explain to you all about Ireland and her National Museum . . . . You have no idea how backward in all cultural matters we here are.'[49]

He told Bender that although there were many fine objects in the museum, they are 'intermingled with [the] worst rubbish', and pointed out that in the museum's collection of traditional dolls showing native costumes from around the world, there was one representing the United States which had been made in Woolworth's, and 'is naked except for a banner across its stomach, which reads "USA".'

He was angry with his colleagues, whom he described as being 'insular' and 'years behind'. He told Bender: 'People laugh at my enthusiasm, and I was told by an officer of my own department that it is very undemocratic to work after official hours.' Mahr railed against the government for inadequately funding the institution:

> The Irish government gives only a third of the grant which the English gave, and with a ministry which is full of ridiculous red tape . . . . When the Free State came into being our main block of offices, containing also [the] geology [department], was taken away to allocate [to] the Parliament. Nobody protested. The mahogany cases containing the fine geological collection were built into recesses. As their removal was too slow for the impatience of the supervisor, the cases were sawn to pieces! This happened six years before I came, [so] I cannot blame my colleagues for it. But I dare say that no government would have done it with a collection of which I was the Keeper.

Mahr outlined his personal vision for the institution by saying: 'It is my duty to bring the country which pays my salary up to the standard of the other European countries. It is a very hard job and it takes practically my whole day. Instead of writing learned papers, I have to be an organiser who clears away the mess of his predecessors and who has to do the work they left undone. I will never benefit from it personally and I am only making the bed for my successor.'

Mahr was aware also of the political difficulties of operating within a civil service that was still British in structure but anti-British in outlook. He needed to work closely with his British counterparts for scientific purposes, but also to maintain a distance for reasons of political expediency. Mahr, understandably, refers to the situation as a game:

> My program is to link up Irish archaeology, through the medium of Britain, with European archaeology, and through Europe with the remainder of the world. No British archaeological problem can be solved without Irish evidence, and vice versa. I have to represent the British archaeological interests in Ireland to the benefit of Irish archaeology itself. I have to do it from a sound national Irish standpoint without being an Irishman. I get little support by the local people, who cling to the old English tradition and find it hard to acquiesce with the existing state of affairs in Ireland. I have to be careful not to offend nationalistic feelings thru [*sic*] my close cooperation with my English colleagues. And I have to play this game at a period of economic distress and under an administrative system which, well intended as it may be, is extremely unsuitable for the reorganisation of an old institution by an individualist who constantly is up in arms against the traditional red tape.

The purpose of Mahr's letter was not just to complain; it was also to explain to Bender that the museum should be focused on Celtic archaeology, and that he should channel his philanthropy towards that field:

> For modern Europe, Ireland means very little. It means more to America. But her real world importance is its archaeological heritage, with its bearing on the formation of European civilisation. Irish archaeology is the only thing which can give us a status in European learning. It can be made the pivot stone by which to raise the whole standard of learned work in the country. If I succeed in that *only a little bit* [Mahr's emphasis], I will have done enough, no matter whether I am or am not a well-known man in learning.

In an uncharacteristic move for someone in his position, Mahr urged Bender to stop donating:

But, dear Mr Bender, why shall we go to the trouble to force such a fine Far East collection upon a division of the museum and upon a country which is not yet mature for it? And why should I encourage you in an expenditure if I am perhaps the only man in Ireland who can fully appreciate your gifts? I would act unfair [*sic*] toward a noble and generous benefactor if I did not tell you the truth.

I took the Tibetan banners because I can house them for the time being and because a museum man who refuses such a magnificent gift deserves to be dismissed. If it be united with the already existing stuff, it could be made a good subdivision. But it wants a man (preferably a specialist) and [a dedicated] room. Neither is available . . . . I would propose to you the transfer of the things to another Dublin institution. But the others don't fight as hard as I do and therefore they don't get things done . . . . There are hundreds of museums in America and Europe which are better equipped for a good display of Oriental art than we.

Of course Mahr had another agenda: he wanted Bender's money to be channelled away from Asian art and into research in Ireland:

But we can render services to the whole world which nobody else can do: in the line of Irish archaeology. And if your heart sticks to Dublin, I beg to say that you can achieve the same end with probably less expenditure and with more conspicuous results if you support the only branch of Dublin museum work which means something to the whole educated world, viz. archaeology and ethnology.

We have to build up a comparative continental Celtic collection because we are the only Celtic state in which Celtic art survived. Our ethnography has barely been touched. Hundreds of sites have not been excavated . . . . There are many ways in which you can create a lasting memorial without losing money on transport or other expenditure of a non-productive character (duties, etc). You can build up either an 'Augusta Bender Archaeological Library', or an 'Augusta Bender Room' of archaeological finds by, say, supporting crannóg excavations; you can get a little body of trustees formed who could administer funds which could be called 'Augusta Bender Foundation for Irish Archaeology' and to which other supporters could subscribe.

The letter reveals a passionate and idealistic man brimming with energy but trapped in an institution and a society which, in his own words, were not mature enough for the gift. But it also shows a museum official refusing valuable gifts – something of which his employers would not have approved if they had known about it.

Pat Wallace believes that this letter does not reflect badly on Mahr but, on the contrary, displays his candour:

> Even his worry that the Irish aren't big enough to appreciate a collection of that wonderment is accurate and honest. It still applies that so few people appreciate these things . . . . Don't forget, Ireland was tightening in in those days. We became a more inward and introverted people when we were left to our own devices when we left the British Empire. So we have to see Mahr in context. There would have been no school or college in Ireland teaching the value of an Oriental or Far Eastern collection. But of course Mahr's real motivation was that he wanted the money so he could plough it in to Celtic archaeology, which was the real love he had. He knew that Ireland was the repository of the greatest legacy of Celtic archaeology in the world. And he wanted to enhance that to make the National Museum and Ireland a central focus, to become a central world place of learning, and he probably regarded the Bender collection as being extraneous [to that end].[50]

Most recipients of Bender's generosity were simply glad to get what they did, so Bender wasn't used to receiving suggestions as to where to divert his money. We don't know what his response was, but it seems that he sidestepped Mahr's objections and proceeded with his goal of creating an Asian-art collection in Dublin. Mahr felt compelled to fight Bender's cause in Dublin, and by the end of September 1932 he was able to announce that a room in the museum would be made available for a memorial to Bender's mother after all.

Mahr was to supervise the work personally, and so the 'founding father of Irish archaeology' and the 'patron saint of San Francisco's artists' worked together to present an Asian art collection to the Irish public. They were indeed optimistic times, with the dust of the Great War finally settling, and the 'savants' coming together again.

At sixty-eight years of age, Bender would not make the return journey to Ireland to attend the opening. Instead, he sent Mahr a short list of people whom he wanted to invite. It read like a Who's Who of Dublin intellectual life: Bender had personal connections with everyone on the list. Bender's invitees were:

Dr and Mrs Walter Starkie, Dr and Mrs Gwynn (Provost of Trinity College), Dr and Mrs Oliver St John Gogarty, The Misses Yeats – Cuala Press, 133 Lower Baggot St [sisters of the poet and the painter], Senator and Mrs Wm Butler Yeats, Miss Estelle Solomons, [Jewish] artist [and member of Cumann na mBan during the 1916 Rising], and her brother Dr [Bethel] Solomons [Master of the Rotunda Hospital and former Irish rugby international]; George Russell [Æ], and Kathleen O'Brennan, 24 So. Frederick St [writer].[51]

After four years of gifts and letters from Bender, and targets and setbacks for Mahr, the Augusta Bender Memorial Room of Far Eastern Art was opened on 25 June 1934. Éamon de Valera delivered a long speech thanking Bender, who had, as the Taoiseach put it, 'a public spirit all too rare' and had 'increased the cultural possessions of his native country'. He also extolled the virtues of the museum, including its prehistoric gold ornaments, which came from a time when the 'cultural influence of this little island must have been felt over large tracts of the European continent'.[52]

The event would have been of great importance to Mahr. Even though de Valera did not refer to him directly in his speech, it must have been clear to all concerned that it was Mahr's work that had made the Bender Room possible. Furthermore, it was an opportunity for Mahr to meet not just de Valera, but almost every other leading political figure in Ireland. These included most of the Irish cabinet, the Chief Justice, the head of the Garda Síochána and the Attorney General; the Papal Nuncio and key diplomats in the German, US, French, Argentinian, Czechoslovakian, Italian, Polish, Portuguese, Swedish and Spanish legations; and artists Sir John Lavery and Jack B. Yeats.[53]

Less than a month later, on 20 July 1934, de Valera signed an order promoting Mahr from his position as Keeper of Irish Antiquities to Director of the National Museum. Mahr's salary, which had been £740 per annum, was increased to £840, with £20 extra for each year served henceforth.[54]

So was Mahr's promotion directly related to his establishment of the Bender Room? Did the man who had already become Ireland's top Nazi benefit from the patronage of a Jew? To some extent, the answer is yes. Although the steady stream of artefacts from America could only have enhanced Mahr's standing before his bosses in the Department of

Education, he had also implemented much of the Lithberg Report, and was instrumental in writing the National Monuments Act (1930). As well as promoting the conservation of archaeological sites, he introduced the use of photography for archaeological purposes. His 1932 book *Christian Art in Ancient Ireland* had been well received, and he had stressed the importance of folklife and craft traditions in the National Museum for the first time. Moreover, he had introduced scientific methodology to Irish archaeology through his work with the Harvard Mission.

Shortly before his promotion, Mahr also started work with the Quaternary Research Committee, a group he – along with the naturalist Robert Lloyd Praeger and Tony Farrington of the Royal Irish Academy – set up to investigate the history of bogs in Ireland by counting pollen grains. A substantial proportion of the antiquities uncovered in Ireland are found in bogs, and the group felt that the statistical counting of pollen grains could lead to a dating of the layers building up the bog, and hence to the dating of the antiquities found there.[55] Professor Knud Jessen of Copenhagen was brought over to Ireland for two extended programmes of fieldwork, and together the four scientists used their individual disciplines to enhance Ireland's reputation in the expanding field of studies of sub-fossil plant materials. Jessen's palaeo-botanical skills told Praeger about the history of Ireland's flora; informed Mahr about the ages of objects discovered in bogs; and told Farrington about Ireland's emergence from a former Ice Age.[56]

The acquisition of the Bender Collection, as important and celebrated as it was, was only one of Mahr's many achievements since his arrival in Ireland in 1927. He had been recommended for promotion more than a year before the opening of the Bender Room, in March 1933, when the Secretary of the Department of Education, Seosamh O'Neill, wrote to his opposite number at the Department of Finance, James J. McElligott, stating that Mahr's 'personal qualifications are such as to enable the Minister for Education [Thomas Derrig] to accept him unreservedly as a most suitable person for appointment to the post of Director of the National Museum.'[57]

3

NAZI LIFE, 1933–37

Adolf Hitler was appointed German Chancellor on 30 January 1933, and two months later Adolf Mahr became a member of the Nazi Party. Exactly why an Austrian archaeologist living in Ireland felt the need to join a political party in Germany remains unclear; it would have been of no benefit to his career in Ireland, and it was difficult to see what assistance he could offer the party from such a distant and, at that time, poor country. What is certain is that the Nazis put forward a vision for the German people that dovetailed with Mahr's own hopes.

Gustav Mahr sums up his father's political motivation by saying: 'Coming from a nationalistic academic rearing and career in the Habsburg Empire, he was a convinced supporter of the then emerging Third Reich',[1] but other factors added to the intensity of his support for Hitler. Mahr's Nazism, like that of millions of others, was fuelled by the anger he felt about the terms of the post-World War I treaties of 1919. The South Tyrol area of Austria, where Mahr had been born, was ceded to Italy under the terms of the Treaty of Versailles. More importantly, in the Treaty of Saint-Germain-en-Laye (1919), the Sudetenland, where his family was from, was ceded to Czechoslovakia.[2]

Mahr's father was a bandmaster to Emperor Franz Josef and was stationed in many cities throughout the Austro-Hungarian Empire. When young Adolf was born, the Mahrs lived in Trent, which was then in Austria, but is now in northern Italy. Later they lived in Bregenz, Linz and Krakow.[3] Although Mahr was an Austrian national by birth, his attachment to the South Tyrol was not as strong as that to the Sudetenland.[4] The Mahr parents were Sudeten-Germans, and shared a kinship with the three million German-speaking people who lived in the Sudetenland, representing about one-third of the total Czechoslovak population. The Sudeten-Germans maintained a separate identity from the Czechs; they had their own churches and schools, and many felt persecuted by the majority population. Germans on both sides of the border wished for a reintegration of the Sudetenland into Germany. Hitler understood this and used such nationalistic feelings to win support of Germans everywhere.

On 1 April 1933, the same day that Mahr officially became a member of the National Socialists, the Nazis organised a national boycott of Jewish businesses and professional people in Germany. Jews all over the world understood the danger of this latest development, not least Albert Bender, whose aged cousin Gertrude was a teacher in Berlin. He expressed his upset to Dr Mahr, a learned man whom he expected might have shared his concerns: 'there is something wrong with the world. These are days of chaos and the reversion of an enlightened nation like Germany to fourteenth-century barbarism is so atrocious that one loses confidence in the progress of the human race. Such conduct on the part of Germany is turning the hands of the clock backward for four or five hundred years.'[5]

A more diplomatic man might have sidestepped the issue, but Mahr was always known for his direct manner. Clearly he was sensitive to any criticism of the new developments in Germany and could not resist letting Bender know. His reply, sent on 28 April, was a tirade on the problems and injustices felt by Germans in the wake of the Great War:

> I am very grateful also for your renewed kindness to send the nice postage stamps and cards for my boy and I beg to thank you for them most sincerely. But you make it difficult for me to accept such a present when in practically the same letter you speak of my country in terms like 'fourteenth-century barbarism'.
>
> I am as conscious of my German nationality as you certainly are of your bonds of allegiance and if I look at the different territories which I know rather well, territories inhabited by some 16 million of Germans who are today subject to Czech, Polish, etc., rule under the terms of the so-called peace treaties which were announced as the final readjustment of the 'crimes' committed by the Central Powers, you will perhaps understand that I am thin-skinned and that we cannot well be expected to swallow contemptive [*sic*] terms in addition to the mistreatment which was meted out to us.

I had sincerely hoped that the quarrel between the present German government and Jewry would not have entered our correspondence. I have never alluded to the fact that, after all, there was a thing called the Balfour Declaration (1916) [*sic*] by which international Jewry was enlisted to support the anti-German cause and I have never alluded to the fact that the Germans have a very great grievance against America in the question of the 'fourteen points' which were most flagrantly turned into their very opposite without scruples of conscience.

But you are not Mr Wilson or Mr Trotzky [*sic*] and I am not Mr Hitler. Why can we not discuss more pleasant things in which we both take a common and purely human interest?

The Irish have filled the whole world for several centuries with their grievances. Could anybody expect that a people, twenty times as numerous, would silently rot away in misery and humiliation in order as not to disturb the equanimity of the powers and people that are responsible for the 1919 'treatises' [*sic*], that were offered at the point of the sword after a most inhuman blockade which was carried on for half-a-year after armistice, and which put hundreds of thousands of children, old people, etc, etc, to death?[6]

Mahr was clever enough to avoid telling Bender that he was a member of the same party as those who were attacking Bender's co-religionists in Germany. But he was foolish to send such a letter; it could have jeopardised his relationships with both his benefactor and his superiors (it was written on official museum notepaper). Apart from that, his analysis of Germany's grievances was thorough, and he might even have underestimated the numbers who had died in the months after the armistice. Modern estimates put the number who died as a result of the food blockade, which went on for eight months after the armistice, at more than one million lives.[7] Mahr's final paragraph is particularly chilling, since he seems to predict accurately another world war:

> If there is anything wrong in Germany, the main responsibility rests with the powers which promised they would bring about the golden era and which have only succeeded in plunging the world [into] a latent war, infinitely worse than the late war . . . .

The hapless Bender, who had dedicated his life to kindness and helping others, was obviously upset. Mahr had always signed his letters 'A. Mahr', and although his last name is spelled differently, it is similar to the

Irish names 'Meagher' and 'Maher'. So until Bender received this letter from Mahr, he could only have assumed that the senior staff member at the National Museum of Ireland, who had such a deep understanding of Ireland and a strong command of the English language, was an Irishman. One could only imagine Bender's surprise when he realised he was writing to an Austrian. Bender was so flustered that he wrote not once, but twice to Mahr the day he received his letter. The gentle philanthropist, 'the greatest humanitarian I have ever known', according to Oliver St John Gogarty,[8] tried to make amends. The Jew apologised to the Nazi over his comments about Hitler's Germany:

> I cannot allow the day to pass without acknowledgement of your letter of April 28th. It was a great surprise to me, and yet when I consider it, I readily concede your right to consciousness of German nationality, as well as my own right to an opinion on anything relating to Governmental affairs in this chaotic world of ours. The truth is that I was unconscious of the fact that I was writing to a gentleman of foreign origin, but it must be clear to you that I had no wish to interpolate into our friendly correspondence any subjects of controversy. There is no need for it. At the worst it was a slip of the pen, as one might say, on my part for which I wish to tender you herewith my sincere apology. The last thing on earth that I would want to do would be to offend any man on account of something over which he has not the slightest control. I make it a rule to keep away from such subjects but I suppose at some time or other a man is off-guard. It should be remembered that where there is not the slightest intent to wound there can be no real grievance. You are quite right in saying that the world is full of injustices and no nation is exactly in a position to assume a spot-white mantle.[9]

Later in the day Bender sent a second letter because he 'was so distressed this morning' that he forgot to enclose two items relating to the ongoing project to create the Bender Room in the National Museum. Bender finished the letter by saying: 'Once more let me express my regrets at having unconsciously hurt your feelings. This is the first time in my life in which I have been the culprit for such an offence – that it was unconscious should be my best excuse.'

Mahr, a domineering man who was not often burdened by guilt, at first was conciliatory with Bender, but soon he could not resist a second airing of Germany's grievances:

Let me first assure you that there is no question of offence, or mutual excuse or the like. I was not offended, nor did I for a second assume that you had any such intention. It goes without saying that I quite understand your attitude in the matter – what I am concerned with is only the possible repercussion of such controversies on my own relationship to non-Germans, and in that I have ever, and will ever, follow the old principle 'right or wrong, my country'.[10]

This final phrase, one that he uttered many times throughout his life, offers an important insight into Mahr's politics. In his family and military background a high value was placed on a man's discipline and obedience, and that implied loyalty to one's country in the good times as well as the bad.

Adolf Mahr continued to Bender:

The cruelty with which the French have tried to annihilate Germany, under the connivance of most other nations; the world-wide atrocities [sic] propaganda; the political dismemberment of nearly all frontiers; the breach of the fourteen point promises; the moral humiliation crowned by the enforced war-guilt onus; impoverishment, unemployment and the communist threats have created a frame of mind which is completely different from what Germany once was.

Again, Mahr sent a chilling warning to Bender about the rise of Hitler, and the failure of democracy: 'Few people yet understand it and the newspapers do their best to distort it. But it is a fact that the new outlook of the present Government constantly gains in followers and nothing will stop this development which goes away from the old democratic ideal of the nineteenth century. The number of Europeans who will believe in democracy is dwindling.'[11]

Mahr had rejected the idea of democratic government, and would continue to hold this belief until late in his life. Once in a political discussion with his son, he displayed his contempt for Gustav's political liberalism, referring to him as a 'shit democrat'.[12] Mahr also took issue with what he called 'International Jewry'. The Balfour Declaration of 1917 was a promise by the British government to the Zionist Federation for the establishment of a national home for the Jewish people in Palestine. Adolf Mahr felt that the Zionists were repaying this debt by joining with American capitalists in an effort to crush Germany again.[13] He believed

Jews wielded disproportionate power in America, and that they ruled the communists too, so in his view the Jews were ruling both the world's most powerful political ideologies, and steering them upon a collision course.[14] Gustav also attributes his father's views to a fiercely anti-Semitic environment in Vienna. 'He was an idealistic man, reared in Vienna, which had a violently anti-Jewish atmosphere; one of the worst in the world. The Austrian Nazis were far worse than the German ones,' he says.

During his student years in Vienna, Adolf Mahr was a member of his university's duelling club, which in the best tradition of student societies was largely a drinking club. Even then, before World War I, his club refused to duel with Jews.[15]

Another episode – one relating to Mahr's conversion to Protestantism – illustrates the depth of distrust for the Jews in early twentieth-century Austria. Mahr was reared as a Catholic, but became an atheist and left the church as soon as he reached adulthood. His wife, Maria van Bemmelen, was a member of the Dutch Reformed Church, but she too was not religious. Neither was keen on christening their children, but in the sectarian atmosphere of Austria at the time, an unchristened child was sometimes suspected of being Jewish. Mahr once said: 'I don't want a church, I don't need a church. But if you have children and they don't belong to either Catholic or Protestant churches, they are automatically considered Jews.'[16] So Mahr converted to Protestantism and made sure Gustav and Hilde were baptised into the Protestant faith. This move away from Catholicism made life more difficult for Adolf Mahr in the post-war years.

There were other elements in Mahr's early adulthood that may have made him more susceptible to Hitler's call. He had first-hand experience of the crippling impoverishment and unemployment that he mentioned to Bender. The economy was so poor in Austria that Adolf and Maria needed the financial support of her parents from the earliest days of their marriage. Writing in Dutch in a 1921 letter to the van Bemmelens, Mahr thanked them for their recent gift of Dutch florins, which he richly appreciated because German and Austrian money was deflating so quickly. His salary from the museum was already low, but decreasing owing to the rapid inflation. He had resorted to selling books from his library to pay for food, but found the inflation so severe that the next day the money he had received had lost half its value. 'You get paid and immediately run to the store to buy bread, because next day it is worth nothing'.[17]

In this desperate time, the Jews were seen as part of the cause. Maria Mahr wrote to her father in Holland, describing the influence of the Austrian Jews as being 'terrible'. 'Although they are only a small part of the population they have everything under control.'[18]

In 1923, a year after Gustav's birth, the situation had still not improved. Adolf Mahr wrote to the van Bemmelens:

> Maria is losing weight badly. I'm not sure if it's from bad food, or that she was still breastfeeding the boy. I hope that she will recover quickly now that she has stopped breastfeeding . . . . Maria deprives herself of food in order to give Gustav and me enough. She has no appetite herself and the doctors are afraid she might be developing TB. Fortunately this is not the case; it is because of a lack of good food. She has been a full year and a quarter in the house all the time with the baby. It is time she changes her surroundings. It is too depressing all the time to be locked up at home . . . . I think it's my duty to tell you that Maria is in a bad state. We have to get her out of town for a while so she can have milk and food in the countryside, and doesn't get too depressed about the situation.[19]

Maria Mahr had enjoyed a comfortable background in Holland, and was just twenty when she married the thirty-four-year-old Dr Adolf Mahr. They moved to Vienna at a time when Austria was suffering the effects of Germany's hardships. Austria had less industry than Germany, and relied on tourism from its neighbour to bolster its economy. When this dried up, the Austrian economy joined the German one in a downward spiral. The rapid inflation left city people particularly vulnerable. Rural people could always grow food, but an archaeologist was reliant upon his salary only, and this was decreasing in real terms by the day. Maria was twenty-one when Gustav was born, and Adolf noted that in the year that followed she was like 'a bird in a cage':

> She is becoming too much the slave of the child. I am sorry when I see her looking out the window longing for the long distance and views she would see in Holland. Here, she only sees the dirty backyards of the next houses . . . . Maria has lost 7 kilos since February [it was now July]. We thought she would stop losing weight, but it continues. Although she has stopped breastfeeding, she still loses weight. We are wondering if it is that she's depressed . . . . I am stronger against the hardships: we

Austrians have learned since 1919 how to endure all these hardships. We have more strength. But a Dutch woman like Maria is more upset about this than I am. I always want to give her more of my optimism, and try to make more money with the books, but I'm not always successful.[20]

Under the circumstances, it should not be surprising that a year later, in the sixth month of her second pregnancy, Maria miscarried.

Two other episodes in Mahr's young adulthood may have hardened his attitude, and made him more susceptible to Hitler's call. In 1906, Mahr did voluntary military service in Salzburg, where he was awarded the rank of lieutenant in the Kaiser's army.[21] But later, during his student days, while engaged in a duel with a Croatian student, he suffered a sword injury to his right elbow. Some important ligaments were cut and Mahr was never able to straighten that arm again. His wounded arm prevented him from being called into active service during the Great War, something that may have led to pent-up nationalistic feelings. Coming from several generations of military men, and having trained in the Kaiser's army, Mahr was probably disappointed to have missed his chance to serve his country in war, and may have tried to compensate by being extra-nationalistic in later life. Incidentally, the duelling injury probably saved Mahr's life. Most of the regiment to which he had belonged was drowned in a battle along the Danube near Budapest.[22]

The second episode relates to his romantic life. Maria Mahr was Adolf's only wife, but not his only fiancée. Long before he met Maria, he had courted a woman in Vienna during the years of the Great War. At the time, an army man (even ex-army men like Mahr) needed to prove they were financially strong enough to support a wife and children before they could get permission to marry. This wasn't possible for Adolf Mahr, who had chosen a scientific career, which in the Vienna of the time did not pay well. It seems that any union between Adolf and the woman was also strongly opposed by the Mahr women, principally his mother and older sister, probably because they believed her to be beneath his social station. She wasn't good enough to become Mrs Adolf Mahr. Adolf eventually ended the relationship, and as a consequence, the woman drowned herself in the Danube. From that time, until the end of his life, he always wore the watch she had given him while their relationship was still strong.[23]

Despite Adolf's Nazism, and opposition to 'international Jewry', he did not seem to have difficulty in dealing with individual Jews. He maintained friendly relationships with Bender and many other Jews, while still perceiving 'international Jewry' as an enemy group. 'There was, he felt, an international Jewish conspiracy against Germany,' says Gustav Mahr. 'They were the enemy. But Mr Bender was not international Jewry; he was doing other things, and was a good man. And my father tried to be a good man too.'

In the Mahr home at 37 Waterloo Place, Hilde's Jewish friends were welcomed. 'I had lots of good school friends and all of them, except for Terry Meagher, were Jewish children,' says Hilde. 'I felt the same as them, and my parents never objected that I brought them home, and that we played together.'

But wasn't there a conflict between this and her father's political standpoint? 'He would not let us feel a conflict,' she says. 'He would say the Jews are a big group that influence world politics, and also German politics, but he also respected every Jew as a person.'

This two-tiered approach may have seemed logical in the early years, but as the Nazis stepped up their violent campaign against Jews in Germany and Austria, where did Mahr's allegiances lie?

'If he lived in Germany there is a possibility that he would have recognised what was happening,' says Gustav. 'But you must remember that there were very many Germans and Austrians who right into the 1930s, and right up to the beginning of the war, were absolutely convinced that Hitler was the best answer that we could give. And at last we were again respected everywhere because we built up a large army, and we were somebody again.... He went along with Hitler but so did most of the world too, including [British prime minister Neville] Chamberlain. And that was in 1938. So before that time, what else could you expect from Mahr?'

The Nazi issue was never again mentioned in the Bender-Mahr correspondence. Bender went on making his donations, and Mahr continued to form them into a special collection. Bender invited Mahr to California and Mahr responded thus:

I wish I could adopt your suggestion and drum up some excuse to go to California, but I am afraid it will not materialize in the present year and probably not within the next few years. Sooner or later, however, I hope to annoy American audiences in several towns with a very bad lecture. As soon as the present economic depression is over, and there is a more hopeful prospect of entering into negotiations, I shall apply to a few friends in different American towns to see whether a lecturing trip could be arranged. I would like to do so because I dare say there is a lot to learn from American museums in the way in which they attract visitors, serve public and science alike and carry out their research and techniques.[24]

Mahr, of course, was far too busy to go on a lecture tour of America. His museum work, which had always filled his life, now had to share his energies with his political work. In 1934 he and some others from the German colony set about creating the Irish branch of the Nazi Party. There was a small but growing number of Austrians and Germans living in Ireland during the 1930s. Most of them, like Mahr, had been brought to Ireland by the Irish government to fill professional roles. The community numbered about five hundred, and about thirty (approximately half the adult males) joined Hitler's party.[25] The membership was predominantly male, in line with the male-dominant ethos of the Nazi Party. So although Maria Mahr was married to a Nazi, she herself was not a member. The female party members were usually students visiting from Germany, often having joined in order to qualify for student grants.

Mahr and other Dublin-based Nazis formed the Irish branch of the Nazi Party in 1934. The group elected Colonel Wilhelm Fritz Brase as its first chairman. But when Brase, a German who was director of the Irish Army School of Music, wrote to his military superiors seeking permission to lead the group, the reply carried a suggestion that make a choice; either the Irish Army or the Nazi Party. Brase chose the former,[26] which cleared the way for Mahr to become the group's first *Ortsgruppenleiter*, or local branch leader.

Other prominent members of the group included Wolfgang Hahn, a consulting engineer based in Fitzwilliam Square, Dublin; Karl Krause, representative of the AEG company in Dublin; Franz Winkelmann, director of the Irish Glass Bottle Manufacturers Ltd; Otto Reinhardt, director of the forestry section of the Department of Lands; Robert

Stumpf, a radiologist at Baggot Street Hospital; Oswald Müller-Dubrow, a director at the Irish section of the Siemens-Schuckert company; Karl Kuenstler, a technician at Siemens-Schuckert; Helmut Clissmann, who was head of the German Academic Exchange Service, which arranged most of the study trips to Ireland by German university students; the Dutchman Henri Broekhoven, who was a director at the German-owned Siemens-Schuckert company; and Heinz Mecking, a manager at the Turf Development Board, who arrived in Ireland in 1936.[27] The group's meetings were mostly conducted in a German social club behind the Court Laundry in Dublin, although individual members also frequented the Red Bank Restaurant, which was owned by a German couple, Mr and Mrs Schubert. Another favourite gathering place for the Nazi group was the Kilmacurragh Park Hotel in County Wicklow, which was run by another German, Charles Budina.[28]

The Irish Nazi group fell under the auspices of the British Nazi organisation, lead by Otto Bene, a German shampoo salesman who had been based in London since 1927. Bene had first heard about Hitler while on holiday in Germany in 1930, and had been particularly impressed that the Nazis were interested in recruiting Germans who lived abroad. He joined the fledgling London chapter in 1931, and within five months he became *Ortsgruppenleiter*. The following year, Bene became *Landesgruppenleiter* – leader of the Nazi Party in Britain and Ireland. This was a full-time salaried position, which allowed him leave his job with the chemical company and devote his time to building the Nazi organisation in Britain.

Showing great flair in his new role, Bene expanded membership in Britain from around a hundred to roughly 350 in 1936. By then, he had helped to establish chapters in Ealing, Birmingham, Bradford, Manchester, Liverpool, Cardiff, Doncaster, Hull, Glasgow and Dublin. Bene visited Ireland at least twice: in 1933, when the Nazi group was formed in Dublin; and in 1935, when he was photographed beside Mahr at the sixtieth birthday party of Colonel Brase, at Brase's Sandymount home. The same year, the Irish Nazis seceded from the British body so as not to offend the new de Valera government, which was unhappy about any Irish organisation being subservient to a British one.[29] This shift did not lessen the close contact between Mahr and Bene, however, and the two remained friends for many years.

Despite the popular notion that the role of a Nazi abroad was to recruit citizens of their host country to the National Socialist cause, one of Bene's roles in Britain was to prevent non-Germans from joining the group. The Nazi Party in Britain was a German organisation for German immigrants and for 'old Germans' (British people of German descent), rather than for 'alien' nationals or races. And while Bene had contact with leading members of the British Union of Fascists, such as William Joyce[30] and Sir Oswald Mosley, he saw to it that ordinary Nazi members did not, as he put it, 'fraternise with members of fascist organisations' in Britain.[31]

Nevertheless, by April 1936, the security services in Britain had become concerned about Bene's expanding organisation. One secret report from the Foreign Office to Sir Russell Scott of the Home Office said that it was the organisation in general, rather than the individual at the head of it, which was dangerous: 'While I think you will agree with me that the chief danger of such an organisation would arise in time of war, yet I do feel very strongly that we should consider and decide on a policy with regard to it in normal times.'[32]

The Home Office was particularly concerned about the 'old Germans', who, as naturalised British citizens, might be ideal for espionage: 'In the event of war between Great Britain and Germany, after all German subjects had been deported, the "old Germans" . . . would remain in this country as ready-made machinery for the organisation of sabotage and espionage work.'[33] Home Office officials were also concerned that Bene was 'working for the creation of a pro-German feeling in Great Britain . . . done as part of a policy whose ultimate object is to neutralise Great Britain and separate her from France.'[34]

Mahr had not yet prompted such concern among the security authorities in Ireland. He strengthened his political position by becoming head of the *Auslandorganisation* (AO) in Ireland, an international organisation founded in 1931[35] for the promotion of trade links between Germany and other countries. After the Nazis took power, it became a special agency of the party responsible for the supervision of Germans abroad,[36] and was the most important agency for gathering information from other countries.[37] Although it was not a secret organisation, its functions included monitoring political developments and German nationals in the host country, and providing suitable candidates for espionage.[38] Every AO district leader, including Mahr, was responsible for drawing up a monthly report on the local political situation. These reports were forwarded to the Foreign Office in Berlin.[39]

Mahr had one more hurdle to clear before becoming the dominant German figure in Ireland: the German Legation. Under normal circumstances, the minister (ambassador) at the Legation, as the leading representative of the state, would have had greater power than Mahr, who was merely the local leader of Germany's ruling political party. But as Hitler gradually abolished the political opposition to him, the party and the state became synonymous; for Mahr, this provided the opportunity for the *Ortsgruppenleiter* to outrank the minister.

Mahr is believed to have played a part in the demotion of two members of the Legation staff. The first was Dr Georg von Dehn-Schmidt, whose stay in Dublin finished in 1934. Shortly before he left Ireland, Dr von Dehn-Schmidt made the usual round of farewell visits to diplomatic colleagues. When saying goodbye to the Papal Nuncio at the nunciature in the Phoenix Park, he knelt to kiss the Nuncio's ring. The incident was photographed by a press photographer, and Mahr forwarded a copy to the notorious Julius Streicher, a virulent Nazi who was later found guilty of crimes against humanity at the Nuremberg Trials, and was executed.[40] Streicher published the photograph in his racist newspaper *Der Stuermer*, which, he often claimed, Hitler always read from the first page to the last. The Führer called in von Dehn and dismissed him from his new position in Bucharest, saying that, by kissing the Nuncio's ring, he had acted in a manner unworthy of a German representative abroad.[41] Mahr later denied any involvement in von Dehn's dismissal. 'In fact, no Éire [Irish-based] German had [been involved in von Dehn's dismissal],' he said.[42]

Von Dehn's replacement in Dublin, Wilhelm von Kuhlmann, fell ill, and was superseded briefly by Dr Erich Schroetter in 1936/37. Dr Schroetter, too, somehow fell foul of Mahr, and was removed from office.[43] The next in line to assume the top job in the German Legation was Dr Eduard Hempel, who took over the position in 1937 and remained there until Germany's final military defeat eight years later. He would have been aware of the fate of two of his predecessors, and Adolf Mahr's role in their downfalls. Hempel's position was further weakened by his not being a true Nazi, if he was one at all.[44] He joined the party in the summer of 1938 – probably only to advance his career. Adolf Mahr, it seems, was now Hitler's top man in Ireland.

Mahr, through his frequent trips to London, was on good terms with the new German ambassador to Britain, Joachim von Ribbentrop, a senior Nazi who later became Hitler's foreign minister. In May 1937, Mahr was the official guest from the Irish-German community at the coronation of King George VI in London.[45]

With a branch of the Nazi Party established, the members decided to involve their children too. Many of the expatriate German and Austrian members were concerned that their children were growing up in an English-speaking environment where they lost touch with the German language and customs. The most obvious way of remedying this situation was to establish a Hitler Youth movement in Ireland.

Hitler Youth, and its female equivalent, the League of German Girls, were established in 1933, and all German youth clubs existing at the time were brought under its control. By 1935, close to 60 percent of German young people were members: children were expected to apply for membership by 15 March of the year of their tenth birthday. Special attention was paid to a child's 'racial purity', as well as the background of their family, before they could gain admittance to the Jungvolk (junior division). They would remain there until the age of fourteen, and then could become full members of the Hitler Youth or the League.[46] The Mahr children were in the *Jungvölk* section; although by 1936 Gustav was old enough to progress to full Hitler Youth membership, he did not make the changeover. The rules about membership of these organisations were more relaxed in Ireland than in Germany.

Hitler wanted the Hitler Youth boys to have 'a violently active, dominating, brutal youth'. He said: 'I will have no intellectual training. Knowledge is ruin to my young men.' In contrast, the girls' training prepared them to be 'carriers of the National Socialist world-view'. They were to dedicate themselves to comradeship, service and 'physical fitness for motherhood'.[47] Despite Hitler's ambitions for a 'brutal youth', many of the organisation's activities were closer to those of the ordinary youth clubs that pre-existed the Hitler Youth: activities in which members took part included arts and crafts, making model planes, journalism and music. Camping trips and visits to foreign countries were also arranged.

In Ireland, the organisation consisted of about a dozen children who, in the beginning, met in a shed behind the Mahr home, and later gathered at the German Legation. The leaders were German students who had come to Ireland to study, and who, according to Gustav, were 'Nazi infected'. The girls in the group were led by Trinity College student Nona Keitel, the tall, blonde daughter of General Wilhelm Keitel, Hitler's chief military adviser during World War II. Her boyfriend, Bruno Wagler, also a Trinity student, looked after the boys.[48] The highlights of the Hitler Youth calendar were the annual two-week-long camps, which took place in Hampton Hall, Balbriggan, County Dublin, from 1935 until 1938, and in Charles Budina's hotel in Kilmacurragh, County Wicklow, in 1939. Hampton Hall, situated about thirty kilometres from Dublin and adjoining what is now the public park at Ardgillan, was a large, run-down mansion on a derelict country estate, flanked by rolling hills to the west and the Irish Sea to the east. The estate was then owned by a German firm that made the premises available to the German Association. When the Nazis tightened their grip on all things German after 1933, the company provided the estate free of charge to the Hitler Youth group as well. The group went on night hikes, sat around campfires, sang traditional German songs and learned how to march.

Gustav was sometimes put on night duty, where his responsibilities were to ensure that the fire stayed lit and to look out for intruders. 'And we did a lot of bathing and dashing around, cooking and exercising with sticks,' he says. 'The leaders tried to imbibe us with the culture of Nazi Youth of the time. But it was pre-military training in a harmless fashion.'

'It was more fun than anything else,' says Ingrid. 'I was the youngest. They would carry me on their shoulders during walks, and took me swimming . . . . The older ones saw Leni Riefenstahl's film about the 1936 Berlin Olympic Games [*Olympia*], and I'd hear them all bawl "Heil Hitler". My brother had to look at it, but me, a brat of six, seven or eight, would have disturbed everyone, so I was allowed play outside.' Ingrid was the family rascal, and one night she crept down into the building's pantry to steal oranges!

Photos of the Irish Hitler Youth camps illustrate how much out of line the Irish organisation was from its parent organisation in Germany. They show Irmgard Schubert, a half-Jewish German child who had been adopted and raised by the Schubert family, which owned the Red Bank restaurant, a favourite haunt of ex-pat Germans. Dora Hayek, whose mother was a daughter of a rabbi, also went on the camps, as did Guenther Stumpf, whose mother was Jewish.[49]

In Easter 1936, the British Hitler Youth group came to visit its Irish counterpart. The two groups of young Hitler supporters stayed at Hampton Hall, where they took part in drills, hikes and other activities. After a few days in Balbriggan, the group embarked on a 'cultural tour' of Ireland, led by Dr Mahr. The Nazis liked to emphasise the Celtic blood of Germans, and Ireland, the great reservoir of Celtic archaeology, made for a most suitable classroom for the two groups. Mahr took the children to the passage tomb of Newgrange and to the fifth-century monastic settlement at Monasterboice.

The British group was numerically stronger than the Irish one, and they had full Hitler Youth uniforms, whereas the Irish group wore only blue scarves with a knot. The Irish-based children did not wear uniforms because their parents were lukewarm about the indoctrination of Hitler Youth: according to Hilde Mahr, they wanted to keep it more like an ordinary youth club. She says that her mother was also unwilling to put her children in uniform because of the costs involved, and that her father did not care for uniforms either, believing that children should not be indoctrinated. He felt that children should be given 'more freedom to find out for themselves . . . . He wanted us to know and learn German, and feel German, and also Dutch. He didn't like to see me going to the Brownies because he said that is [indoctrination by] the English High Church,' she says.

Such a gathering of young Nazis will surprise many of today's readers, but no secret was made of it at the time. The *Irish Press* reported on the meeting of the Irish and British groups under the headline 'HITLER YOUTH – COUNTY DUBLIN HOLIDAY CAMP ENDS':

> A party of Hitler Youth who had been in camp for a fortnight at Hampton Hall between Skerries and Balbriggan, County Dublin, dispersed yesterday when German Legation officials paid them a farewell visit. The party numbered about twenty-five boys and girls, most of them children of Germans living in Dublin, some from England, and a few from Germany. Herr Bruno Wagler, a German student, was in charge. A portrait of Hitler hung inside the house, while over the porch the crossed flags of Germany and the Hitler Youth were entwined with palm.[50]

Christmas was a particularly important time for the Germans, and also for the Dutch, who celebrated the feast of St Nicholas on 6 December each year. The Mahr children enjoyed the two sides of their heritage by celebrating both occasions. Every year their house at Waterloo Place was decorated with a large Christmas tree that was laden with hand-made sweets and silk paper. Presents were placed under the tree, and the room was then locked for three days before a grand family opening on St Nicholas' Day.

The Mahr home became a meeting house for Germans and Austrians studying or working in Ireland. At Christmas, there were always several German students who couldn't get home, and they became guests of the Mahrs instead. Ingrid says that friends of the family often called their house 'Café Mahr', because there were so many people coming and going. Maria Mahr made a Santa Claus costume, and it was worn by one of the students each year. The children best remember the tall Hans Hartmann wearing it; he arrived from Germany to learn the Irish language in 1937. Outside the home, the Mahrs celebrated Christmas with the rest of the German colony at elaborate parties in two of Dublin's grand hotels, the Gresham and the Royal Hibernian (the latter now gone). The *Irish Times* gave an account of one such party in 1936. The report shows how open the German Association was at the time, and how strongly it was influenced by Nazi ideology:

> A very enjoyable Christmas party was held by the German Association in Dublin at the Royal Hibernian Hotel, Dublin yesterday afternoon. It was a real family gathering and the spacious salon of the hotel was crowded to its utmost capacity by pleasantly excited German children and their parents and other adult visitors. They were welcomed by Herr Müller-Dubrow, President of the Association, and were then entertained to tea.
>
> Afterwards there was a musical programme. A delightful Christmas play was prepared by Frau Mahr, was acted cleverly by the children of the colony, while women of the colony sang 'We Three Kings'.
>
> The Reverend Wilhelm Tanne [whose house in Malahide the Mahrs rented during the summer months] said that when a German saw green leaves at Christmas time or smelt the spicy Christmas cakes he began to weave the dreams of a thousand years. Germans felt that they must gather together at this festival time. They could be glad, he said, that

their country was not only strong and united again today, but that there was no room for bitterness there. At one time some fifty thousand Catholic and Protestant nuns looked after the poor at Christmas time, but one million of their compatriots were collecting today, so that no one would be cold or hungry in Germany at this season. If a stranger asked how that had been done, and what was the recipe for it, one must answer that there was only one recipe for a German – Adolf Hitler, who had put into effect what could not be done by books, and certainly not by newspapers.

The proceeds of the lottery held that evening would go towards the Winter Help Fund and everyone would be glad when that money would find its way to the Führer to save the poor of Germany from cold and suffering.

He said that they should look at the lights on the Christmas tree which they saw in that room as the children looked at them. The children understood the spirit of Christmas, but the grown-ups were apt to forget it. They had souls, into which the light came through Christmas, and that was why they sang the Christmas hymns with all their hearts.

The children were presented with toys and gifts.

The party concluded with the singing of 'Deutschland über Alles' [the German national anthem] and the 'Horst Wessel Lied' [the official marching song of the Nazi Party].

Among those present were: Dr A. Mahr and Frau Mahr, Colonel Fritz Brase and Frau Brase, Herr K. Schroetter (German Chargé d'Affaires) and Frau Schroetter, Herr R. Wensel (Consular Secretary, German Legation), Frau Wensel and Fraulein Wensel, Herr F. E. Muller (Chancellor, German Legation), Dr and Frau Stumpf, Fraulein von Caprivi, Mr and Mrs Broekhoven, Dr Micks, Commandant Sauerzweig, Mr R. M. Smyllie [editor of the *Irish Times*], Herr and Frau Joebges, Mr B. Muntz, Herr Schubert, Herr Clissmann, Mr D. Devlin, Mr Seán O'Cuiv, Mr T. Forbes and Mr P. Kirwan.[51]

The photos showed Santa Claus distributing gifts to Hansel and Gretel, represented by Master Gunther Stumpf and Miss Ingrid Mahr.

It is unfortunate that the newspaper style of the era did not include the name of the reporter beside the report; furthermore, it is written in such a way that it is difficult to know where the Reverend Tanne's opinions end and those of the reporter begin. It can be assumed, however, that the editor of the *Irish Times*, R. M. Smyllie, wrote the piece: not only is he listed as one of those who attended the event, but he was also a

German-speaker. The speeches, according to Hilde Mahr, were all delivered in German.

Robert Maire Smyllie was born in Scotland and educated at a school in Sligo, and at Trinity College Dublin. He was on a tour of Europe when World War I broke out and was interned in Berlin – a sojourn that he claimed had completed his education. While in Berlin, he learned German, and later covered the Versailles Treaty talks as a journalist.[52] Adolf Mahr must have been very interested to hear Smyllie's first-hand accounts of this important conference. The *Irish Times* had always regarded itself as 'the newspaper of record'; at the time, it was owned and run by an Anglo-Irish elite. From the report of the Christmas gathering, it seems that he was still by that time under Hitler's spell, but during the war he became anti-German and pro-British.

Hilde Mahr recalls the parties as being great fun for the children. 'Apart from the plays, which I didn't like, there [was] lots of singing, games, treasure hunts and raffles,' she says. 'But I couldn't stick that indoctrination. And as you see here – "the strong and united Germans", "no room for bitterness" . . . – that's indoctrination.'

The Christmas party in 1937 followed a similar formula, but differed from the earlier one in some important respects. Both the *Irish Times* and the *Irish Independent* reported on the celebrations, which took place in the Gresham Hotel on O'Connell Street. In excess of two hundred people attended and, once again, the event was hosted by the German Society 'for members and their Irish friends'. The Nazi Party was not mentioned in the reports. The *Irish Independent* reported that 'the Swastika and the Tricolour draped the balconies', and the *Irish Times* said: 'smaller flags embossed with the Swastika were evident along the balconies and on the tables.'

Following tea for the adults, and lemonade and sweet cakes 'to gladden the hearts of the children', the gathering was entertained by a reading in verse about Christmas, childhood and fairyland by Herr E. Boden of the German Legation. A group of the children then performed 'A Christmas Dream', written especially for the occasion by Fraulein Wenzel. The cast included Helmut Clissmann (head of the German Academic Exchange Service), the three elder Mahr children and several other children; the performance was accompanied on piano by Colonel Fritz Brase.

The German Minister, Herr Edward Hempel, welcomed the guests, thanked the members of the cast, 'and asked those present to rise and salute the Leader and Chancellor of the Reich. With right arms raised in the Nazi salute, the gathering sang 'Deutschland, Deutschland über Alles', the 'Horst Wessel Lied' and 'A Soldier's Song'.'[53]

It is difficult to believe that Éamon de Valera and his advisers would not have noticed this public display of support for a foreign power. Those in attendance were listed in the newspaper reports; the attendees included several high-ranking civil servants and other people whom de Valera knew personally, including Adolf Mahr, Fritz Brase, Eduard Hempel and other members of the German Legation; Otto Reinhardt, and Michael McDunphy, whom the *Irish Times* described as 'Secretary to the new President of Ireland'; R. M. Smyllie; Friedrich Weckler, who had worked on the Shannon hydroelectric scheme during the 1920s, and then at the state-owned Electricity Supply Board; and Miss L. Dalton, Secretary of the Belgian Consulate.

Perhaps de Valera felt that this group did not constitute a threat to Ireland at that time. Mahr's Christmas parties were not illegal, and there were no apparent links between Mahr and the IRA, or any other subversive groups in Ireland. The Nazi persecution of Jews and other groups on Continental Europe had not carried over to Ireland, and, while Hitler had announced his plans to dominate eastern Europe to his closest aides at the Hossbach Conference only a month earlier, publicly he was talking peace.

Both Mahr and de Valera could be forgiven for not seeing the grave dangers posed by Hitler's rise to power. After all, millions of Europeans had also failed to spot the signs. Although Hitler threatened Germany's neighbours, it was credible that he intended only to undo the Treaty of Versailles. As he was to demonstrate, much of this could be achieved without bloodshed. In 1933, Hitler stated that to have a war would be 'infinite madness', and that 'no European war could improve the unsatisfactory conditions of the present day'. He also said that a new war would cause Europe to 'sink into Communistic chaos'.[54]

Of course the Machiavellian de Valera, who lived the maxim 'keep one's friends close, and one's enemies closer', may have felt it prudent to maintain good relations with Hitler's top man in Ireland. By this time, Dev's son Ruairi was working in the National Museum. Dev and Mahr worked in adjacent buildings, attended some of the same functions, and shared an interest in politics and archaeology.

De Valera was also careful to maintain a good working relationship with Minister Hempel. Germany was at the time squaring up for a fight with Britain, and de Valera probably adopted that other maxim: 'my enemy's enemy is my friend'. De Valera may have reasoned that a showdown between Britain and Germany might help to bring about a united Ireland – as long as Germany won.

For his part, Mahr may have felt that, by being so open about his activities, he could not be accused of anything sinister. And why shouldn't he display his affiliations? At the end of 1937, Hitler had been in power for nearly five years, during which time Germany had once more become a major power. Germany now had a powerful voice on the international stage, and the Führer had declared an end to the Treaty of Versailles a few months earlier. As Hitler's star rose, so did Mahr's; for as long as Germany was not threatening Ireland, Mahr's career was under no threat. It appeared that he could successfully work for one country while swearing allegiance to another. But as the world moved closer to war once again, dark clouds were gathering on the horizon. So far, Mahr had managed to ride two horses, but he would soon have to choose one, or fall off both.

4

IMPENDING WAR, 1937–39

In early 1936, German troops occupied the previously demilitarised Rhineland – a move denounced by Britain, France, Italy and Belgium – and later that year the Italian and German governments signed a mutual-defence pact. In November 1935, Hitler had introduced the Nuremberg Laws, which restricted Jewish political and social life. He promoted a bitter anti-Semitic campaign that stirred up hatred against Jews, encouraged violence against them, and campaigned for the picketing and closure of Jewish businesses. When this caused a public outcry abroad, there was a movement to boycott German goods in several countries. The German government retaliated by organising a boycott of Jewish businesses. Jewish doctors and judges were also dismissed from their positions, Jewish students were removed from universities, and German citizenship was withdrawn from persons of 'non-German blood'.

The Nazi Party in Ireland was out of step with its parent group in Germany. The German colony would have been left in a particular dilemma. Ever fastidious about their food, the German community found the commonly available Irish soda bread too coarse for their palates and preferred German rye bread. This caused a difficulty because, while the group was bolstered by leading academics and corporate directors, there wasn't a baker in its midst. The expatriate Germans and Austrians soon realised that the only place they could get bread that was to their liking was at the German bakers of Dublin's Jewish community.

Mahr, because of his Nazi Party membership, could not be seen to be buying goods from a Jew, or have other party members know that he was dealing with a Jew, so Gustav was often sent over to the Clanbrassil Street area, the centre of the Jewish community in Dublin. Gustav says that the

Jewish baker often joked bitterly that, if he had wanted to kill the entire Nazi Party in Ireland, all he had to do was poison their bread.

Life continued as normal at the National Museum. In line with further restructuring, Mahr handed over care of the Bender Room to the Keeper of the Art Division, a Mr Westropp, in 1935, and so there was little need for him to be in direct contact with Albert Bender. Nonetheless, Mahr suggested that they stay in touch as friends: 'I will consider it a privilege if by continued direct correspondence between you and me, I will be afforded the facility to uphold our personal touch, because not only is it incumbent upon the Director to carry on in such important transactions with the donor personally, but it gives me also the pleasure to keep you informed about whatever progress our work makes.'[1]

Divesting himself of the Bender Room did little to lessen Mahr's workload. Now close to fifty years of age, he was showing the strain of juggling both an archaeological and a political career, the travelling that these roles entailed, the demands of rearing four children, and being a heavy smoker and coffee drinker. In the spring of 1936, he fell ill and was confined to bed for several months. Mahr loved to drink milk fresh from the cow when he was travelling in the countryside, and it is thought that he contracted a virus from drinking unpasteurised milk. In June 1936, he dictated a letter to Bender to explain that: 'I am now a sick man and it is now six weeks that I am laid up, but it looks as if it would take about the same time until I can go abroad for a convalescence . . . . The collapse, by the way, as I can see now, did not come of a sudden. All during the last eighteen months or so my ability to work was on the wane and the feeling of being unable to cope with my work has been a great moral pain to me throughout this time.' He thanked Bender for the 'beautiful kimono' that he had sent to Mrs Mahr, and concluded by saying: 'I can only hope that you are keeping well, and I am looking forward very much for the time when our correspondence will again be more regular than it has been during the recent past.'[2] Bender, now aged seventy, was also ill, probably with gout, and the Mahrs sent their best wishes to him for a complete recovery.

In July 1936, Adolf Mahr was still too ill to work, and instead dictated his numerous letters each day to Maria Mahr, who also found her time taken up with keeping relatives informed of his recovery, attending to visitors, and entertaining the Harvard excavators, who visited every

Sunday with news of their digs. 'It is their fourth and last season in Ireland . . . ' said Adolf Mahr, through his wife. 'We are sorry that the cooperation is coming to an end because it has been such a stimulating feature in the scientific life of the country during the past years.'

It was now high summer, and Maria expected her husband to be well enough to take a Continental holiday in August: 'We want it badly, because this July in Dublin is characterised by most abominable weather. Had this country only Californian sun it would be a paradise.'[3]

Although Mahr returned to work in August 1936, his correspondence and other duties were still in arrears as late as December. He, his department and others in his immediate circle adopted a system whereby they systematically tackled a certain portion of the backlog each day. He explained some of his difficulties to Bender:

> To make matters more awkward one of my assistants [Raftery] was promoted Keeper in another Division, and another assistant [O'Riordain] has been elected to fill the newly established Chair of Celtic Archaeology in University College Cork. I feel I have reason to be proud that it was a pupil of mine who won this distinction, because it shows that the Museum is not only doing normal museum work but is even fulfilling the functions of a University. But all the same it means that my staff has been reduced from three to one at a time at which I scarcely know how to do the most urgent work.[4]

In April 1937, a German battleship, the *Schleswig-Holstein*, sailed into Dun Laoghaire Harbour. Built in Kiel in 1905, she was one of the few big cruisers that Germany was allowed to keep after World War I; the rest of its fleet was scuttled in Scapa Flow, off the coast of Scotland. The ship had been reconstructed in 1926 and was in use by the new German government as a training ship for cadets. It stopped in Dublin for five days on its way back to Wilhelmshaven after visiting ports in Central and South America. Thousands of people lined the shore in Dun Laoghaire to see the warship. The *Irish Press* described the scene:

> As soon as the warship anchored, she hoisted the Tricolour and boomed a salute of twenty-one guns. This was replied to by a battery of artillery from the Free State Army at the East Pier, and, the return salute completed, the battleship hoisted the German flag with the Swastika insignia in the centre.[5]

The German ship rested in Scotsman's Bay just outside the harbour. Several officers came ashore and were met by Herr Schroetter, the German chargé d'affaires; Captain Eamonn Butler, the liaison officer with the Irish army and father of the well-known wildlife film-maker Eamonn de Buitléar; and Captain Richard McGurk, acting harbourmaster at Dun Laoghaire. Over the next four days, ten thousand people were brought aboard by motorboat to inspect the ship,[6] including Terry de Valera, another son of Éamon. Terry de Valera recalls seeing the captain, who looked 'so handsome, resplendent in that attractive German naval uniform complete with his decorations. Over his shoulders he wore a black cloak with red lining.'[7] Ireland's Hitler Youth members were also invited on board. They were fed cake and drinks, and had a competition to see who could eat the most cake – which Gustav won![8]

That afternoon, Captain Krause, the commander of the ship, called at the General Headquarters of the Free State Army at Parkgate Street, where he was received by Minister for Defence Frank Aiken and Major General Michael J. Brennan, Chief of Staff. They also visited the Lord Mayor of Dublin in the Mansion House.[9] The following day, Captain Krause and officers were met by de Valera at the Offices of the President of the Executive Council.[10] It was a brief meeting – it lasted just fifteen minutes – and it seems that Dev did not pose for photographs with the men. Meanwhile, the German Legation gave a tea party in the Royal Marine Hotel in Dun Laoghaire for about a hundred and fifty of the ship's crew. Adolf and Maria Mahr attended, along with many other members of the German colony.

On the third day of the ship's visit, Mahr got his chance to entertain. Three hundred of the ship's officers, cadets and crew were taken by the German colony by bus and car to Glendalough, County Wicklow. The group picnicked near one of the lakes, and heard a talk by Mahr, presumably on the subject of the monastery that St Kevin founded there in the sixth century. In the afternoon, they went for tea in Charles Budina's Kilmacurragh Park Hotel, where they danced to music performed by the ship's orchestra. The following day, Mahr led eighty-five cadets on a tour of Monasterboice and Newgrange[11] – the same places he had brought the Hitler Youth groups a year earlier.

On 13 April, the Dublin soccer team Bohemians played a team from the German warship at Dalymount Park. The score was Bohemians 2,

Schleswig-Holstein 1, with goals from Barry Hooper and Kevin O'Flanagan for the home side, and Herr Bischaf for the visitors. The *Irish Independent* suggested that the Irish won because the Germans 'had no big guns in the for'ard turrets'.[12] On the final day of the group's visit, Frank Aiken, Secretary of the Department for External Affairs Joe Walshe and other government officials were present at a lunch on board the warship. The Mahrs also attended, along with others from the German colony. Two thousand people lined the front at Dun Laoghaire to watch the ship's departure.[13] Just before the ship sailed, the Free State tricolour was lowered and the Swastika raised again as the band played 'Deutschland über Alles' and 'The Soldier's Song'.[14]

The *Irish Times* said of the visit:

> The obvious friendliness, of officers and men alike, induced a response which should do much to make the younger Germany better known and more clearly comprehended than has been possible in the absence of such visits .... Whatever views the citizens of Saorstát Éireann may have upon the political philosophy of contemporary Germany – and we do not think that there is much doubt on that score – they demonstrated in the clearest possible way that politics are not permitted to interfere with the cordial – even enthusiastic – reception of our German guests .... For a week these young seamen, many of whom will be the officers of the German Navy of the immediate future, have been with us and of us: we hope they remember us kindly and come again.[15]

Just over two years later, the *Schleswig-Holstein* again made news, this time while paying a courtesy visit to the Polish garrison island of Westerplatte, a sea fort located at the mouth of the Vistula near the city of Danzig (modern Gdansk). Although the garrison was a strategic point on the Baltic Coast, the Poles allowed the 'training ship' to come deep inside its defences because it seemed to be only marking the anniversary of the Battle of Tannenberg. At 4.47 AM on 1 September 1939, the ship opened up its massive main guns, firing at near-point-blank range and zero elevation at the fortified island. Shortly afterwards, a hidden cargo of Marine assault troops disembarked and launched their main attack on the garrison. At the same time, thousands of German troops were pouring over the border into Poland. It was the first day of World War II: the *Schleswig-Holstein* fired the first shots of the six-year campaign.[16]

Bolstered by the visit of the German warship, Mahr's strength recovered sufficiently for him to write what many regard as his finest piece of work; indeed, the current director of the National Museum, Pat Wallace, describes it as 'the greatest paper ever written by an Irish archaeologist'. In 1937, Mahr had become president of the British Prehistoric Society, one of the most distinguished roles in archaeology and prehistory. Neither before Mahr, nor in the years since his tenure, has the position been held by an official from an Irish museum.[17] Mahr's presidential address to the Society in October 1937, entitled 'Some Aspects and Problems in Irish Prehistory', was an account of the archaeological work that had been done in Ireland over the previous ten years. More specifically, it was an account of Mahr's work during that period, and showed him to be a scholar of world standing. He wrote to Bender: 'I had anticipated that the text in printed form would run into something like 30 or 40 pages, and I sat down immediately to write it, but it is already now 120 closely typewritten pages, and it will run into something like 130 or 140 printed pages . . . . I am concentrating every free quarter-of-an-hour upon it.'[18]

Professionally and politically, life could hardly have been better for Mahr. After ten years in Ireland, he was now an internationally recognised Celtic scholar, and in just five years the Nazi Party had made Germany a powerful nation again. In March 1938, German troops marched into Austria and brought about the Anschluss, the union of the two countries. The move, which reversed the Treaty of Saint-Germain-en-Laye and flew in the face of the Treaty of Versailles, must have delighted Mahr, but it terrified Austria's Jews. The Nazis immediately closed Jewish community newspapers and confiscated Jewish homes, and within a month all Jews had been ejected from their jobs. Vienna, the city where Mahr had studied and worked before coming to Ireland, had been home to 165,000 Jews, the third-largest Jewish community in Europe after Warsaw and Budapest. By September, some 60,000 of the city's Jews were destitute, and there was a wave of suicides in the Jewish community.[19] The Jewish community in Vienna could trace its history back to the twelfth century, and had produced several figures of world renown, including Sigmund Freud, his fellow psychoanalyst Alfred Adler (who originated the concepts of the inferiority complex and overcompensation), the composer Gustav Mahler and the writer Stefan Zweig, who, despairing of what he saw as the end of civilisation, fled the Nazis and committed suicide in Brazil in 1942.[20] Now leading Jews, including the Chief Rabbi, were forced to scrub the streets of their native city.

The Anschluss was not mentioned in Mahr's correspondence with Bender. Shortly after the event, he told Bender that his wife had developed gall-bladder, appendix and hernia problems, and that she required an operation. 'As you have always been so very kind and full of human understanding,' he wrote, 'I thought I [would] let you know of my worries just as a friend.'[21] On Mahr's part, this was of course a case of ignoring the elephant in the room. He must have been mindful of Bender's dire prediction, made in 1933, that the rise of Hitler indicated a reversion by Germany to fourteenth-century barbarism.

A week after Mahr's letter to Bender, a plebiscite was held on the 'reunion' of Austria and Germany. Voters had to answer the question: 'Do you agree to the reunion of Austria with the German Reich carried out on March 13 and do you vote for the [Reichstag] list of our Leader, Adolf Hitler?'[22] As local party leader, Mahr gathered together the adult members of the German and Austrian colony on a hired boat, and sailed from Dun Laoghaire Harbour into international waters three miles offshore. There, in the Irish Sea, with Ireland and its capital city still in view, the members of the colony voted 99 percent in favour of the union of Germany and Austria – a result that was similar to that of the German plebiscite.

The annexation of a small nation by a larger, more powerful one should have sounded alarm bells for de Valera and his government. The Chief's own newspaper, the *Irish Press*, stated in its editorial on the Anschluss that Hitler 'had wiped from the map a Nation with a history going back for more than a thousand years, and he is convinced that he can do so with perfect impunity'. It continued by saying that there 'is not one of the smaller States which do [*sic*] not feel that their security, if not their very existence, is threatened.'[23] Despite these fulminations, Mahr and his Nazi Party seemed to be under little pressure to cease their activities in Ireland. It is possible that Dev felt political sympathy with Mahr: the fact that Germans had been cut off from their homeland by artificial boundaries drawn up just twenty years before had parallels with the nationalists in Northern Ireland. Indeed, Mahr wrote in 1938 that the Irish had 'their own Sudeten in Northern Ireland'.[24]

Two months after the Anschluss, the continued closeness of de Valera and Mahr was illustrated in an incident described by Mahr's assistant Howard Kilbride-Jones:

> The sum of £200 had been set aside to cover the examination of the mound at Drimnagh, but after one month's digging I realised the sum was totally inadequate for a complete examination. Since Mahr was on holidays with his family at Youghal, I went to see Robert Corish [sic], the Minister for Finance. He was most unsympathetic. He told me that I must make do with the £200, whereas I estimated that the sum required to complete the excavation was £600, so I sent a telegram to Mahr. He arrived by the first train next morning and over lunch he asked me for a full explanation of why I wanted the extra money. Satisfied with my account, he said 'we will go and see Mr de Valera', who was then Taoiseach. We knocked on Dev's door at 4 PM and Mahr related the whole story, starting with Mr Corish's refusal. At 4.30 PM we left with Dev's personal cheque for £400. As we left, Mahr turned and asked: 'Is this coming out of your pocket?'
>
> 'No,' replied Dev, 'I shall get Mr Corish to reimburse me.'
>
> We left laughing. Next morning I walked into the Bank of Ireland in St Stephen's Green and presented the cheque. The cashier looked at me as though it were a hold-up.[25]

It is difficult to imagine such an event happening in modern times; the sum involved was the equivalent of about half a year's salary for Mahr. The conclusion that must be drawn from this episode is that, even though de Valera was leader of the country and Minister for External Affairs, he seemed to have little concern about the remilitarised and expanding Germany, or about Dr Mahr, its local organiser in Ireland.

With Austria annexed, Germany now surrounded Czechoslovakia on three sides. The Czech government understood that it too was in danger of being annexed, not least because nearly three million ethnic Germans – the Sudeten-Germans – lived within its borders. The Sudeten-Germans had been separated from their homeland by the Treaties of 1919 and had had many grievances against the Czechs ever since. For a Sudeten-German like Mahr, this must have been an exciting time: Hitler had won back most of his native Austria, and now his sights were set on his ancestral home, the Sudetenland. In a show of strength, the Czech government mobilised its army on 20 May, on the pretext that Germany was on the point of invading. This had not been Hitler's intention, but he retaliated by drawing up plans for a real invasion of Czechoslovakia, and set an invasion date of 1 October. The world held its breath at the prospect of yet another war in Europe. Into the breach stepped British Prime Minister Neville Chamberlain, and throughout that summer diplomatic efforts were made to avert war.

As international public opinion turned against Nazi Germany, Mahr must have seen the potential problem for the Irish government of having a prominent Nazi in the ranks of its civil service. In July 1938, he wrote to the Secretary of the Department of Education, Joseph O'Neill, to say that he was resigning his position as local leader of the party in order to avoid embarrassing his superiors:

> I beg leave to notify you in a semi-official way that I have sent in to Party Headquarters in Berlin my resignation as leader of the very small local group of the German National Socialistic Party.
>
> I have always held the opinion, and I cling to it, that in occupying this position I have undertaken nothing which, even in the slightest degree, ever could be incompatible with the oath of allegiance which binds me as a civil servant of this country, a country which has honoured me significantly by entrusting me with the custodianship of its national treasures.
>
> On the contrary, the National Socialistic outlook on life implies that a German citizen living abroad, who submits to party discipline, is a more desirable guest of the country of his sojourn than a German who shuns such voluntary discipline. The Party rules strictly forbid any interference with matters political abroad and prescribe a codex of honesty and straightforwardness also in private matters, which is wholly praiseworthy and contains nothing sinister or detrimental to mutual goodwill amongst decent men. In my particular case I was able to obtain 'Humboldt studentships' for some fifteen Irish students at German expenses, amounting to some £1,500.
>
> Hence I have a perfectly clear conscience as to the time during which I was the 'Dublin Nazi No. 1' or, as some people may now prefer to call it, 'Public Enemy No. 1'.
>
> But I am not blind to the fact that this position of mine might conceivably embarrass the Minister, and thereby the Government, at a time at which an almost apocalyptic foreboding of international disaster is deliberately fomented for the purpose of psychologically preparing another crusade against the liberty of a great nation.

> Hence, I think it is now my duty to remove what some people may think to be an incompatibility, in order to show my sincere wish not to put a Department, which has so far trusted me, any longer in a position which they may think unfair to them.
>
> This is no council of fear. I am perfectly aware of the fact that nothing I may or may not do at the present moment can obscure or undo my openly professed adherence to the Party. But it may ease off ill-feeling which may exist if I resign of my own free will from the local leadership and if I do not turn a deaf ear to hostile comments, which might not stop short of talking of ministerial connivance.
>
> I beg to acknowledge gratefully that the Government was punctiliously fair towards my natural national feelings in never having raised the matter. For this I tender my most sincere thanks. It confirms my conviction that the incompatibility does not exist as far as fair-minded people are concerned.[26]

Mahr's letter concluded with a request that O'Neill notify the Taoiseach in his capacity as Minister for External Affairs, and also bring his resolution to the attention of the Minister for Education. O'Neill duly forwarded the letter to the relevant departments.[27]

It is important to note that Mahr offered to resign only as 'Dublin Nazi No.1' – that is, as leader of the Nazi Party in Ireland. He did not offer to resign from the party, or the *Auslandorganisation*, or from any other related group. Moreover, he did not rule out the possibility of becoming 'Dublin Nazi No. 2' or 'No. 3'. It is difficult to understand why the Irish government failed to insist that he resign from the Nazi Party altogether. No member of the civil service was allowed to be a member of an Irish political party; should the rule not be extended to all political parties? Had the government curbed Mahr's political activities, it might inadvertently have done him a big favour, given what was to follow. As in the case of Colonel Fritz Brase, Mahr might have been able to leave the organisation in an honourable manner, and live a relatively trouble-free life as a museum man, safe from the prying eyes of the Garda Síochána and Military Intelligence.

Instead, it appeared that Mahr remained Dublin Nazi No.1, something that cast him as a liar as well as a political risk. Four months after his 'resignation' letter to O'Neill, in a memo marked 'secret', an unnamed Garda told 'Joe' [presumably Joseph Walshe, Secretary of the Department of External Affairs]: 'Evidence shows that Mahr is again acting as *Ortsgruppenleiter* of the *Ortsgruppe* of the *Auslandorganisation*. [We] don't suggest action at this stage as evidence could not be used if he denies it.'[28] The garda also added that a letter from Mahr to Helmut Clissmann about books was signed: 'Heil Hitler, Dr Mahr, Party Group Leader'.

The Garda's findings make it look as though Mahr had lied to O'Neill in his July letter. In truth, it seems that Mahr had genuinely tendered his resignation but that it took many months before the resignation was ratified in Berlin. That December, a senior *Auslandsorganisation* director, Admiral Menske, visited Ireland to arrange a replacement for Mahr as head of the AO. Heinz Mecking, chief adviser to the Turf Development Board, was to be the new leader of the Nazi Party in Ireland.[29]

Two months later, Ernst-Wilhelm Bohle, the AO's founder and leader, wrote to Mahr to formally accept his resignation:

> Party comrade Dr Mahr,
> From your different notes and letter from Jan 3, 1939 this year I have seen that it is no more possible for you to remain leader of the *Ortsgruppe* Dublin.
> I release you herewith from your post of *Ortsgruppenleiter* Dublin, and thank you for the work you have done in this occupation in the best possible way, as *Stuetzpunkleiter* [key person], a position you held for five years.
> With best wishes for your future, and comradely greetings,
> Heil Hitler!
> Bohle, Gauleiter[30]

Mahr appears not to have informed his superiors when his resignation was ratified in February 1939; they understandably continued to believe that his July 1938 letter was a sham. As far as Irish Military Intelligence was aware, Mahr was still the local leader of the party, and was therefore in breach of a promise to his employers that he would stand down. Not surprisingly, they stepped up surveillance of Mahr's movements and his mail.

In October 1938, under the terms of a peace agreement imposed upon the Czech government by Germany, Britain, France and Italy, the Sudetenland was ceded from Czechoslovakia to Germany. It was a great victory for Hitler: with no loss of life, and through his personal determination and cunning, he had united nearly three million Germans in the Reich. He was now the master of central Europe; he toured the Sudetenland, where he was received by large, cheering crowds.

Chamberlain also received a warm welcome when he returned to England. He stepped off his plane and waved a piece of paper, which had been signed by Hitler, and announced that he had brought 'peace in our time'. It seemed that Chamberlain's diplomatic skills had averted another war in Europe; although he had made several important concessions to Hitler, he had received assurances that Germany had no further territorial ambitions. Around the world, people breathed a sigh of relief. Mahr, too, must have been relieved: he had averted any difficulties with his employers by resigning from his political activities; the threat of war had been lifted; and his ancestral home, the Sudetenland, had been secured for the Reich. If only his impressions had been matched by the reality.

There was little cause for optimism for Jews living under Hitler's rule. Some 50,000 fled Austria between April and November 1938,[31] while more than that number were trying to emigrate – to any country that was willing to take them. The problem was exacerbated by the anti-Semitic regimes that existed in neighbouring countries: the Polish authorities blocked the return of about 20,000 Polish Jews from the Reich in the spring of 1938; the Romanian authorities passed a law that stripped 225,000 Jews of their nationhood, and Hungary also passed a series of anti-Semitic laws. Mussolini ordered all foreign Jews, about 20,000 in number, to leave Italy. Even the Czechs, living in fear of their country being further dismembered by Germany, dismissed Jews from the universities and the professions.[32]

The President of the United States, Franklin D. Roosevelt, called an international conference at Evian-les-Bains in France in July to devise ways to deal with the various refugee crises. Thirty-two countries were represented; Frank Cremins, Irish envoy in Geneva, led the Irish delegation. Cremins told the conference that Ireland was effectively closed to refugees. He explained that Ireland's new industries were 'not yet capable of absorbing the regular increase in our population' and that the country could make 'no real contribution to the settlement of refugees'.[33]

Later that year, de Valera 'relaxed' the rules regarding refugees. He permitted visas to be granted, but only to those who could produce evidence that they would be allowed to re-enter their native countries at a later date. This clause effectively excluded the vast majority of Jewish asylum-seekers: Hitler's government was hardly going to promise to readmit expelled Jews at some time in the future. Furthermore, de Valera left the matter of German refugees in the hands of the Irish Minister in Berlin, Charles Bewley, a strong supporter of the Nazi regime and an anti-Semite.[34] In practice, Ireland was closed to Jewish refugees.

Ironically, in a desperate attempt to get into Ireland, one of Mahr's former colleagues in Austria, Dr Alphons Barb, asked him for help in escaping the Nazis. True to Mahr's seemingly complex attitude towards Jews, in October 1938 Mahr sent Albert Bender a most unusual letter in which he (a Nazi) asked Bender (a Jew) to help his friend Barb (a Jew) to escape from the Nazis:

> I beg to appeal to you today in a matter of human appeal.
>
> As you may remember I came over to Ireland eleven years ago from Vienna, where I spent all the earlier periods of my scientific education and work. During the last years of my stay in Vienna I had a very considerable amount of co-operation with a Jew whose name was Dr Alphons Barb. I had a very high opinion of this man's abilities, and I watched myself the earlier stages of the development of a small local museum into an all-embracing provincial museum which was practically solely due to his energy and ability. When I saw the local collection first in 1921 it had been a business of a small single room; when I left Vienna in 1927 it consisted of five rooms; when I saw it again in 1932 it was a building with some twenty exhibition galleries containing Archaeology, Art History, History and Folk Collections and Natural History Collections. Today, I dare say, this Museum must be even larger and better.
>
> Dr Barb started as a goldsmith's apprentice and then turned to classical and prehistoric archaeology, and took his degree finally in classical archaeology. This is now many years ago and since then he has become a truly encyclopaedic worker. I have a great opinion of his work and ability, and I like him also personally. He married in about 1930 (a Hungarian Jewess) and has two children. Recent developments in Austria deprived him of his career, and recent developments all over Europe preclude any possibility of finding for him a position anywhere in Europe. I have tried very hard in many countries to find some position for him, and all efforts were in vain.

Dr Barb is willing to take any job and so is his wife, who would not mind becoming a cook or domestic servant, or, indeed, anything in order to provide for the children. Dr Barb has a good command of the principal languages and would be of very great value to any employer, be it a Museum or another scientific institution, or even in any ordinary business.

I beg of you most sincerely to think it over whether you think anything could be done for this man.[35]

One can only guess at how desperate Alphons Barb must have been when he solicited help from Mahr: it is likely that he knew of Mahr's party affiliations. Likewise, one can only wonder at Mahr's dilemma. The removal of Jews from public life in Europe might have seemed agreeable to him when they were nameless and faceless people hundreds of miles away, but what must he have thought when his own friends were the victims? Even if Mahr disagreed with Hitler's anti-Semitic measures, there was little he could do to change them. There was no mechanism for protest within the party, and resigning from his position would have made life difficult for him if he ever wanted to live or work in Germany. Perhaps he reverted to one of his favourite sayings, 'My country right or wrong', or another, which seems particularly appropriate in the context of purging a new territory of one's 'enemies': 'When you plane wood, you get shavings'.

On 20 November, Mahr wrote to Bender again, this time including this letter from Barb:

Dear Dr Mahr,

Many thanks for your most recent letter and all the trouble you take in my case. I am writing also to Mr [Robert] Briscoe [a Jewish Fianna Fáil TD] as suggested by you, be it for no other reason but not to neglect even the slightest chance.

A few weeks ago I have written to the Relief Committee in New York and have asked [them] to secure for me any position whatsoever which could enable me to enter American soil. The reply was very friendly, but they said that it would be against the law to secure a position for a foreigner before he is in the country. I would have to be first in the possession of an immigration certificate; an affidavit is required. The Relief Committee asked whether I had any relatives or good friends in [the] USA. They further said that, if I mentioned these addresses, the

Committee would get in touch with them, in order to secure an affidavit for me.

I have neither relatives nor friends in [the] USA. Can you think of anybody whom one could persuade to give such an affidavit on my behalf? I am sure I would not be any financial burden for the person who signed an affidavit for me, because I would certainly find some sort of a job.

Yours sincerely,
Dr Barb

It is not known what help, if any, Bender provided to Barb, or whether or not Mahr's intervention was of any practical value to the Jewish archaeologist. Barb, his wife and their children got to England in the spring of 1939, with the help of the Warburg Institute in London, which then employed him. The Institute was, and remains, home to a famous German art collection that had been assembled by the art historian and collector Aby Warburg of the Jewish banking dynasty. Warburg had created a library of more than sixty thousand books in his native Germany, but with the advent of the Nazis, the Warburg Library was transferred to London, where it is said to have revolutionised the study of art history in Britain.[36]

Another of Mahr's Jewish acquaintances wasn't so lucky. Dr Arthur Kohn of Vienna contacted Mahr, who in turn got in touch with Frederick May, a composer who lived in Donnybrook and who campaigned on his behalf. May told Mahr in a May 1939 letter:

> The Irish government wouldn't allow him [Kohn] take up a musical or business position, even supposing he could obtain one . . . the only conditions of his residence here are that [he and his family] must be temporary, that he must do no work here, and that somebody must guarantee his maintenance . . . . I just had an idea that you might know some rich philanthropist who specialises in such work; though if such a person existed in Ireland I should be as astonished as I should be pleased.[37]

The same week, Erich Stadlen of the Society of Friends (Quakers) German Emergency Committee in London wrote to thank Mahr for his efforts on Kohn's behalf, and explained that Kohn was likely to get a visa to the United States within two years. He pointed out that Kohn's 'position is desperate', however, and that 'anything you can do to find a guarantor [would be] much appreciated.'[38]

It is not known if Mahr was able to help Kohn, but a month later a delighted Kohn wrote to Mahr to thank him for his efforts:

Dear Friend,
   Today I merely take time to report that the miracle has happened and that a Reverend in a little English locality has undertaken to harbour myself and my wife until my departure for America. I have heard from Herr May meanwhile that you also were making other efforts on my behalf and I thank you very sincerely accordingly. We will in this way hardly see each other again but I hope that you will write to me once more. I will hardly get away from here before two or three months.[39]

This letter is particularly poignant because it is dated 14 June 1939. The 'two or three months' that Kohn needed before making his departure to England, and from there to America, coincided with the outbreak of war and the closure of shipping lines to Britain on 3 September. He was rounded up in Vienna, and transported to Theresienstadt concentration camp in September 1942. He died there in April 1944, aged fifty-four.[40]

Despite pledging peace internationally, Germany continued its campaign of terror against groups of its citizens domestically. On 7 November 1938, a Polish Jew assassinated a senior civil servant in the German Embassy in Paris, and in 'retaliation' the Nazis ordered the destruction of all Jewish places of worship in Germany and Austria. The attack had been prepared long before; the assassination simply provided a pretext for it.[41] On 9 November, in a period of just fifteen hours, a hundred Jews were murdered, and more than 170 synagogues and 7,500 Jewish-owned businesses were destroyed. Streets were covered in broken glass, and as a result the day was named 'Kristallnacht' – 'crystal night'. It was decided that the Jews would have to pay for the damage they had 'provoked'. The six million marks that insurance companies paid for destroyed Jewish premises were confiscated by the state.

The writer and diplomat Hans Bernd Gisevius suggested that the word 'pogrom' was not strong enough to describe what had happened on Kristallnacht. 'Not a Jewish home remained unmolested, not a Jewish business unplundered, not a synagogue unburned,' he said, by a mob that 'vented its emotion on defenceless people.'[42]

Although the attacks provoked worldwide condemnation of the German government, Gustav Mahr does not recall them being discussed in the Mahr home: 'I was sixteen years old, and I can't tell you anything about them. I did not hear about that. He [Adolf] kept that absolutely away from us.' It is understandable that he spared his children such news, but the question remains whether Adolf Mahr was aware of the severity of anti-Semitism in Germany.

Gustav contends that the poor state of communications left people in Ireland unaware of many of the happenings in Europe; he also notes that his anti-Semitic relatives in Austria had little interest in raising the alarm: 'All these things were hidden; we didn't see that from Ireland. We didn't get news, nobody warned us what was going on. Our relatives in Austria were delighted with the situation, and others didn't write anything [to us].'[43]

Moreover, the Jews themselves were eager to avoid international criticism of their government. A case in point involved Julius Pokorny, who had been dismissed from his chair of Celtic Studies in Berlin University in the wake of the passing of the Nuremberg Laws of 1935, but was eager to avoid public criticism of the move.

Pokorny was born in Prague in 1887, and in 1920 became Professor of Celtic Studies in Berlin University. He was both a staunch German nationalist and an Irish nationalist, and was a propagandist for the Gaelic League in Ireland in the years before independence. James Joyce honoured him by making him a character in *Ulysses*, and he also appears in poems by Myles na gCopaleen and Osborn Bergin.[44] Pokorny was a Catholic, born to Catholic parents, but in 1933 it emerged that his maternal grandfather 'had not been Aryan'. This led to Pokorny being dismissed from his position in the wake of the promulgation of the Nuremberg Laws in 1935. He sought help from the Irish government, through his friend Richard Best, Director of the National Library. Even though he described his case in detail to Best, he implored him not to discuss the contents of his letters with anyone, 'as it may land me in prison'.[45] He warned Best:

> Now, in replying, please be careful not to say anything that may hint at the suspicion that I had complained about Germany. Also, for heaven's sake, be careful in talking to friends – a little slip, and they have spies everywhere. Nobody ought to guess that I am not completely happy. It is too dangerous.[46]

In his comments about spies, Pokorny was probably referring to Mahr. Best, in his capacity as Director of the National Library, would have had a close working relationship with Mahr: their offices were barely a hundred metres apart.

In January 1939, Pokorny again wrote to Best, this time telling him that he had, so far, defied the new law which compelled Jews to have the letter 'J' stamped on their passports. The procedure was intended to make it more difficult for Jews to escape into Switzerland, and this was one of Pokorny's last hopes: 'By the way, please be extremely careful in talking about my being "on the run", for fear that Mahr may hear of it. Also, I am supposed to have given up my passport long ago. If they find me out I'll go to prison at once.'[47]

The cloak of secrecy that surrounded the treatment of 'non-Aryans', in which the victims themselves were often complicit, suited both the German and Irish governments. Secrecy ensured that there was little public pressure on the Irish government on this issue, and as a result not a great deal was done to provide practical help to anyone in Pokorny's position. The Irish government eventually provided a visa for Pokorny, and he was able to escape into Switzerland in 1943, but the help was very little, and very late. Pól Ó Dochartaigh, in his biography of Pokorny, wrote: 'The treatment of Pokorny is a case study in Official Ireland's studied avoidance of the burning European issue of the 1930s and 1940s, with only one or two individuals prepared to do anything, and then only for Pokorny their friend rather than for refugees as a whole.'

Albert Bender must have wondered about his friend in the National Museum, who had so strongly defended the German government just five years earlier and was now trying to help Jews defy that same government. It would have been an appropriate time to refer to some of Mahr's old letters and ask him for an update on the 'misery and humiliation' suffered by the German people after the Great War, and whether or not 'international Jewry' was being defeated by the persecution of tens of thousands of ordinary Jews. Perhaps he should have reminded Mahr of his meeting with other anthropologists in 1932, when he had concluded that 'the present national and racial boundaries are a thing of very late origin and that the boundaries which separated mankind in the Stone Age are probably more important than the make-shifts of our present politicians.'

Instead, Bender sent a cheque to the playwright Kathleen O'Brennan in Dublin so that she could buy a Christmas gift on his behalf for Maria Mahr. O'Brennan used the money to buy Mrs Mahr a fur cape, saying: 'As you sent so much money I wished to get her something which she would appreciate, and so I found that her heart's desire was a fur.... As I knew you wished to give her the utmost pleasure I did so, and now the lady is arrayed in a fur cape, that was her dream for some time.'[48]

Bender's cheque also covered a present for O'Brennan, who bought a new rug for her flat, where she was due to have a party to celebrate the Abbey Theatre's acceptance of her new play. The play was scheduled for production in February 1939, but she worried that she had 'not been sent the contract yet, and they are such erratic people at the Theatre that I never believe anything until I have it sealed and closed.'[49]

O'Brennan did not refer to political events in Europe, or to Mahr's Nazi activities, which were well-known in Dublin, but she did shed light on their mutual friend Oliver St John Gogary, a prominent literary figure in Dublin social circles at the time:

> I suppose you know he has left Dublin for London. His big libel case nearly swamped him, in the sums against him. Of course he will never stay in London. He belongs to Dublin and I don't think he liked going in the end. Unfortunately, his wife is a bit of a snob, and she believes that the daughter may have opportunities over there, which she would not in Dublin. She was not popular here.... But we all expect him back, as he went over before, and returned pretty quickly. He has no business capacity. He opened a big hotel in the West of Ireland [Renvyle House Hotel in County Galway], or rather with his wife's money, for she is fairly well off. With anyone else it would have been a success, but with Gogarty, who could never forget he was one of the wits of Ireland, he just spent his time wandering about with the Lords and Earls.[50]

Meanwhile, the Irish security services broadened their surveillance of the German community in Dublin. On 26 November 1938, Garda Superintendent T. Maher noted that 'the following Germans gathered at [Heinz] Mecking's house, "Nanville" on Beechwood Road [in Ranelagh] and remained in conference for seven hours: Karl Kuenstler, 58 Merrion Square; Karl Krause, 58 Merrion Square; Robert Stumpf, 25 Pembroke Park; and Dr Mahr, 37 Waterloo Place.' He also noted that, at the Nazi Conference in London held over the weekend of 29 November, Mecking, of the Turf Development Board, was selected to represent the Nazi Party of Dublin. Regarding Mecking's return to Ireland, Maher said he 'arrived in Dun Laoghaire from Holyhead on a mailboat with Max Civtor Francis Trankner, a British subject, son of Oskar Paul Trankner, a German national of 20 Lower Pembroke Street.'[51]

In February 1939, the secretary of the Department of External Affairs, Joe Walshe, wrote a secret memo to Éamon de Valera. The memo was prompted by a visit Walshe had received from the German chargé d'affaires, Henning Thomsen. Walshe told Dev that Thomsen 'began by remarking that, although he liked the nice spring weather, he found the people not so congenial as the Norwegian people amongst whom he had just been living. The reason for that was that the Norwegians were a Protestant people, and the Irish were almost exclusively Catholic, and, for that reason, dominated by the Clergy.'

The point of Thomsen's anger was a newspaper report on a comment by Bishop Brown of Galway, 'who accused Germany of violence, lying, murder and the contemning of other races and people'. Thomsen contended that Dr Brown had no right to discuss Germany's affairs, and also protested about a leading article in the *Irish Press* which attacked the anti-Christian element in Germany. Thomsen asserted that the government should accept some responsibility for the attacks, because the paper 'was controlled by the government party'.

Walshe pointed out to Thomsen, and relayed to de Valera, that:

> the existence of a Nazi organisation in Dublin, no doubt representing the views he had expressed to me in the course of our interview and having as its chief member and organiser an employee of our State [Mahr], was not calculated to improve relations between our two Governments. I could hardly imagine his Government tolerating a similar organisation in Germany. He answered, not quite in so many words, that the Nazi organisation in Dublin was really none of our business.

Walshe said that he had predicted for three years that the measures that had been taken against the Catholic clergy in Germany were bound to cause antagonism in Ireland and that when the position of Dr Mahr 'as head of the Nazi Cell in Dublin became a matter of public controversy', the government would be placed in an awkward situation. He said that, although Mahr had indicated his intention to resign as head of the 'Cell' in July of the previous year, Dr Hempel had told Walshe that he 'had not yet resigned his position owing to unforeseen difficulties, but was about to do so immediately, and that he was to be replaced in that position by Herr Mecking, who is an employee of the State under the Turf Board.' Walshe concluded by saying that 'no ordinary Civil Servant is allowed to be a member of a political organisation, and it could not be regarded as an injustice if Dr Mahr were ordered to cease his membership of the Nazi Cell.'[52]

Even though Walshe had been concerned about Mahr's activities since June 1937, it is unclear whether his concerns were ever relayed to de Valera; or, if they were, whether or not de Valera had acted upon his advice. In sending this memo, Walshe put on record the clear conflict of interest Mahr had created for himself: as a member of the civil service, he owed a loyalty to the Irish State, but as a member of the Nazi Party he had sworn allegiance to Adolf Hitler and the Third Reich. Mahr contended in his letter to O'Neill in 1938 that there was no conflict of interest, but as war loomed it was clear that he would have to decide if his loyalty was to Germany or to Ireland.

Mahr and other civil servants who were also members of the Nazi Party had made things difficult for the government, especially since it hoped to chart a course of neutrality in any war. The Nazi group had had three leaders, all of whom were civil servants: the first, in 1933/34, was Fritz Brase, an Irish army colonel; he handed over to Mahr, who in turn handed the reins to Heinz Mecking. To the British, the fact that such Nazi figures enjoyed civil-service positions could be interpreted as meaning that the Irish government was pro-Nazi. Not only was this embarrassing, but it put Ireland in danger of being invaded by the British should relations deteriorate between Britain and Germany.

Following Walshe's memo, the Garda Special Branch and Army Intelligence (G2) stepped up surveillance on Mahr and his group. Letters to his home and the museum were intercepted, copied, resealed and delivered. The Mahr family believe that their parents knew that this was happening, and it contributed to a feeling that they might soon have to leave Ireland.[53] The optimism for 'peace in our time' did not last long after the Munich agreement. On 16 March 1939, German troops occupied Prague, signalling the collapse of Czechoslovakia. Even Chamberlain now felt that war was inevitable. He abandoned his policy of appeasement and called for Britain to rearm.

In Dublin, teachers instructed schoolchildren to pray that there would be no war. Ingrid Mahr recalls that, one day, her teacher in Tullamaine School, Miss Cairnes, made the class 'kneel in front of a newspaper cutting of photographs of Mussolini and Hitler, and we had to pray that these two men wouldn't make war . . . . It was very anti-German.' She told her mother about it, but Maria Mahr said: 'Don't say anything, and do as you're told.'[54]

A week after the occupation of Prague, an unsigned G2 memo said that a German academic in Trinity College, Dr Friedrich Merkel, had been going through the 1937 Shipping Statistics of Éire: 'He made no secret of this and left the book lying around in Trinity staff common room . . . . Both Von Marwych and Merkel admire [the] Roman Catholic Archbishop of Cologne for opposing Hitler'; the writer of the report concluded that they were not violent Nazis. In contrast, the report stated that: 'Mahr is the most ardent Nazi in Dublin.'[55] It also mentioned the case of a German student, Martin Plass, who had arrived in Ireland to work on his PhD on George Russell (Æ) but had neglected to report to Mahr, as all visiting Germans were expected to do. 'He was severely ticked off last year for not reporting to him,' it said.[56]

Given that Adolf Mahr was now a security concern for the Irish government, it seems bizarre, if not comical, that he was called upon to make plans for the protection of the national collections in the event of war. On 23 March 1939, the Irish government set about making plans for its national treasures in the event that Ireland was bombed or occupied by a foreign army. The ARP (Air Raid Protection) meeting was held under the auspices of the Department of Education to discuss alternative accommodation for the treasures in the National Library, National Gallery and National Museum. Captain Lawlor represented the ARP team, and the heads of the three institutions were also present.

The two most likely armies to invade Ireland were Germany and Britain, and yet those that decided the secret hiding place for Ireland's national treasures included Hitler's top representative in Ireland, Adolf Mahr, and George Furlong of the National Gallery, who worked for British Intelligence. The third director, Dr Richard Hayes of the National Library, an expert code-breaker, also worked for Irish Military

Intelligence. Even the head of G2, Colonel Dan Bryan, in his report on the meeting, said he considered it 'funny' that Mahr should arrange ARP protection for the museum against an invading army. Mahr told the meeting that an invasion was unlikely, and that if one did come to pass 'it would be by a highly cultured nation who [sic] would value articles of art, culture etc., as much as we did'.[57]

Bryan added that Mahr wanted a tunnel to be dug under Kildare Street to hide the treasures, but was later convinced that this approach might not offer enough protection. He noted that Mahr had a deep knowledge of Ireland and of aircraft: 'Mahr displayed a surprising and detailed knowledge of the geography of the country; knew all about villages in the west that Drs Best, Furlong, etc. knew nothing of. This can be explained by travel in connection with archaeological, etc. work.'[58]

G2 had an intelligence source, in one of the universities, who was code-named 'Paris'. That source reported in May 1939 that Germans in academic circles had become very unpopular. The three reasons cited were as follows:

> When Professor Mary Macken of UCD and [Irish Times editor R. M.] Smyllie were to speak at a lecture of a visiting German, objections were raised because they were anti-Nazi; when a German in favour of the Nazis lectured, the whole colony was marshalled to attend; when a German Jew gave a lecture, the German colony was ordered not to attend, but Mahr came and sat where he could see all present, his sole purpose being to spy on those who attended.[59]

Surveillance of Mahr's mail yielded little of use to Military Intelligence in the spring of 1939. Some of the correspondence made reference to the trip the family planned in the Ostmark (the name applied to Austria following the Anschluss) that summer. Adolf had secured official leave from the museum to go on an eight-week sojourn in Germany. He was to be a delegate to the Sixth International Congress of Archaeology in Berlin, the sort of event he loved, where 'the savants' could come together and 'lose all interests in what is today miscalled "politics"'. Following his presidential address a year earlier in London, Mahr could expect a warm reception from the delegates, who included top archaeologists from across Europe and beyond. It would be the Mahrs' first family holiday to Adolf's native Austria: the visit represented a chance for them to meet their Austrian relatives for the first time, and to feel German on what was by then German soil.

The third reason for their trip was to allow Adolf Mahr to attend the Nuremberg Rally, which was due to take place during the first two weeks of September. It is unlikely that he told his employers about this when applying for official leave; he had received letters from top Nazi officials, who were looking forward to their great gathering.

In May 1939, Mahr received a letter from his good friend Otto Bene, the former head of the *Auslandorganisation* in London; Bene was by then in Milan, where he was Consul General for Northern Italy. His main project there was to move South Tyrolean Germans out of the area and relocate them in areas of Prussia that Berlin wanted to 'Germanise'. This was part of a plan by Hitler to integrate another three million Germans into the Reich, while avoiding conflict with Mussolini. However, the South Tyrolean Germans were not eager to swap this most scenic area for the flatlands of modern-day Poland, even to join the Reich. Bene was in sympathy with them and, according to Gustav Mahr, successfully delayed the process that he had been employed to expedite. The South Tyrolean Germans did not leave Italy, and the area remains German-speaking to this day.

There is another, more sinister, side to Bene, and this side of him taints Adolf Mahr, if only by association. Although Bene was never charged with war crimes, it is clear that, as the German Foreign Office representative in Holland during the war, he was involved in the deportation of more than a hundred thousand Jews from Holland to the extermination camps in the east, mostly in Poland.[60] G2 intercepted two letters from Bene to Mahr in the spring and summer of 1939. In a letter dated 13 May, Bene accurately predicted that 'Danzig will soon come into the Reich and the Colonies will fall due next year' because 'Ours are better nerves . . . .' He also wrote: 'The thought that one has been able to take part in the great work is very pleasing. I have always felt myself somewhat to blame for the defeat [presumably in the Great War], I mean because I could not do anything to prevent it.' The letter is signed off: 'Heil Hitler'.

Bene's letter of 2 July showed him to be eager to bring his Nazi comrades together before the Nuremberg Rally: 'Please let me know where yourself and [Max] Funk will be staying. . . . As I have since obtained a special engagement I will probably be located during the next two months in Bolzano [in northern Italy] . . . . We should meet at Bolzano or Merano.'

Max Funk was one of the top Nazis in Britain, and wrote to Mahr from his home in Birmingham in June: 'Glad plans coincide . . . . Did you write to PC [Party Comrade] Bene at all? . . . . We will reach Karnten [in the former Austria], about 12th August . . . . For the rest, everything here is in the butter [i.e. 'good']. Politically our malicious minds are satisfied at the moment.'

A long letter arrived in June from Frieda Hayek in Austria. Mrs Hayek was Czech-born, and married to an Austrian, Theo Hayek, who had been managing director of the Irish Sugar Company. When they were living in Dublin, from 1934 until around 1937, the Hayeks had been friendly with the Mahrs. The Hayeks were now retired and living in Gmunden in Austria, and looked forward to the arrival of the Mahrs for a long visit. Frieda Hayek reminisced in her letter about how, when it rained in Dublin, she would often pick up her knitting and 'go to the Mahrs because you were always so friendly and good-hearted.' The Mahrs planned to stay at a lakeside hotel at Millstatt-am-See in Karnten for three weeks, and after that they intended to rent an apartment, in order to keep down costs. The Hayeks were happy to help them find an apartment. Mrs Hayek suggested that Maria and the children should come to her home in Gmunden when Adolf was at his Congress: 'You can play the piano and we'll find other stuff to do . . . . But if you prefer to go to Bad Ischl [a beautiful spa town in the former Austria], then I'll understand.'61

Mrs Hayek went into detail about how much it would cost to cater for five or six people in Austria at that time, and gave prices for coffee, tea, butter, milk and other commodities. She said: 'Come live as Germans among Germans for a while.'

Many people have felt that Mahr's departure from Ireland was not only a holiday but that, in fact, he was fleeing the country, under pressure from Irish security agencies. But in Mrs Hayek's letter, and several others, there is no suggestion that the Mahrs were thinking of anything other than a two-month hiatus. In July, a letter arrived from Auguste Hoernisch, Adolf Mahr's youngest sister, who lived in Bad Ischl. She was married to Franz Hoernisch, a local doctor and Nazi official. The couple had acquired a villa from a Jewish family who had been expelled from the area two years earlier, and that would be the Mahrs' holiday home for the summer. Auguste Hoernisch told her brother:

We began cleaning up the villa yesterday. I never thought I would have to clean up tons of muck after Jews. For two years after the Jews went in 1937 nothing was done. The landlady was such a fool that she let everything go to rack. . . . I have cleared out the villa and the place will be very neat for your visit. I hope you and Maria won't be annoyed if curtains for the windows are lacking. . . . I can always manage four . . . and if necessary the two little ones can sleep on the sofa.[62]

War in Europe had loomed for at least two years: was it not foolhardy to go to Germany amid such uncertainty? Hilde insists that her father did not expect war:

My mother was very much afraid that war would break out. But Dad had met with his friend Herr Funk, who was . . . the Nazi boss in England. Funk said No, there's not going to be war. Hitler is not going to make war. So Dad said we are going on holidays. I remember hearing my parents discuss it before we went. Dad said: 'We are going this summer. Last year we couldn't go because of the Sudetenland annexation, the year before it was the Austrian occupation, and this year we are going because Gustav will be finishing school and then he has to go to study in Germany . . . . When he goes to Germany he has to do his military duty. I don't want him to see his home country for the first time as a soldier. We will go there this summer and meet our relatives, whom we had never met before.

On 19 July 1939, the Mahrs left Ireland and sailed to Germany. Unknown to the family, it would be a holiday from which they would not return. Adolf Mahr sent a postcard to their housekeeper in Dublin, saying: 'We had a splendid sea passage. Hamburg receives us with thunderstorm and torrents of rain . . . . In Donegal we would have got that, but much cheaper.'[63] The Mahrs first stayed at Hotel Lindenhof in Millstatt-am-See, an alpine lake resort in Karnten in southern Austria, near the Italian and Slovenian border. It was no doubt a great time for the children: they met their Austrian cousins for the first time, swam in the Austrian lakes and hiked in the hills. Adolf Mahr's Nazi friends Herr and Frau Funk of Birmingham and Herr Bene from Milan also came to visit. Mahr planned trips to Berlin, to Stettin and Kiel in northern Germany, and finally 'Party Day' on 4 September, according to Maria Mahr's letter to her housekeeper in Dublin. 'I'll probably go to Vienna with the children,' she wrote.[64]

Other correspondence intercepted by G2 suggested that the Mahrs would return at the end of the summer. There was a letter, written in both German and English, to Gustav Mahr, c/o Hotel Lindenhof, from his friend Arthur Forster on 12 August which confirmed they were due to meet up on the steamer *New York*, which was to leave Germany for Ireland in September:

> Thanks for your letter . . . . I am answering quickly so you can write back before I go to Wartheland . . . . In two weeks we go to Germany; Hamburg and then Dresden by train. Then to Saxony, the hive of Germany industry . . . . We will see each other again on the *New York*, and have high jinks. All the best, Heil Hitler, Arthur.

One document that arrived at the Mahr home while the family was away shows Adolf Mahr in a particularly bad light. The German Legation kept track of Germans who arrived in Ireland, those who were leaving Ireland, and those who moved address while they were in Ireland. An updated list was sent to Mahr. Those who were Jewish had the word 'Jude' typed after their name, in addition to male Jews having 'Israel' inserted into their name, and female Jews having 'Sarah' inserted, according to the Nazi edict.[65] In light of the fact that the Nazis kept lists of the names and addresses of Jews all over Europe, and used this information when gathering them for deportation to death camps, this information-gathering appears to be particularly sinister. The Germans knew that there were about four thousand Jews in Ireland. Had there been a German invasion of Ireland, it appears that they would have had up-to-date information on where to find these people.

The list, dated 16 August 1939, showed mostly Jews entering Ireland:

Adressenveraenderungen [changing address]
Herr and Frau J. Marckwald, c/o Mr Concannon, Galway
Karl Lanzendoerfer, Sandymount
Herren H. Israel Heymann, c/o J Neville, Leeson Park (Jude)

Abgaenge [leaving]
Karl Meixner
Frl. Dorothea Kraus
J. Hoven
H. & F. Broehl

H. Krull
Frl. Resi Dorn
Pater Wilhelm Schulze
Pater Friedrich W. Weber

Zugaenge [entering]
H. & F. Gerhard Israel Rosenberg, Terenure (Juden)
Herr Philipp Israel Moddel, Rathmines (Jude)
Herr Gerhard Israel Schloss,
 c/o Irish Steel Ltd, Haulbowline, Cork (Jude)
H. & F. Wilhelm Luz, Crumlin
Herr Dr Stefan, Israel Lendt, Mountjoy Sq (Jude)
Herr Siegmund Israel Liffman, c/o Mr Mewey, 18 Belgrave Sq (Jude)

The racist magazine *World Service* arrived in Mahr's mail while they were away; as advertised on the masthead, it was 'published in seven languages, non-profit' for the purpose of 'accurate distribution of news items collected from the press of the entire world, which deals with the dangerous and subversive activities of international Jewry.' The article headlines included: 'How Jewry agitates for war', 'France begins to see through the Jewish warmongers', 'The Archbishop of York – Warmonger!', 'Jew-lover Ethel Mannin admits Jewish Warmongering' and 'England, the Defender of Jewry'. Most disturbing was a piece about the distribution of Jews in Poland; this article used the official census of 1931, which showed the population distribution of Jews in each district:

	TOWN	LAND
Warsaw	34.7 %	3.8 %
Lodz	31.6 %	2.6 %
Kielce	29.6 %	4.2 %
Lublin	42.9 %	6.0 %

The article noted that 'Jews are scantily represented on the land', explaining this by saying: 'They feel the strain of hard work and drift back to the cities, where they can indulge in usury and other shady tricks.'

Although *World Service* and the list from the Legation hardly reflect well on Dr Mahr, it is conceivable that the magazine arrived unsolicited. Another item of mail, however, was very damaging. A letter from SS officer Friedrich Maier von Weinertsgruen, translated from the German, read:

> Honoured Herr Doctor,
> Many thanks for last letter and I thank you from my heart for your recommendation to Chief Group Leader Schmauser.
> I hope the desired result will ensue.
> As regards myself I may tell you that a certain change has occurred in my mode of life in as much as I have become a head official of the SS since 1st June and am with the Reserve Command of the R.u.S. [Race and Resettlement Office] head office of the Prague Topographical Office.
> The questions referred to are therefore now of greater importance than ever. At all events I thank you sincerely for your efforts.
> Please convey my compliments to your much respected wife and also to the Hoernisch family.
> I remain thanking you once more,
> Heil Hitler,
> Yours,
> Friedrich Maier von Weinertsgruen.[66]

As Ireland's leading archaeologist, Mahr had access to detailed topographical maps, showing rock structures, bogs and other details that would not be included on a common tourist map but would be useful to an invading army. A letter from an SS officer in a Nazi topographical office thanking Mahr for his efforts may have confirmed G2's worst suspicions about Mahr – that he had used his time and position in Ireland as a Fifth Columnist, preparing a German invasion plan for Ireland. The sentence 'The questions referred to are therefore now of greater importance than ever' must have seemed particularly sinister while Europe teetered on the brink of war. This interpretation of the letter informed many people's opinion of Mahr both during this period and in later years.

The reality, however, is somewhat different. Von Weinertsgruen said that he worked at the Bodenamt, which means Lands Department. The G2 translator took this to mean Topographical Office, which has a more military connotation. The significance of the R.u.S. office was also overlooked. The Race and Resettlement Office was the SS section responsible for organising the settlement and welfare of colonists in the conquered and occupied countries in the east.[67] This office had forced Czechs to move out of the German areas of the former Czechoslovakia, in order to bring in more Germans and fully to 'Germanise' these places. Part of this project involved the replacement of Czech street and town names with their original pre–World War I German names. In order to do this, von Weinertsgruen needed old maps of the area: who better to provide them than Adolf Mahr? It could well be that von Weinertsgruen's letter was simply thanking Mahr for his old Czech maps, and did not relate to Ireland.

An examination of the life and death of Maier von Weinertsgruen sheds light on the tensions between the Germans and the Czechs, the principal motivating factor of Mahr's Nazism. Von Weinertsgruen was married to Adolf Mahr's first cousin Melanie Friedrich. He, like Mahr, was a Sudeten-German – and also a minor aristocrat. Von Weinertsgruen came from a family that had agitated against Czech rule in the Sudetenland, and he and his wife worked with a German secret-service agency during the mid-1930s. Shortly after the birth of their daughter, they were arrested and convicted of high treason by the Czech government and sentenced to ten years in separate prisons. While in prison, Melanie contracted consumption; she died a short time after her release in 1937, at the age of twenty-six. Maier remained in captivity until Germany absorbed most of Czechoslovakia in 1939, and he was set free at around that time.[68]

Now in his early thirties, an alcoholic, and probably still suffering the effects of his four and a half years in prison, von Weinertsgruen began working for the SS. Having trained as a farmer, he was placed in charge of confiscated demesnes in eastern Czechoslovakia, also known as Austrian Silesia. He removed Czechs from the management of the land, replaced them with Germans, and secured food supplies for the Reich. His office was in the newly occupied Prague, where he may well have used his position to take revenge on local Czechs.

In his letter, he told Mahr that he was now an *Einsatzkommando*, which was translated in Dublin as 'a member of the Reserve Command'. The *Einsatzgruppen* were special mobile formations charged with carrying out killings in occupied countries; the individual detachment was called an *Einsatzkommando*.[69] These detachments first emerged in September 1938 in relation to 'the total solution of the Czechoslovak problem'[70] but are mostly associated with the killing of up to two million Jews following

Germany's invasion of the Soviet Union in 1941.

In his letter, von Weinertsgruen thanked Mahr for his recommendation to Chief Group Leader Heinrich Schmauser. Schmauser was probably a police chief in Prague in early 1939, but later became a police chief in Upper Silesia, where he provided security for the Auschwitz extermination camp. Schmauser had a police company of 130 men as a standby force in the area in case prisoners attempted a mass breakout. In such an event, camp guards would man a defence line in the interior of the camp, while Schmauser would provide an outer defence line.[71]

Although von Weinertsgruen mixed in disreputable company, he played little part in the Holocaust. In late 1939, he and another Nazi friend named Hellenbosch got very drunk at the Glembovice estate, of which von Weinertsgruen was in charge. They beat up a Polish Jew who worked there, and then tortured his fiancée, also a Jew, for two hours by whipping her, submerging her in cold water and raping her.

This was too much for even the SS. The two men were arraigned for trial in November 1939. Hellenbosch committed suicide, and von Weinertsgruen was convicted of 'racial shame' and given three life sentences and one year of hard labour. He and his mother applied for a pardon, citing his previous good work for Germany, his previous suffering at the hands of the Czechs, and the fact that he had a seven-year-old daughter who had already lost her mother. The matter was brought before Hitler personally, who dismissed his plea, saying that von Weinertsgruen had disgraced the German race.[72] He died in 1941, presumably executed by the SS.

Most of this was unknown to Adolf Mahr, who had probably never even met von Weinertsgruen or Schmauser. He was simply looking forward to the Nuremberg Rally that summer, the final event of his great trip of 1939. Such an event would have been unimaginable just a decade before: a fellow-Austrian was now the new master of central Europe, presiding over a strong Germany that once again included Austria, the Sudetenland and Alsace-Lorraine. Preparations for the Rally, as elaborate as one might expect for an Olympic Games today, reflected the importance of the moment for Mahr and millions like him. The historian Hamilton Burden describes the preparations:

Thousands of labourers milled about the rally grounds all summer, building ten new tent cities for visitors. Others worked around the clock to finish the new concert hall . . . . The construction workers were fed in five large restaurants that had been set up near the party area. A special force of 26,000 SS men were delegated to keep order along the marching route, direct traffic, and ensure that everything flowed smoothly . . . a new railroad station outside the rally grounds was to be used . . . arrangements were made for the streetcars to go underground for a distance near the party area . . . 150 kilometers of aqueduct were built for new lavatories.[73]

Following the Rally, which would last from 2 to 11 September, the Mahrs planned to return to Ireland on the *New York* on 14 September. But the lives of all the members of the Mahr family were to change that summer, as were those of hundreds of millions of others across Europe. As war loomed between Britain and Germany, the 'Party Day', scheduled for 26 August, was cancelled owing to 'political circumstances'.[74] Perhaps this should have prompted Adolf Mahr to gather his family together and leave for Ireland immediately, but they remained in Bad Ischl. Gustav Mahr feels his father may have 'played for time': 'If the war didn't happen, then staying made no difference. If the war did happen, then they were on the right side of the barrier, and the family was still together.' Even if war did break out, nobody expected hostilities to last long. Gustav feels that his father did not deliberately leave Ireland, but that, when he was in Germany, he did not try in earnest to get back.

Hilde, who was thirteen at the time, says that there is little doubt in her mind that the family was accidentally trapped in Continental Europe: 'Dad tried to get our passports back; they had been taken away in Cuxhaven. He went to Berlin, and tried to get them back sooner, to take an earlier boat, but they were not interested in letting Germans get out of the country again.'

Files at the Irish National Archives show that, as early as 1 September 1939, Mahr visited the Irish chargé d'affaires in Berlin to request help from the British authorities in securing safe passage to Ireland. After the chargé d'affaires had consulted the Departments of External Affairs and Finance, an official letter was sent to Mahr saying that safe passage was not possible but that he was to be granted special leave without pay for the period of his absence, and could resume his position in the National

Museum as soon as circumstances permitted.[75]

Germany invaded Poland on 1 September, and Britain and France declared war on Germany on 3 September. Britain's Royal Navy blockaded German ports, and the ship on which the Mahrs were planning to travel, the *New York*, could not leave. They were stranded.

Those who knew that he was under G2 surveillance would have deduced that Mahr had escaped Ireland just as the noose was tightening. A month before he left, on 13 June, the Irish government introduced the Offences Against the State Act, which was designed to help it crack down more effectively on the IRA. Mahr would have been aware that the same Act could just as easily have been used against German agents in Ireland. There was already enough evidence in Mahr's file to justify his internment should war break out. It is possible that he had received a tip-off from the authorities: leave or be imprisoned. Regarding Mahr's departure, the archaeologist Joseph Raftery told the historian David O'Donoghue: 'Mahr could not have been expected to do otherwise, given his loyalty to the [Nazi] party and the advent of war'.[76]

Around this time, a rumour circulated that persists to this day: Adolf Mahr, a Nazi agent who was under police and army investigation in Ireland, told his employers that he was taking a holiday, and escaped to Germany just before the outbreak of war, taking maps and other important information with him. Soon, much of his mundane archaeological work was seen in a more sinister light. Mahr had introduced aerial photography as a tool for archaeological work, in particular for the Harvard archaeologists. Some people assumed that Mahr's real purpose was to use such photographs for the preparation of a German invasion. If this had been the case, it could hardly have been more embarrassing for the Irish government. Mahr had enlisted the use of Irish army pilots and planes for the aerial-photography projects. Could he really have hoodwinked a nation's armed forces to help plan an invasion of that country?

In his book *Ireland and the Atlantic Heritage*, the former head of the Ulster Museum, Emyr Estyn Evans, included a short section called 'Adolf Mahr: Archaeologist and Nazi Spy'. He said that he had shown Mahr many of the famous sites in Northern Ireland, but 'only later did I suspect that he may have been spying out the land for a sinister purpose'.[77]

In a changed political climate, Mahr's pre-war jokes were now seen in a different light. During the 1930s, he had joked that, following a German victory in a forthcoming war, he would see to it that Evans was made gauleiter (leader) of Ulster.[78] He had seemed to enjoy that particular joke – or maybe it wasn't a joke. Barry Raftery says that Mahr told Joseph and Lotti Raftery that, following a German victory, Mahr would be made gauleiter of Ireland. Historian John P. Duggan, however, says that Franz (Frederick) Winkelmann, a director of the Irish Glass Bottle Manufacturers of Dublin, was reputed to be the gauleiter designate for Ireland.[79] David O'Donoghue believes that the Germans would have given the job to a native Irish person, most likely Seán Russell, the IRA leader who died in mysterious circumstances aboard a U-boat en route to Ireland in August 1940.

With Mahr stuck in Germany, the group of Irish Nazis gathered in Dublin to discuss their options now that war had been declared. They were mostly concerned that, in the likely event of a British invasion of Ireland, they would be interned.[80] Even if Ireland was not invaded, some of them expected that the Irish government might intern them anyway as a precaution.

In a deal organised by de Valera and Hempel through the British Foreign Office, the German colony was allowed to leave Ireland on 11 September 1939. They travelled by boat from Dun Laoghaire to Holyhead in Wales, then through England and by boat to Holland and on to Germany.[81] Fifty Germans left, including Professor Herkner of the National College of Art and Design, Dr and Frau Robert Stumpf, Hans Hartmann, Helene Neugebauer, Harry and Margaret Greiner, Karl Krause, Karl Kuenstler, Herr and Frau Niemann, Herr Lohmeyer, Charles Budina (who left because, as he put it, he needed a 'change of air and did not think the war would last long'), Herr Schubert, Otto Reinhard, Hans Boden, Heinz Mecking and Helmut Clissmann.

Mecking's departure meant that there was no Nazi or *Auslandorganisation* leader in Ireland. Indeed, the departure of the whole colony meant that Germany had few reliable intelligence-gatherers in Ireland for the duration of the war. Over the next six years, German counter-intelligence landed twelve spies in Ireland by parachute and U-boat; they were invariably of little practical use because they lacked on-the-ground knowledge. Furthermore, Helmut Clissmann's departure, apparently at the request of the British,[82] removed the Germans' strongest link with the IRA. J. P. Duggan points out that Berlin later regretted the loss of forty-two key members of the German colony, because 'they could have done more to help the German cause if they had remained in Ireland'.[83] This might further indicate that Mahr's failure to return to Ireland was not intentional.

As rumours circulated around Dublin about Mahr, it is likely that Albert Bender eventually learned of Mahr's Nazi activities. Bender had sent Kathleen O'Brennan a cheque for two guineas so that she could buy Maria Mahr a Christmas gift. O'Brennan replied in late 1939 to say that Dr Mahr and his family had left Ireland before the outbreak of war. She avoided using the word 'Nazi' but said that Mahr was 'regarded as a prominent member of the German colony'. She said that she had no idea of his whereabouts and would wait to hear if there was more news on him before returning the cheque.[84]

The news must have been a crushing blow for Bender. Wasn't this the same Mahr who had written to him about saving an Austrian Jew from the Nazis only a year before? Had all the goodwill and friendship been a lie? It had been eight years since Bender had written to Mahr about 'presenting to the museum twenty-two Tibetan pictures, in the name of my dear mother, Augusta Bender'. Since then, more than 170 letters, and dozens of gifts, had passed between the two men. They had created a precious museum collection together – a civilised act in a world on the edge of barbarity. Now it turned out that he had sent money to Ireland to buy a Christmas present for a woman who was married to Hitler's top man in Ireland?

Bender's anger must have intensified as he thought about his cousin in Berlin who, according to his solicitor brother in London, 'was in a bad way'. Gertrude Bender had been a teacher until 1938. She was now 'in advanced years' and was embarrassed that help was being sought for her. She said she 'wanted only chocolate'.[85] It seems strange that an elderly Jew living in Berlin after nearly seven years of anti-Semitic persecution would want only chocolate. Perhaps 'chocolate' was a code word, or perhaps she, like Pokorny and many others, was afraid of the consequences if she was found to be complaining about Hitler's government.

Bender heard one last time from Mahr, in December 1939. It was the shortest note Mahr had ever written to Bender: a simple postcard showing a snow-covered Bad Ischl. The card read:

A happy New Year to you and all good wishes for 1940. Was caught on leave and could not return to my museum. Hope your health is again OK. A. Mahr.

During the summer of 1940, Diego Rivera arrived in San Francisco again, where Bender had organised a commission for him that involved painting a mural in front of the public, in a project entitled 'Art in Action'. That, at least, was the official reason for his visit; the other was that Rivera was wanted by the Mexican police in connection with an assassination attempt on the exiled Russian revolutionary leader Leon Trotsky.

Following a power struggle with Josef Stalin, Trotsky and his wife Natalia had fled the Soviet Union in 1929, and lived in Turkey, France and Norway, before Rivera's help secured them asylum in Mexico. The Trotskys arrived by oil tanker in the harbour of Tampico in January 1937 and moved into Rivera's house in the Coyoacan area of Mexico City, where they lived rent-free for the next two years.[86] But the friendship between the two couples was damaged when Rivera's wife Frida Kahlo had an affair with Leon Trotsky, possibly in retaliation for Rivera's affair with her sister. The Trotskys moved to a house nearby, which was machine-gunned by a group of Stalinists in May 1940. Because of his much-publicised dispute with Trotsky, Rivera became a suspect in the assassination attempt. As police surrounded his San Angel studio, he escaped with the help of the Hollywood actress Paulette Goddard, and eventually arrived in San Francisco.[87]

In August that year, a young Catalonian 'journalist' named Ramón Mercader joined Trotsky in his office, where the two were to review an essay the younger man had written. Mercader, who used a false name, was actually a Stalinist agent who had been introduced to Trotsky by a mutual friend. He had become a frequent visitor to the heavily fortified house, so much so that the security guards no longer searched him. As Trotsky sat at his desk reading the document, Mercader produced an ice-pick from beneath his raincoat and plunged it into his head.[88] Bender was with Rivera when Kahlo phoned to break the news. 'They killed old Trotsky this morning,' she yelled. '*Estúpido!* It's your fault that they killed him. Why did you bring him?'

But Kahlo herself was culpable: she had befriended the assassin in Paris and had invited him to dinner in her house in Coyoacan. She was arrested, and held for two days, but was not charged.[89] Rivera, fearing that he too was on Stalin's death-list, went into obvious distress, shouting: 'I am next! I am next!'[90] But he knew also that the Mexican police would link him to the murder. Although he was a suspect, he was never charged.

The world must have seemed too crazy a place for Bender. In March 1941, at the age of seventy-five, he passed away after a short illness. The front page of the *San Francisco Chronicle* marked his passing with the headline: 'ALBERT BENDER: A MAN WHO GAVE HIS HEART TO SF DIES'. It listed the collections he had created in many public institutions, including the one in the Dublin museum, where 'he gave a wing in memory of his parents'.

Bender had requested an Irish wake, followed by burial at the Jewish Temple Emmanuel near San Francisco. One of his great discoveries, the photographer Ansel Adams, watched over his body on the final night, and described the wake in his autobiography:

> All during the small hours men and women, singly or in couples, would enter the apartment quietly, many obviously stricken with grief. Some talked about Albert and what kindnesses he had done for them; one elderly man whispered to me, 'Albert helped put our son through college. We shall never forget him.' Practically all of these people were unknown to me. Most were relatively obscure: clerks, garage men, nurses, gardeners, mailmen, garbage collectors, janitors from his office building on California Street, and others who sought a last communion with their friend. These people of the night and dawn revealed to me the scope of Albert's life. I looked for the last time upon him, seemingly comfortable in his casket and serene as if he were dreaming of his good works. His example of nobility and generosity bore fruit in many orchards of the human spirit.[91]

5

NEW LIFE IN GERMANY, 1939–43

At first, the Mahr children enjoyed their extended holiday in Austria. They got along well with their cousins, practised their German, and went hiking in the Austrian sunshine. But as the summer of 1939 drew to a close, they were disappointed to learn that, instead of returning to their own home and their friends in Dublin, they would now have to go to school in Austria. They faced the prospect of an Austrian winter with only summer clothes and sandals. They borrowed winter clothes from their new friends and relatives, and 'Mother sewed an awful lot', says Ingrid. As the temperatures in Austria dropped, Maria Mahr remembered Albert Bender's present of a fur cape the previous Christmas and grumbled: 'My God, if I could only have my fur coat from Ireland.'[1]

The children's command of German was still weak: when the school term started, each child had to join classes where some of the children were two years younger than them. Ingrid, who was ten at the time, was put in a class of seven- and eight-year-olds. The Mahr children also spoke German with Dublin accents, which gave the local children an opportunity to jeer at them. Furthermore, the Austrian accent was so difficult for them to understand that Ingrid once asked her father if the Austrians 'speak German here too'. 'Even the teachers laughed at us,' says Ingrid. 'Our grammar was very bad; I made horrible mistakes. When I had to write an essay, it was read out loud so the whole class had a good laugh.'

Because there was no secondary school in Bad Ischl, Gustav had to move to Gmunden, in the former Austria, where he lived with the Hayeks, former members of the German colony in Dublin who had recently retired to the town. Theo and Frieda Hayek had a large, attractive home, where Gustav enjoyed their hospitality for the winter of 1939/40.

Although he found the transition to German schooling a difficult one, he made the most of his new environment by learning to ski. Later in the war, Hilde visited regularly to receive maths lessons from Theo Hayek.

Things were not so good for Adolf Mahr. Just a few months before, the fifty-two-year-old had been enjoying the fruits of his industrious career. He was highly regarded within his profession, both in Ireland and internationally; his native country was growing in strength, as was his power within its extended political system; his family was healthy and happy. But now, in the autumn of 1939, he was cut off from his beloved museum, and from the power and prestige it had afforded him; he was also separated from his books. He did not even have a set of winter clothes as he faced into a harsh winter in the Austrian Alps. It is little wonder that intercepted letters from Karl Kuenstler in Germany to friends in Ireland reported in October 1939 that 'The Mahrs are very badly off' and that Mahr had 'no job yet'; by April 1940, Kuenstler was reporting that 'I don't see much of Mahr, he turned into a drunkard.'

Dr Michael Quane, one of Mahr's colleagues at the National Museum, wrote to him in November and confirmed what the latter had been told in earlier letters: 'Normal salary paid until the 30th November, and if you are not back by then your absence will be regarded as special leave without pay. The arrangement is on the understanding that you will resume your post in Dublin as soon as circumstances permit you to do so.'[2]

Mahr might have found some solace in Quane's assurances that 'you have nothing to worry about as regards your affairs at this end, and that if there is anything that I can do on your behalf in so far as your personal interests are concerned, I shall do it with a heart-and-a-half. There will be a green, white and gold moon before I forget your kindness to me during my boy's illness in Switzerland.'

It was clear that the Mahrs wanted to get back to Ireland. Writing in December 1939 to Dr Joseph Raftery and his new wife Lotti, Maria Mahr said:

> I pass to the subject of a possible return to Ireland. Can you not help us in this regard? I am always dreaming of getting a flight to Ireland.... My husband however thinks this is impossible and calls me a dreamer. He thinks that surely during light warfare Ireland will establish a neutral route and that we could then perhaps return via such a route by steam ferry. I on the other hand don't believe in such a possibility. Could you

not enquire about an Irish aeroplane that could collect us in Italy? We would be prepared to pay well. Think about it.[3]

Maria Mahr regretted not having given the Rafterys a wedding present the previous summer but hoped that she might hand it to them 'in the not too distant future'. In the meantime, she offered the Mahr home on Waterloo Place to the Rafterys until their return:

> We are of course greatly worried about our house and so we would be delighted if you and your husband would move into it. We could continue paying the entire rent for the time being, so that you would only pay what you would ordinarily pay for an apartment of your requirements. We would pay the rest.
>
> You may, on foot of this letter, go to our landlady Miss A. Crinion, 42 Waterloo Road, and solicitor Arthur Cox at St Stephen's Green, to let them know that we are totally in agreement.
>
> You will find everything that you require in terms of linen and furnishings in the house. Oh, how nice it would be if this were possible and how even nicer if it were possible for us to return.

To add to his troubles, it was clear that Mahr had little chance of earning a living in Bad Ischl. He decided to seek work in Berlin while Maria remained in Bad Ischl with the girls. At least there they had relatives in the town, and their grandmother lived with one of Adolf's sisters about three hours away in Linz. Maria Mahr's sister had married a friend of Adolf's, and they lived in Vienna.

On the political front too, some light could be seen at the end of the tunnel. There was every reason to believe that the dispute with Britain would result in a swift German victory, so it was conceivable that the Mahrs would be back in Ireland within a year. In the spring of 1940, Adolf moved to Berlin, where he got work in a part-time capacity at the Prussian Museum of Prehistory.[4] By May, when he went on a lecture tour of Hungary and Switzerland, his life was coming together again.[5]

The Mahr home in Dublin was kept up by friends, and the German Legation paid the rent on it for more than a year after the family's departure.[6] Eventually, according to Ingrid Mahr, it was ransacked by American and British agents looking for information about Mahr's Nazi activities. After that, Else Brase and Nadja Winkelmann cleared it out. They put the furniture up for auction and placed Adolf Mahr's library and papers into storage in the cellar of the National Museum.[7]

Although Germany was officially at war, the war was still in the 'phoney' period, and life in Berlin went on as usual. Mahr continued his efforts to win back the standard of living he had enjoyed just a short time before in Ireland. He made contact with one of the most powerful men in the German government, his old friend Joachim von Ribbentrop, the former ambassador in London, and now the Reich's Foreign Minister. Presumably through this connection, Mahr began working as an assistant in the Foreign Office in Berlin during the spring of 1940.

That summer, the German air force, the Luftwaffe, began to probe Britain's south coast and to lay mines from the air in the English Channel. Plans were drawn up for an invasion of Britain (code-named 'Operation Sealion') and Ireland (code-named *Fall Gruen* ('Operation Green')). Mahr is sometimes accused of providing intelligence for the latter invasion. If this was the case, he would have to have been involved in the process soon after his arrival in Berlin.

Copies of Operation Green were circulated to top army officials on 8 August 1940. The invasion would have been a hazardous affair, with an initial force of 3,900 troops sailing from the French ports of Lorient, St Nazaire and Nantes, and landing on an eighty-five-mile front along Ireland's south-east coast, between Wexford and Dungarvan. Having captured some small harbours there, light infantry and commando units were to fight their way thirty miles inland. A bridgehead was to be established that would run from Gorey to Mount Leinster through Thomastown, and on to Clonmel and then Dungarvan. Horses were to be used to haul guns ashore from landing craft.[8]

In September 1940, and again in May and October 1941, the Department for War Maps in Berlin issued a text to accompany Operation Green. *The Military Geographical Data on Ireland* is a two-hundred-page book containing photographs, maps and other information about Ireland's coasts. Some of Ludwig Mühlhausen's photographs of County Donegal and surrounding areas appeared in this book,[9] and it is likely that the work of other associates of Mahr were published in it too. It is difficult to link Mahr himself directly to the book, however. *The Military Geographical Data* is very detailed but reads like a school geography book. For example, it contains a diagram of Crookhaven, County Cork, which shows the more prominent landmarks: Couglan Tower, lookout towers and a lighthouse. Cork Harbour is also well illustrated, as are places within Cork city such as Patrick Street, and Dublin and its port areas are well described.

There are obvious omissions, however. There is no mention of the several military barracks in Dublin – something an invading officer would probably like to know about. There is also no reference to the National Museum. If he was involved in the planning for the invasion, Mahr might have been tempted to show the National Museum, even as a location that was not to be bombed. There is an aerial shot of O'Connell Street, and the caption states that there are large hotels on both sides of the street. Mahr would have known there was a large hotel, the Gresham, on just *one* side. In the aerial photo of Heuston Station (then called Kingsbridge), part of the Guinness brewery is shown, but the caption reads that it is 'part of [a] large brandy factory' – an error that Mahr is unlikely to have made. Moreover, there is no mention of Skerries or Balbriggan, places Mahr knew well, although the book's authors clearly had some knowledge of Malahide.[10]

David O'Donoghue believes that several of the mistakes in *The Military Geographical Data* were not mistakes at all but were small acts of sabotage by Belgian typesetters. The documents were typeset and printed in occupied Belgium, where typesetters engaged in passive resistance by inserting minor changes into German government documents.

A review of *The Military Geographical Data* by Irish Military Intelligence in 1946 concluded that the photographs in the handbooks were not the result of a carefully planned and detailed photographing campaign, and that the majority of the photos are 'of an ordinary picture-postcard type . . . they are not properly keyed to the maps . . . and selection of subjects not well defined.' The text, the review said, was mostly information that could be compiled from Ordnance Survey maps, geography books, tourist literature, government reports, and publications such as the Saorstát Éireann Official Handbook. 'The information could probably be got by interviewing people who had visited the country, without giving them detailed instructions before they went,' it said. It highlighted the out-of-date information in the book, such as the Galway–Clifden Railway, which was no longer running, and the boat service on Lough Corrib, which had ceased operations in 1933.

The report asserted: 'the photographs were prepared without

previous assignments; text represents mainly bookwork with some not very thorough checking; but the coastal descriptions were done on the spot by a person or persons specially assigned to the job . . . . Not possible to suggest who was responsible.'[11] This appears to clear Mahr of orchestrating a professional spy network in Ireland, because it seems that one did not actually exist.

From the beginning, Operation Green lacked the decisiveness of Germany's invasions of Denmark, Norway, Belgium, the Netherlands, Luxembourg and France, which had taken place earlier in 1940. Preparations for the English landing were to be given priority over the Irish one, and naval officers in charge of the Irish landing were told to commandeer French fishing and German naval tugs for the purposes of training. The journalist Robert Fisk contended that the indecisive nature of Operation Green suggested that it was to have been a diversionary exercise while the mass of German troops attacked England: 'Only three German divisions were to take part in the Irish invasion, while forty would take part in Sealion.'[12] Fisk further speculated that the German High Command never seriously intended to invade Ireland, and that 'there is evidence that they deliberately publicised Operation Green to stretch British defence preparations in advance of Sealion.' He said that, on 28 June 1940, an instruction was issued that, in order to mislead the enemy, 'all available information media should spread the word that we were preparing a landing in Ireland to draw the net around England tighter and reinforce the "siege".'[13]

The German historian Horst Dinkel believes that there was 'no serious [planned] attempt to land German troops in Ireland'.[14] Kurt Haller, a close associate of the Foreign Office's coup d'état specialist Edmund Veesenmayer, agreed, saying: 'The Foreign Office never had any intention of starting a major action in Ireland. As a neutral, whose neutrality was in the interests of the German war effort, Ireland raised no acute problem.'[15]

This was not the general belief in Ireland, where many expected a German invasion that year. The writer David Marcus, who was raised in the Jewish community in Cork, remembers the fear at the time: 'a Nazi invasion of Britain was thought imminent and many experts believed that Ireland, Britain's "back door", would be its springboard. As speculation grew, one particular dawn was pinpointed by military analysts as likely to offer the invading armies the most suitable climatic and marine conditions for a successful sea journey and any one of the many coves in the vicinity of Cork harbour a perfect landing place. I spent all the previous night sitting up in bed, staring at the clear, starry sky and waiting in terror to hear the streets resound with the rumble of tanks and the stamping of storm troopers' boots.'[16]

The civil servant León O'Broin, who was Regional Commissioner for Galway and Mayo at the time, recalled a fear shared by officials in his position that, in the likely event of a German invasion, they would all be shot. The feeling was that the gauleiters would shoot them if they refused to collaborate, and that the common people of Ireland would do the same if they *did* collaborate. 'Yet,' he said, 'there would have to be some measure of collaboration in the interests of the people we were appointed to serve.'[17]

In the autumn of 1940, Operation Sealion was postponed. Germany was losing the Battle of Britain and, without air superiority, Hitler had no choice but to postpone the invasion of Britain.[18]

The autumn of 1940 saw Gustav leave Gmunden and join his father in Berlin.[19] Adolf had found a school in the city which catered for German children who had been raised in other countries. They were mostly from South Tyrol, which had become part of Italy in 1919. It suited Gustav to be surrounded by students whose German was as weak as his own: he joined the school for three months, during which time he sat his final school exams.[20] Then he was drafted into the *Reichsarbeitsdienst*, the State Labour Service, where youths were required to work on farms or in factories. The State Labour Service was originally a means of reducing unemployment in Germany, but Hitler also saw its authoritarian regime as a good foundation for military life. Gustav was sent to work on roads in east Prussia.

Maria Mahr and her daughters lived in Bad Ischl from 1939 until January 1941. They then moved to Berlin to live with Adolf. A friend of the family – a journalist who was working with a German paper – was sent to cover events in occupied Norway. He left a large apartment in Berlin for the family's use.[21] The girls' German was now strong, after a year and a half spent in Austria, but in Berlin they were the butt of jokes again – this time for speaking with Austrian accents. Once again, they joined the Hitler Youth.

Soon after seizing power, the Nazis had identified the strong propaganda potential of radio, and the Reich's Propaganda Ministry attempted to broadcast its message to every corner of the world. Josef Goebbels, the Minister for Public Enlightenment and Propaganda, was prepared to use minority languages such as Irish, as well as the international languages, to achieve this, and through the RRG (*Reichsrundfunkgesellschaft*, or Reich Broadcasting Company), his department was transmitting programmes in twenty languages by the end of 1939. In 1941, this increased to thirty languages, and two years later the Germans were broadcasting in fifty-four languages.

Professor Ludwig Mühlhausen, the chair of Celtic studies at Berlin University, was asked to set up the service that would broadcast to Ireland; it would be called Irland-Redaktion. Before the war, he had travelled extensively in Ireland, particularly in Cork and Kerry, where he spent several summers learning Irish.[22] He stayed on the Blasket Islands off County Kerry while they were still inhabited, and in 1932 studied local Irish dialect and folklore in Cornamona, County Galway.[23] In 1938, he shared a house in Teelin, County Donegal, with León O'Broin, who was there to learn the local Irish dialect. He recalled that Mühlhausen took photographs constantly, and local people observed that, when returning to Dublin, he did not venture through British-controlled Northern Ireland but instead went the long way round, via Sligo.[24] Mühlhausen was a member of the SS, and was later described by G2 as an 'enthusiastic Nazi' and a spy.[25] The chair he occupied in Berlin was given to him only after Julius Pokorny had been unseated because of his Jewish ancestry.

Mühlhausen started the Irish radio service near the end of 1939. Initially, the service consisted of a fifteen-minute talk in Irish by Mühlhausen on Sunday nights; it had a large audience, of around sixty thousand. However, this was mostly because his programme 'piggybacked' onto the end of the broadcasts by William Joyce (Lord Haw-Haw), which had a popular following in southern Ireland, as well as in nationalist areas of Northern Ireland.[26] A G2 report said that Mühlhausen spoke good Irish, with a mixture of Kerry and west of Ireland dialects. In one of his typical talks, he said that it was a pleasure to talk over the air to his Irish friends, imagining himself seated '*cois na tine agus boladh na mona im' shron*' ('by the fire, and with the smell of the turf in my nose'). He discounted reports of the persecution of Czech and Polish Catholics and reminded listeners of the atrocities that had been committed in Ireland by the Black and Tans and the Auxiliaries.[27]

In 1940, Hans Hartmann – formerly Father Christmas at the German colony's Christmas parties in Dublin – joined Irland-Redaktion. He had been taking a doctoral thesis on Irish folklore under Mühlhausen's supervision, and was invited to contribute a fifteen-minute broadcast each Wednesday night, in addition to Mühlhausen's Sunday-night talk. Around the same time, the writer Francis Stuart, who lectured in English at Berlin University, started working in the RRG as a scriptwriter for Lord Haw-Haw.

Adolf Mahr, now working in the Foreign Office, was aware of Hartmann and Mühlhausen's talks on the Irish radio service, but did not like them. He did not get on with Mühlhausen and thought that it was a waste to devote so much time to the Irish language. Instead, he developed a plan for von Ribbentrop which contained proposals to transform the Irish radio service. His fifteen-page report, *Rundfunkpropaganda nach Irland* ('Radio Propaganda to Ireland'), was submitted to von Ribbentrop's office on 18 March 1941.[28]

Mahr's report started with an assessment of Ireland: its population, the border, and the political allegiances of the various communities. It acknowledged that 'democratic ideologies are strong, as well as respect for America' and that 'there is little understanding of, and absolutely no sympathy for, National Socialism, mainly for reasons related to the Church.' It also suggested that nationalistic sections of the population support Germany's fight against the English, in accordance with the old saying: 'England's difficulty is Ireland's opportunity.'

Mahr estimated the number of wireless receivers in 'Éire' at around 250,000, and stated that listeners were 'largely restricted to urban and rural intelligentsia'. He estimated that only around 5 percent of the population spoke Irish, and as a result that the Irish-language broadcasts 'do not reach the older generation of nationalists (who were unable to learn Gaelic) and . . . do not reach the nationalists in Northern Ireland at all.' But he suggested that Irish-language broadcasts be maintained because 'language enthusiasts amongst the educated sections of society' see 'a nationalist political factor in the language'. He wanted to expand Irland-

Redaktion to a nightly service, but with an emphasis on English-language programmes, while at the same time maintaining Irish-language programmes.[29]

Mahr believed that Germany could tap into a huge worldwide anti-British audience by targeting programmes at the Irish diaspora, which he estimated to number around ten million people. He wanted to attract some of the estimated 1.5 million Irish people living in British cities such as London, Liverpool and Glasgow, as well as the estimated 250,000 in Australia, the 150,000 in Canada, and the five to six million in the United States. The last group, the American-Irish, Mahr describes as 'de Valera's prestige trump card, nationally and politically.' Mahr wanted to set up secret transmitters to target these people so that they would lobby against US entry into the war.[30] Mahr called for German support of Irish neutrality, 'which is of advantage to us', and suggested that the new service use declarations by Irish bishops and statements by de Valera to bolster the case for Irish unity, and to criticise 'the Ulster injustice'. Topics covered would include: English cruelty to Ireland, Cromwell's scandalous deeds, the persecution of Catholics, and the Irish War of Independence.[31]

Mahr suggested the use of a transmitter in Rome, since it would 'find a certain receptive spiritual atmosphere in Ireland', which 'can be beneficial for talks on Catholic religious tendencies . . . .' Mahr did not call for any anti-Semitic messages; the only mention of the Jews was when he referred to the current war as the 'English-Jewish war'. Suitable speakers would be recruited from among the ranks of Irish inmates of prisoner-of-war camps in Germany.

There was a heavy Irish republican tone to much of Mahr's report. During his twelve years living in Ireland, he showed scant interest in the issue of a united Ireland, and there is little evidence to link him with the IRA, but his plans for Ireland read like a de Valera or an IRA manifesto. In short, he now seemed to be a passionate Irish republican:

> Éire's neutrality is therefore not pro-German or pro-Italian. Neither is it anti-British. It is simply pro-Irish. It is genuine neutrality and strives to shorten all the suffering. With that Éire also helps to alleviate the suffering of her Northern Irish brothers.

Conspiracy theorists might wonder whether Dev was his co-scriptwriter, but David O'Donoghue, who first published the document, believes it was written with the help of Francis Stuart, an avid republican, and the senior IRA man Frank Ryan, who were both resident in wartime Berlin.

Mahr's report concluded:

> The overthrow of British imperialism is unavoidable since it has afflicted Ireland with so many crimes. With it, it will bring Ireland's reunification so that [Ireland] can sever all remaining connections to the British Empire. Then Ireland will see the fulfilment of its indefeasible right to total sovereignty. Only then will the reconstituted sovereign Irish nation be able to fully contribute, in friendship with all peoples and without link to other powers, to the rebuilding of the true international community of people which has been destroyed by England's plutocratic and unchristian imperialism.

Aside from his political rants, the breadth and accuracy of Mahr's proposal showed once again his intellectual grasp of Irish history. This contrasts with the trite observations about Irish towns in *The Military Geographical Data on Ireland* – and again suggests that Mahr had little to do with that document. His clearly stated opposition to any interference in Ireland's neutrality further supports this view.

Gustav Mahr, referring to his father's blueprint for radio propaganda into Ireland, says that it showed that he was so strongly in favour of Irish neutrality that he would not have supported any proposal to invade Ireland: 'He could see that the only chance of keeping Ireland out of war was to refrain from all attempts to invade the country, or use it for espionage purposes. That would ruin everything . . . . Father discouraged getting Ireland involved, as it would only backfire. He even realised that his only chance of getting back to Ireland would be if Ireland was not involved in war.'

O'Donoghue points out that the two ideas are not mutually exclusive, and that it suited Germany to support Irish neutrality publicly, while secretly drawing up invasion plans: 'They broadcast in favour of Irish neutrality, but during the war they sent a dozen agents to Ireland, which was a flagrant breach of our neutrality'.[32]

Von Ribbentrop approved Mahr's plan for the revamped Irland-Redaktion on 23 May 1941. Mühlhausen was dropped; Mahr assumed charge of the station later that year, and took it on a course that closely followed his blueprint for the station. He did not talk on air himself – his German accent was still too strong – but he wrote many talks that were delivered by members of his presentation team.[33] He put Hans Hartmann in charge, and the programme format included 'lots of jigs and reels, Irish music, war communiqués, praise of the German leaders, predictions of a German victory, and a glorious unified Europe after a German victory, anti-partition, anti-English, anti-British Empire, and an extreme Irish nationalist slant; normal, standard Nazi propaganda,' according to O'Donoghue. Later in the war, Irish-language content increased to one hour per week.

This version differs slightly with the account of Elizabeth Clissmann, the Irish wife of Helmut Clissmann. She met Mahr several times during the war, and says that Mahr was 'only an overseer of the radio station'. Gustav Mahr agrees, saying that his father 'never wrote any talks for the radio station. He was only [there] in an advisory capacity.'

On 22 June 1941, Germany invaded the Soviet Union. This marked the end to any hope of a swift conclusion to the war. In the words of the historian Enno Stephan, 'the step from war to world war had been taken'. The invasion, codenamed Operation Barbarossa, was one of history's most audacious and terrifying military actions. German confidence was already high following recent victories over Poland and France, and in the Balkans, when some three million German troops, along with close to one million soldiers from pro-Axis countries, invaded the Soviet Union. They attacked along a line stretching from Finland to the Black Sea, and had at their disposal 3,350 tanks, 7,000 field guns, and more than 2,000 aircraft. The force also used more than 600,000 horses to tow guns, ambulances and ration wagons.[34]

This massing of forces had gone largely unnoticed by Moscow, and the defending Soviet army was no match for Hitler's blitzkrieg. In the great Stalin purge of the Red Army, which began in 1937, more than 36,600 officers had been executed, imprisoned or dismissed. This left the army bereft of leadership, and especially vulnerable to Germans' swift, well-co-ordinated air and land attacks. It also fuelled Hitler's belief that, once the country was attacked, the 'rotten structure' of the Soviet Union would come 'crashing down'.

By the end of the second day of fighting, the Luftwaffe had destroyed 2,000 Soviet aircraft, many of which had never even left the ground.

Those that did fly into battle were often piloted by inexperienced soldiers, who felt that 'they were corpses already' when they took off.[35] Within a week, more than 300,000 Red Army soldiers were trapped and 2,500 tanks destroyed or captured. In the north, General von Manstein's Panzer Corps smashed through Russian lines and was advancing towards Leningrad (St Petersburg) at a pace of almost fifty miles a day.

After just three weeks, the Red Army was in a desperate position. It had lost 3,500 tanks, more than 6,000 aircraft, and nearly two million men.[36] It seemed inevitable that Hitler would achieve what Napoleon had failed to do, and conquer Russia. But the Russian invasion marked a new departure for the German army, one that would stain its reputation for ever. At a secret meeting in March 1941 with his top military command, Hitler had explained the manner in which the war against Russia would be fought:

> The war against Russia cannot be fought in knightly fashion. The struggle is one of ideologies and racial differences and will have to be waged with unprecedented, unmerciful, and unrelenting hardness. All officers will have to get rid of any old-fashioned ideas they may have. I realise that the necessity for conducting such warfare is beyond the comprehension of you generals, but I must insist that my orders be followed without complaint. The commissars hold views directly opposite to those of National Socialism. Hence these commissars must be eliminated. Any German soldier who breaks international law will be pardoned. Russia did not take part in the Hague Convention and, therefore, had no rights under it.[37]

The Commissar Decree (also called the Commissar Order) marked a departure from the traditional rules of war. Soldiers were given a free hand to treat Russian captives as they pleased, and were exonerated from criminal charges even when their activities included murder, rape and looting. Furthermore, other 'special orders' called for Soviet political officers, Jews and partisans to be handed over to the SS, or the Secret Field Police. The resulting slaughter shocked even some senior army officials, but Hitler's orders were carried out without protest. The *Einsatzgruppen* (the mobile task force charged with carrying out liquidations in occupied countries) alone shot thousands of Jewish civilians every day as Germany advanced into the Soviet Union.

The Commissar Decree backfired for two reasons. First, it increased the resolve of the Russian people to defeat Nazism. Soldiers who might otherwise have surrendered during a losing battle simply fought to the last bullet, because they expected that dying was better than being taken prisoner by the Germans. Second, when the tide of the battle turned and Russian forces overran German territory, they took revenge not just on German troops but on millions of German civilians. Hitler's attack on the Soviet Union also marked a reprieve for Britain and Ireland. As German armies eventually got stuck in the quagmire that was Stalingrad, Hitler could never again muster enough forces to consider launching an invasion from his western front.

Gustav Mahr, still in the Labour Service, served on the border of Lithuania and east Prussia during the summer of 1941. He was stationed there for several weeks waiting for something to happen, but expecting to have to cross into Russia. On the night before Barbarossa, he helped build ramps to allow tanks to drive from street level up an embankment on to a railway bridge. This would enable them to cross the River Memel into Lithuania, and from there move on towards Riga, with the eventual goal of taking Leningrad. In order to attract as little attention as possible, Gustav's team worked under cover of darkness and mostly by hand. Several trains arrived with a cargo of rocks and other materials, which they unloaded and used to create the ramps.

Since he was not a soldier, Gustav did not take part in Operation Barbarossa. Instead, on the morning of the invasion, he was taken to barracks, where he was told to stand guard over about a hundred injured Russian soldiers. Later that day, he and his group were sent on bicycles in pursuit of the advancing front. They cycled to the city of Memel (now Klaipede) along the Lithuanian coast, and then inland towards Siauliai. He saw few corpses but was fearful of reprisals and partisan attacks. 'We only had rifles, which were not much use,' he says. 'I think we had one machine-gun between about twelve of us.'[38]

That night, as they camped out, news filtered through that a German army motorcyclist had been found dead nearby, with his genitals cut off. 'That really got us going,' says Gustav. The next day, they cycled to Siauliai. Gustav found a city that was 'on fire from one end to the other, and almost flattened'. They turned north towards the Latvian capital, Riga, and passed by many disarmed Russian troops 'wandering about looking for a prison camp'. From Riga, they headed for Pskov, a city on the Soviet side of Lake Peipus, which formed part of the border between the Soviet Union and Estonia. In this forested area, they found few roads and railroads, but instead muddy tracks formed by tanks and other heavy vehicles. They began to build roads using tree trunks.

By September, three months after the invasion, the Germans laid siege to Leningrad, and in October they launched Operation Typhoon, the offensive against Moscow. In Berlin, Hitler announced the extent of his victory over Stalin: 2.5 million prisoners taken, 22,000 guns captured, 18,000 tanks destroyed and 145,000 Russian aircraft eliminated.[39] Few could have doubted that Hitler was anything other than a military genius, and that the fall of the Soviet Union was imminent.

Gustav continued to build roads all summer. In late October, he was ordered northwards again, and cycled first to Narva, which lies on the Gulf of Finland, and then east to Leningrad, where he stopped just a few kilometres short of the Russian front. As the harsh winter tightened its icy grip on men and machines, it became clear that Gustav's services were no longer required. Now in the city of Volosovo, near Leningrad, he was close enough to hear the fighting, but too young, and insufficiently well-trained, to take part. The roads were no longer quagmires; they were frozen solid, and there was little point in working on them until the spring. His group was loaded onto a train and sent back to its base near Memel.

Gustav could not have known how lucky he was to be leaving the Soviet Union that November. Hitler was at his zenith; now, instead of building on the great military successes, he was about to make the mistakes that would eventually lead to the defeat of Germany. In late November, the German drive towards Moscow began to falter. Troops were hungry, sick and tired after a five-month campaign. Furthermore, they were ill-equipped for a winter campaign, and were slowed by heavy rains and the severe frost.[40]

In early December, two events indicated that the tide of war might soon change. Far from being on the verge of collapse, the Red Army counter-attacked on 5 December, using reserves who were fresh from training in Siberia. They had sheepskin coats, quilted pants, fur hats and felt boots, and so were able to travel quietly and for long periods over the snow. During the second week of December, the Siberians broke through near Klin, on the outskirts of Moscow, and killed 3,000 German soldiers.

To the south of Moscow, another counter-attack forced the Germans to retreat around 200 kilometres.[41]

On 7 December, the focus of the war changed once again as the Japanese attacked Pearl Harbor. Four days later, Germany and Italy declared war on the USA, in solidarity with Japan. It was a tactical error. A country of Germany's size could not expect to defeat the Soviet Union, Britain and the United States all at once. Moreover, Hitler had always felt an affinity with Britain and the United States. There was little to gain, even if victory was possible.

Adolf Mahr, who shared Hitler's dislike of various groups, including Czechs, Communists and 'international Jewry', must have fretted over the declaration of war upon America. This latest development created additional difficulties in relation to Ireland's neutrality. The Irish were positively disposed towards America, and would show less resistance to her using their ports than they would to either Britain or Germany doing so. Perhaps stemming from this fear, one of the announcers on Irland-Redaktion warned that Irish bases given to the USA would be seen as the equivalent of bases handed to Britain, and would therefore be targets for German bombers.[42] O'Donoghue has noted that Mahr's carrot-and-stick approach towards Irish neutrality can be clearly seen in the broadcasts of this period: 'If Ireland remained neutral, the prize of reunification would be hers once England was defeated, but if England or America occupied the Treaty Ports or elsewhere in the Twenty-six Counties, Ireland would immediately become a legitimate target, with all the terror and destruction that implied.'[43]

In autumn 1941, Gustav returned from Labour Service to his family in Berlin. The reunion was short-lived: he was immediately drafted into the army. He became a private first class, a rank below officer level. He says that he was happy about this and never wanted to become an officer: 'I probably wouldn't have been a very good one. Perhaps this was a rather instinctive stand-offish position; I didn't want to get very involved with the whole show. I didn't want to become an officer, or to lead troops. I did my duty, but more or less half-heartedly,' he says. Was he indoctrinated? 'Yes, but always an outsider.' Gustav spent Christmas 1941 in the infirmary of his infantry regiment in Kostrzyn, near Berlin. He was covered in boils, 'probably from malnutrition, from my summer in Russia'. It was to be a brief respite: in the New Year, his regiment was destined for front-line action against the Red Army.

Although the imprisonment, sterilisation and murder of Jews, Slavs, gypsies, homosexuals, the disabled and the mentally ill had been going on for several years, the German authorities believed that there was still a lot of work remaining before they achieved a racially 'pure' Germany. Twenty-seven different agencies were involved, but from a Nazi standpoint the system was too muddled and slow.[44] Hitler believed that there were around eleven million European Jews who had not yet been dealt with. A meeting was called in the lakeside resort of Wannsee near Berlin, bringing together fifteen top civil servants, SS and police officials. There was only one item on the agenda: to plan for the 'Final Solution of the Jewish Question' – the blueprint for the Holocaust.

The Wannsee Conference, which convened on 20 January 1942, was chaired by Reinhard Heydrich, administrator of the concentration camps, who was tipped by top officials as a natural successor to Hitler. His deputy, Adolf Eichmann, head of the Jewish-evacuation department of the Gestapo, and Under State Secretary Martin Luther of the Foreign Office, were among the delegates.

Upon the annexation of Poland, its 2.5 million Jews had been herded into ghettos. This was merely a temporary solution: even feeding so many people was unsustainable for a country at war. Until the invasion of the Soviet Union, forced emigration to the island of Madagascar seemed to be the most likely prospect for Europe's Jews,[45] but at Wannsee this and other emigration possibilities were found to be unworkable. The delegates discussed the prospect of sterilising all Jews, but no decision was taken on that subject either. Instead, the group agreed on a policy of 'evacuation to the east', a euphemism for removing Jews to the death camps in Poland. There they would be used as labour, 'in which task undoubtedly a large number will fall through natural diminution'. Those that survived the labour gangs 'must be treated accordingly . . . in case they should succeed and go free'. Delegates were told about a new design of gas chamber that could kill up to sixty thousand Jews a day. This was the *Endlosung*, the 'Final Solution'.[46]

Europe was to be 'combed from west to east' for Jews. A chart was drawn up which indicated the Jewish populations that had yet to be evacuated. Ireland's 4,000 Jews were on the list, as were Britain's 330,000, and the Soviet Union's five million. The list specified thirty-five jurisdictions, which were divided into occupied countries and districts, and unoccupied countries. The number of Jews intended for 'deportation' came to more than eleven million.⁴⁷ Within weeks, the first poison-gas chambers were built in Poland, and the whole mechanism of genocide was streamlined. Up to that point, less than 10 percent of the Holocaust's victims had died, but in the frantic year that followed, half of all the Jews who were to die in the Holocaust perished.

Gradually, the news of the Final Solution seeped into the ranks of the bureaucracy. How much a man knew depended on his proximity to the operations and on his insight into the nature of the process.⁴⁸ Mahr worked in the Foreign Office, which was heavily involved with the Final Solution, and was a particularly insightful man. Does that mean he would have known about the Final Solution?

Mahr's friend Otto Bene was now the Foreign Office official representative in Holland.⁴⁹ The destruction of Holland's estimated 140,000 Jews was under way, and Bene sent reports to head office in Berlin on the 'deportations to the east' during that summer. His correspondent in head office was Martin Luther, the man who had represented the Foreign Office at Wannsee.⁵⁰

On 22 June, Adolf Eichmann informed the Jewish Affairs Department in the Foreign Office that arrangements had been concluded with the railways for the deportation of 100,000 Jews from the Netherlands, Belgium and occupied France to the Auschwitz camp in Poland. The Dutch quota was forty thousand. The Foreign Office replied that, for certain 'psychological' reasons, the diplomats desired that the first transports be composed of 'stateless' Jews. There were, according to a note from Bene to the Berlin Foreign Office, 25,000 'stateless' Jews in Holland. These were mostly German Jews who had escaped to Holland in the years after the Nazis came to power in Germany, and before Germany occupied Holland.⁵¹ The German authorities were apparently concerned about interventions by the Swedish government on behalf of Dutch Jews, and also about protests by the Dutch public, so the deportation of 'stateless' Jews was a ploy to start the deportations while avoiding outside interference.

The best known of the 'stateless' Jews was Anne Frank, the teenager who kept a diary of her two years spent hidden in a secret apartment in her father's Amsterdam factory. The Franks were German, and all Anne's uncles had fought for Germany in the Great War. But her father, Otto, saw the warning signs when Hitler came to power, and moved his family to the perceived safety of Amsterdam in 1933. When the war began, he expected that Holland's neutrality would not be violated,[52] but in May 1940 the country was invaded and, once again, Otto Frank had to act quickly. He organised a secret six-room apartment to hide eight members of his family and friends, and this became their home for the next two years.

On 17 July 1942, Bene proposed to Berlin that all Jews should be divested of their nationalities, as a means of preventing future interventions by Sweden, which had taken some Dutch Jews as refugees. Although this proposal was not introduced, Bene was able to report to Berlin on the same day that the first two trains of Jewish deportees had left Holland, and that there were no 'incidents'.[53] Nazi propaganda claiming that the deportations were true 'resettlements' had been successful, and at the end of July Bene reported: 'In Jewish circles the opinion is widespread that the Jews who are fit for labour service are being deported to prepare the necessary quarters for the Jews in the East.'[54]

Although the Dutch population was uneasy about the latest developments, only the Protestant and Catholic churches protested. In order to placate them, Bene wrote, converted Jews and Jews in mixed marriages were exempted from deportation for the moment.[55] By 16 November, this special status was dropped, and Bene reported that the 'converted Jews were among the first to be seized'. Jews in mixed marriages also lost their immunity, although some retained it if they could prove that they had been sterilised. According to Bene, 2,256 Jews had submitted such proof; hundreds of them had acquired it by subjecting themselves to an operation.[56]

The destruction of Dutch Jews was one of the Nazis' most successful operations. Holland was bounded on the east by the Reich, on the south by occupied Belgium, and on the west and north by the open sea. Holland itself is a flat country, with few woods or mountains where people could hide. Moreover, the Jews lived in compact communities in a few large cities. 'It was,' says the historian Paul Hilberg, 'as though the Dutch Jews had already been placed in a natural trap.'[57]

The spring and summer of 1943 saw the last large-scale round-up of Jews in Holland. The small towns and countryside were cleared of Jews, and Bene observed that 1,302 Jews had reported 'voluntarily': 'With the aid of the Jewish Council, the deportations from the provinces proceeded without a hitch.' In June that year, the last big deportation of Jews from Holland took place, as the police rounded up 5,500 for deportation from the Jewish ghetto of south Amsterdam. Now that the large populations of Jews were liquidated, the drive against Jews in hiding intensified. Bene's reports to the Foreign Office suggested that as many as 11,000 Jews were in hiding in February 1944, down from 20,000 in June of the previous year.[58]

On 4 August 1944, the Gestapo broke through the door of the Frank family's annexe. Five agents rushed in and arrested the occupants. The group was sent to Westerbork in north-east Holland before being transported to Auschwitz, and from there some went to other camps. Otto Frank survived, but his wife had died shortly before the camp was liberated. Anne Frank and her sister Margot had died of typhus in the Bergen-Belsen camp.[59] A year later, Otto Frank returned to the annexe and found his daughter's diary on the floor, where an SS man had thrown it during the raid. *The Diary of Anne Frank* was eventually published in thirty-two languages, and became a successful stage play and film.[60]

Bene's activities during the war do not necessarily associate Mahr with the murder of Jews; indeed, in the post-war trials Bene himself was not convicted of involvement in the Final Solution. But considering the two men's close friendship, and the fact that they were working for the same organisation (the Foreign Office) at the same time, it would be surprising if Mahr had not known about the 'deportations', and what that euphemism meant.

Adolf Mahr's sister-in-law also worked for the Nazi regime in Holland. Jozien (pronounced 'Usine') van Bemmelen was a secretary to Artur Seyss-Inquart during his time as Reich Commissioner for the Netherlands from 1940 to 1945. Seyss-Inquart had previously helped organise the Anschluss from the Austrian side, had been Deputy Governor General of Poland immediately after Germany's invasion in 1939, and had remained so loyal to Hitler that the latter proposed him as Foreign Minister during his final days in power in 1945. At the Nuremberg trials, Seyss-Inquart was accused of having participated directly in the deportation and shooting of hostages, and he was later hanged.[61]

Like her older sister Maria, Jozien had married an Austrian, and the couple had moved to the Indonesian island of Sumatra after the Great War. There, they lived an idyllic life with their three children, until both her husband and her little boy contracted a tropical fever and died. Jozien returned to Europe with her two daughters, but instead of settling in her native Holland, she moved to Vienna and lived among her late husband's large National Socialist-supporting family. She became a university lecturer and soon got to know Seyss-Inquart, who was then the pro-Nazi Minister for the Interior. When he left Austria for Holland, where he became the official in charge of the German occupation, Seyss-Inquart needed a secretary. He hired Jozien, who was fluent in Dutch and German.

The Nazi occupation of the Netherlands split the van Bemmelen family. While Jozien worked for a Nazi official, and Maria was married to one, their brother Jaap was active in the Resistance. He had been a member of the Dutch High Court and was a professor of criminality at Leiden University. (After the war, Holland's Queen Beatrix was one of his students.)[62] He and other academics rebelled against Nazi rule by refusing to oust their Jewish colleagues and by taking strike action. They were arrested and detained in a concentration camp, but Jaap was not badly treated because of his family connection in Seyss-Inquart's office. His teenage son Hans also worked for the Resistance and spent many months on the run, evading arrest several times.[63]

When the Mahrs' apartment in Berlin was destroyed in an air raid during the summer of 1943, Hilde and Ingrid moved to their Aunt Jozien's empty apartment in Vienna for a while.[64] Soon, however, Jozien needed her apartment back. Her Dutch friends and relatives had made it clear that they saw her as a traitor because of her work for Seyss-Inquart, and this had prompted her to give up her job and return to the less hostile environment of Vienna. Adolf Mahr visited the city during this period, because Hilde and Ingrid were now staying with their cousins and grandmother nearby. It seems likely that he met Jozien on a visit and discussed what was going on in Holland.

Despite the fact that Mahr almost certainly knew about the deportations, he did not necessarily know the fate that awaited the deportees. Elizabeth Clissmann, who lived in occupied Copenhagen at the time and regularly visited Berlin, where she met Mahr, says that she did not know about the gas chambers until after the war. She feels that Mahr probably did not either: 'you knew the Jews were having a rotten time, they were being arrested and transported to the East. Maybe even worked to death, but not part of a policy of destruction. . . . People might have learned things from soldiers in the East. But I didn't live a sheltered life and I didn't hear about the gas chambers.'[65]

Mahr's loyalty to the Nazi Party, while maintaining personal relations with individual Jews, again caused him difficulty during this time. He had maintained a strong friendship with the Hayeks in Gmunden; they had been especially helpful to Gustav during the winter of 1939/40. During the winter of 1943/44, when Hilde lived in Austria, she received maths lessons from Theo Hayek. The difficulty arose because Frieda Hayek was Jewish, and as such was scheduled for removal to the Theresienstadt concentration camp, about fifty kilometres from Prague.

Theresienstadt had opened in late 1941 and was originally regarded as an especially humane detention centre.[66] Jews from Prague, who were taken there in their thousands, believed that they were safe in a 'model ghetto'. Some even bribed Gestapo agents for the privilege of being sent to Theresienstadt.[67] Among the Jewish inmates were elderly men and women, war veterans, and Jews who were married to Aryans, like Frieda Hayek. Soon after the Wannsee Conference, Heydrich designated Theresienstadt as a transit station for trains on their way to Auschwitz and other extermination camps. Mahr, his brother-in-law Dr Franz Hoernisch, and Theo Hayek understood that every effort should be made to keep Frieda Hayek out of the camp.

The Nuremberg Laws on Citizenship and Race of 1935 defined Jews according to whether they had four Jewish grandparents, two Jewish grandparents, or just one. The *Mischlinge* (individuals of mixed race) were given a status above full-Jews, and on a par with full-Jews who were married to Christians. At the Wannsee Conference, an attempt was made to reclassify *Mischlinge* and Jews married to Christians, but the matter was not resolved, and so by law they were not to be deported. Many Jews who fell into this category were unaware of this loophole in the law and presented themselves for 'removal' when they were called upon to do so. Ingrid Mahr says that her father knew the law and argued on Frieda Hayek's behalf that her detention would be illegal: 'He would have said: "She is not allowed to be deported. She is married to a Christian citizen, and it is only people who are separated or widowed who must be deported." Because he knew this law and he had enough connections, he could prevent this from happening.'

Under the Classification of Intermarriages Act of 1938, it was easier for a Jewish woman in a mixed marriage to avoid incarceration than it was for a Jewish man in a mixed marriage. This was largely, though not exclusively, to do with 'ownership' of the family home, which usually rested with the male. A Jewish woman married to a Gentile was deemed to be living in a Gentile home, but a Gentile woman married to a Jewish man was deemed to be living in a Jewish home. Such a 'humiliating' position for an Aryan was unacceptable to the regime, and was likely to result in the deportation of the Jewish male partner.[68]

According to Hilde, Adolf Mahr came to Austria from Berlin every two or three months and made regular contact with the authorities on Mrs Hayek's behalf. Despite his best efforts, she was arrested and taken to a concentration camp in February 1945.[69] Adolf Mahr and his brother-in-law Franz Hoernisch, both Nazis, campaigned for her release. They contacted Adolf Eichmann directly; Eichmann ordered her release after six weeks of captivity.[70]

This must have given Mahr a great sense of satisfaction. He had made similar efforts on Alfons Barb's behalf some years earlier, and although Barb escaped the Nazis, it is unclear whether or not the credit for this is due to Mahr. His efforts on behalf of Arthur Kohn were unsuccessful: less than a year earlier, Kohn had perished at the Theresienstadt concentration camp. By contrast, his efforts to secure Mrs Hayek's release were successful. The story is slightly marred by Frieda Hayek's own political allegiances. Despite her being the daughter of a rabbi, and her experiences of trying to avoid arrest, and of incarceration, she remained a strong supporter of the Nazis.[71]

There was another Jew living nearby in Berlin whom Mahr could have tried to help had he known she was there: Albert Bender's seventy-four-year-old aunt, Gertrude Bender, who had been a teacher in Berlin until 1938 and had since then felt the wrath of the Nazi government. Albert had been worried about her for several years, although her name had not arisen in his letters to Mahr. In January 1942, she was deported from Berlin to Riga.[72]

Riga, the capital of Latvia, had been home to a 43,000-strong Jewish community before the war. During the summer of 1941, when Latvia was overrun by Germany, thousands of Jews were killed or imprisoned, and 32,000 Jews were herded into a ghetto. In November of that year, when Gustav Mahr left the region to return to Berlin, the Germans separated the ghetto inhabitants into two groups: working Jews were put into the 'small ghetto', while non-working Jews remained in the 'large ghetto'. The large ghetto was 'liquidated' in late November and early December, and some 20,000 Jews were shot and buried in the Rumbula forest. During the first half of 1942, the large ghetto was filled again when 16,000 Jews were taken from the Reich to Riga. Fourteen thousand of them were later murdered.[73] Gertrude Bender was on a transport that left Berlin for Riga on 19 January 1942, and, it seems, she was murdered soon after her arrival there.[74]

In early 1942, Adolf Mahr became head of the Irish subsection of the political-broadcasting department of the Foreign Office.[75] His station, Irland-Redaktion, was going well, and in March Hans Hartmann persuaded his Berlin University colleague, Francis Stuart, to give his first talk on air. Stuart had previously written talks for William Joyce, but this was his first broadcast. He told listeners: 'Ireland belongs to Europe, and England does not belong to it. Our future must lie with the future of Europe and no other.'[76]

Just as their home had been a meeting place for Adolf Mahr's workmates in Dublin, the Mahr apartment in Berlin hosted many of the people who worked in both the Irish- and English-broadcasting services. The children became friendly with two of the men who worked on Lord Haw-Haw's programmes, and Margaret Joyce, William Joyce's wife, tested Gustav as a potential speaker on the radio service. Being able-bodied, he was prohibited from joining the team, and had to remain in the army.[77] However, fate intervened, and Gustav was given the opportunity to work in a deciphering team, far removed from the front. He believes that this move saved his life: it was a result of the efforts of Ulrich Tanne, son of the Reverend Wilhelm Tanne, in whose Malahide home the Mahrs used to spend their Irish summers. In February 1942, Ulrich, who worked in the German command as a decipherer, visited the Mahrs in Berlin. On hearing that Gustav was about to be called up to an infantry regiment, he said he would try to prevent this. He managed to get Gustav removed

Adolf Mahr as an archaeology student in Vienna, c. 1906.

Young Adolf with his father, a bandmaster in the Kaiser's army, Salzburg, c. 1900

From left to right: Hilde, Ingrid and Gustav, c. 1930

All photographs on these pages are reproduced courtesy of the Mahr family

From left to right: Hilde Mahr, Karin O'Sullivan, Pronnséas O'Sullivan, Gunther Stumpf, Ingrid Mahr and Donal O'Sullivan on South Strand, Skerries, County Dublin, c. 1937

Ingrid on her first bicycle, c. 1939, with Brig

Adolf Mahr holding the newborn Brigit in 1933, with Hilde, Gustav and Ingrid (holding doll)

Maria and Adolf Mahr at the Giant's Causeway, County Antrim, 12 July 1930

The Mahr home, 1927–39, at Waterloo Place, now Upper Leeson Street, Dublin

Adolf and Maria Mahr at home in Dublin, *c.* 1934

Christmas in the Mahr home, 1930

Mahr (left) with an unknown official and Otto Bene (right). The picture was taken soon after Hitler's ascent to power in 1933. At the time, Bene was leader of the Irish and British Nazi organisations; he later worked for the German Foreign Office on the deportation of Jews from Holland.

The German colony at the German Legation in Dublin, on Hitler's birthday, 20 April, c. 1933. Adolf Mahr is seated third from left in the second row; Otto Bene is standing immediately behind him; Col Fritz Brase, the first leader of the Nazi Party in Ireland, is to Bene's left; Oswald Müller-Dubrow, a d tor of the Siemens-Schuckert Company in Ireland, is the bearded man seated on the extreme right.

Dr Adolf Mahr, *c.* 1947

Mahr wearing a Nazi badge, *c.* 1938

...ing the Nazi salute at the Hitler Youth camp at Hampton Hall, Balbriggan, County Dublin, probably ...5. Adolf Mahr is on the left: he was unable to straighten his arm owing to a duelling injury sustained ...ng his student days. Ingrid and Hilde give the salute from the steps (partially hidden, second and ...l from left, respectively). Gustav is fourth from the left in the row of standing boys.

The raising of the Swastika at the Hitler Youth camp at Hampton Hall, *c.* 1936. Hilde and Ingrid Mahr are saluting from the steps on the right of the picture, and Gustav and Adolf Mahr are on the left.

Hitler Youth camp at Hampton Hall, probably 1935. Gustav Mahr is in the front row, fourth from right

mbers of the Hitler Youth at Newgrange, County Meath. Dr Adolf Mahr, Director of the National seum of Ireland, gives a lecture on the 3200 BC burial chamber during a visit by the Hitler Youth up of Britain to Ireland in Easter 1936. Note that the British Hitler Youth members are in uniform.

Irish Hitler Youth gather at the entrance to the burial chamber at Newgrange. Note that the famous lightbox above the door has not yet been rediscovered, and is still blocked by stones. Adolf Mahr is second from left at the top; Gustav is second from left at the bottom.

At an archaeological excavation in Lough Crew, County Meath, July 1928: Adolf Mahr (extreme left), Maria Mahr (centre) and the Austrian expressionist painter Oskar Kokoschka (extreme right, standing

The arrival of the German battleship *Schleswig-Holstein* in Dun Laoghaire, County Dublin, in 1937. Thousands of Dubliners line the harbour, hoping for an opportunity to board the ship.

German sailors chat as the ship's tender enters Dun Laoghaire harbour under the Nazi flag.

The good days. Adolf and Maria Mahr in County Wicklow in 1937. Financially, professionally and politically, Adolf Mahr had never had it so good.

Adolf Mahr explains the history of the famous Irish High Cross to the crew of the *Schleswig-Holstein* at the fifth-century monastic settlement in Monasterboice, 1937.

Gustav Mahr in the German army, c. 1941

Gustav Mahr in army uniform at Meissen, 1942

In Dresden, also in 1942. Gustav is third from right.

Gustav Mahr (left) and his schoolfriend Wolfgang Hahn on a Dublin beach *c.* 1934 and, below, near Dresden, in 1942. Gustav is on the left and Wolfgang is in the centre.

...git (third from left), Hilde (second from right) and Ingrid Mahr (holding dog) visit their friend Mona ...se (centre) in the Berlin suburb of Teltow in 1941. Brase, daughter of Colonal Fritz Brase, grew up in ...olin but, like the Mahr girls, was trapped in Germany in 1939. Mona Brase was looked after by the ...erly Baczkowski couple (on left) for the duration of the war. In 1945, as Berlin fell to the Red Army, ... Baczkowskis and Mrs Baczkowski's sister (also pictured) committed suicide by taking an overdose of ...ping pills.

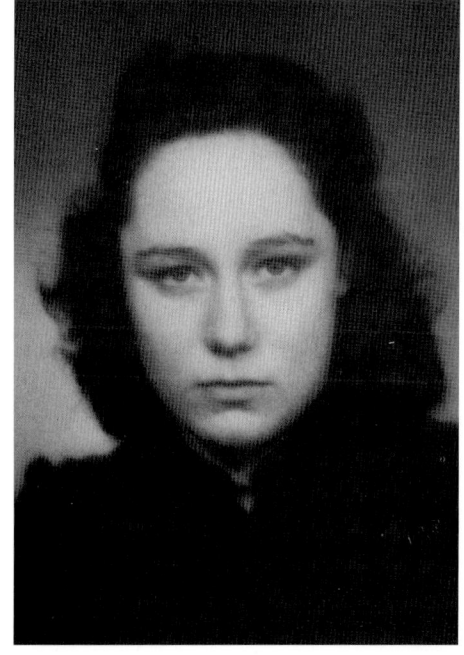

Ingrid Mahr at Bad Ischl,
February 1944

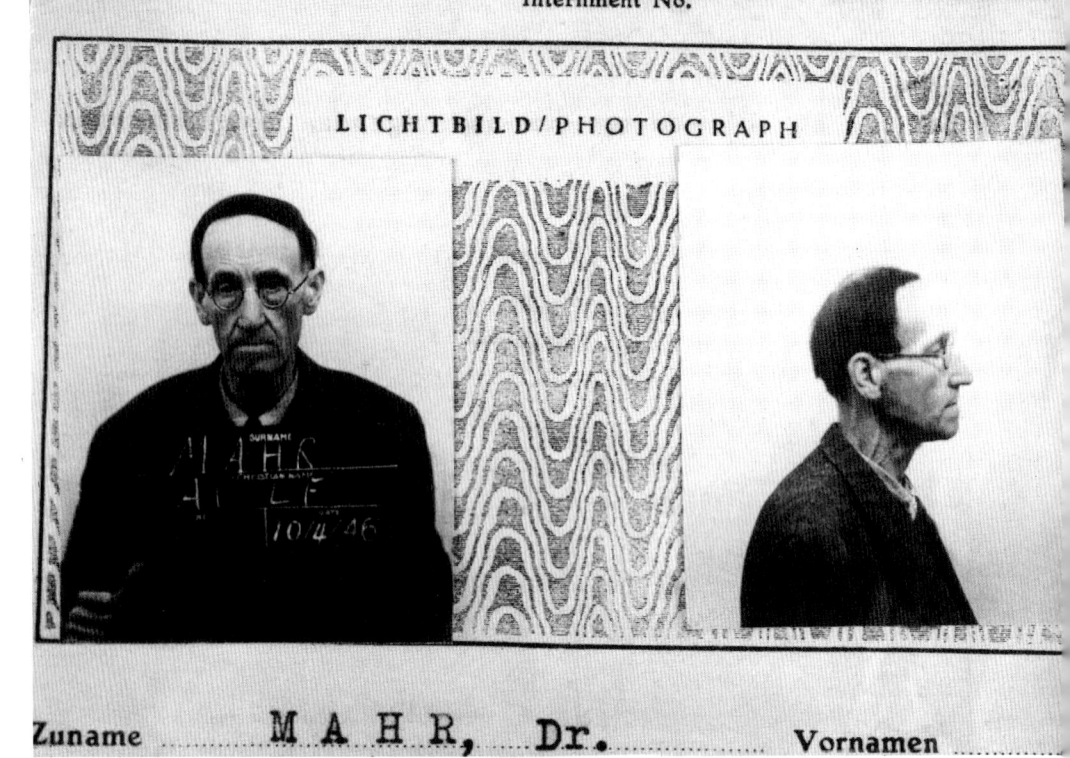

Adolf Mahr in a British prisoner-of-war camp, April 1946

Hilde Mahr (left) at her workcamp in Mecklenburg, shortly before it was overrun by Russian forces in the spring of 1945

family reunited, summer 1946. Adolf Mahr, still recovering from his prison-camp ordeal, celebrates ty-five years of marriage with Maria and the couple's children in Augustfehn in northern Germany.

The Mahr children celebrate St Patrick's Day in Berlin in 2005. From left: Brigit, Gustav, Ingrid and H

Adolf Mahr placing a gold torc from the National Museum's collection around the neck of an unide woman, late 1930s

from the infantry division, and into a division for men who spoke several languages, where he could be used in translation and interrogation work. 'This saved my life,' says Gustav, 'because as long as I stayed in Berlin, I didn't have to do any fighting. I wasn't actually a coward, but I didn't feel like fighting, as most people do not. And I wasn't keen on fighting English people, or Irish people, like my old school friends; many of the Wesley boys fought in the British army.'

That St Patrick's Day, the Irland-Redaktion team and other members of the former German colony in Ireland were guests of the chargé d'affaires, William Warnock, at the Irish Legation in Berlin. Even though the Irish government did not welcome their broadcasts, the station's talks on neutrality were consistent with Irish government policy, so there appeared to be little difficulty in bringing over the staff of the service for a drink. Later in the war, Warnock allowed Stuart to listen to Radio Éireann programmes on the Legation's radio set, and thereby, unwittingly or otherwise, helped him keep his talks up to date with events back home. In addition, Warnock's secretary, Eileen Walsh, regularly delivered Irish newspapers to Stuart so that he could keep up to date on events in Ireland.[78]

That summer, Gustav was sent to Meissen on the River Elbe to train as a signalsman, and after that he was transferred back to Berlin for courses in deciphering. This gave him the twin benefits of serving in the military without having to fight, and being able to live with his family. He had lots of free time and was even able to take a holiday in Austria. But during this relatively happy period, Gustav also saw Jews being rounded up in Berlin. In the early morning, as he was going to work in his army uniform, he often saw old women carrying feather beds and dragging trunks of belongings to take with them for their 'new lives' in the east. He remembers an antiquarian bookstore, around the corner from the Mahr home, which was crammed with Hebrew literature, presumably left there by Jews divesting themselves of their books before deportation. Neither he nor the Jews knew what lay ahead, but he could feel that it was an 'ominous time'. 'The official line was that they were being interned, that they were no use to the war effort, that they were being put to work elsewhere,' says Gustav. 'I don't know what I could have done. It's very difficult when you're integrated into a totalitarian state. It was like *1984* by George Orwell.'

The younger Mahr children were hardly even aware of the deportation of Jews. 'I didn't gather that they were deported. I must have been asleep. I was too busy with myself, it seems,' says Hilde.

There were still thousands of Jews in the city: those who had avoided arrest because they were in a mixed-race marriage, those working in armament factories, and others in 'privileged' groups. In Berlin, the Mahr children still bought goods from a little Jewish-owned shop, and the local Jewish doctor, Dr Neumann, opened his practice each day, even though he was allowed to treat only other Jews. Gradually, his patients were so reduced in numbers that it was hardly worth his opening at all.

Maria Mahr's support for the Nazi cause seemed to be wavering at this time. When Ingrid had an inflamed eardrum, Maria sent her to Dr Neumann. The thirteen-year-old remarked to her mother that he seemed to have no other patients: nobody else was sitting in the waiting room. Her mother told her that the other patients must already have left for the day. She forbade Ingrid from telling her friends that she had gone to Dr Neumann.[79]

Ingrid says that, when her father went to local Nazi meetings, her mother visited a local Jewish family and gave them food.[80] 'Mother used to often go in the night-time to visit them. She went down the backstairs, across the yard and up to their door,' she says. 'In every house there was a member of the party who had instructions to see what was going on in the house and who was there. You had to be careful.'

During the freezing winter of 1942/43, Ingrid befriended a Jewish boy who lived in the same building. The two children shovelled snow together on the street, one wearing a yellow Star of David. Maria Mahr went to the grocer's across the road and came out with two oranges. 'She put the two oranges into my pocket,' says Ingrid, 'and told me to give one to him. I did. You weren't allowed to talk to these people, but I liked taking risks, so I gave it to him.'

That winter, the Nazis made a final push towards a 'Jew-free' Berlin. Not long after the boy had shovelled snow with Ingrid, he and his parents were taken away. 'Where they went to, we didn't know,' she says. 'They were fetched in the night-time . . . . He was about ten or twelve years old, slightly younger than me. It was the beginning of 1943, and the boy was "fetched".'

The Mahrs lived in west Berlin, which had been a rich Jewish area.

Many of the small shops in the area were Jewish-owned, and two elderly shopkeepers lived nearby. Maria Mahr sent Hilde and Ingrid over to their house occasionally to help them stick ration stamps on to pieces of paper. 'Don't ring at the door, only knock', they were told. 'Mother never said they were Jews,' remembers Ingrid, 'but one day we looked out to see that the old couple's shop was closed. Mother just said, "Yes, they were old, they had to retire." But we knew that they must have been "fetched" too.'

Another Jewish woman lived alone on the same floor as the Mahrs. 'We only ever saw her at the window, but when she saw us, she would go back inside,' says Ingrid. On the night the trucks came to take the woman away, the soldiers forced their way into her apartment, only to find that she had hanged herself.

Did the children see the trucks arrive? 'No,' says Ingrid, 'we never saw that. Mother must have known, but we never saw. She must have opened the door and seen the old woman hanging. But we were in bed, and if we woke she would just say "Don't worry, it's nothing. Go to bed."'

Inge Deutschkron, a young Jewish girl living in one of Berlin's fashionable quarters, explained the scene as her aunt and uncle were taken away that winter:

> Two Jewish orderlies wearing the yellow star went into the house. They reappeared minutes later behind my aunt, who was lugging the heavy backpacks. She walked quickly, as though eager to get it over with. My uncle followed haltingly. They didn't look back as they stepped into the car, not a single backward look at the city that had been their home for almost thirty years. . . . [My mother and I] were the only ones on the street. Strange how the Berliners knew when to make themselves scarce so as not to have to see what was happening in their streets.[81]

During the autumn of 1942, Gustav was still living with his family in Berlin. By now he was working on a team deciphering British messages that had been sent in the Mediterranean area. It was a 'calm before the storm'. There was still little evidence of war in Berlin, although the family knew of the disaster in Stalingrad, and its implications. There was 'a sense of foreboding,' says Gustav. The diplomat Con Cremins, who met Adolf Mahr at the Irish Legation that autumn, said that Mahr was now 'very doubtful about the prospect of a German victory. I was quite struck by his air of depression.'[82]

The German public was prevented from knowing the full extent of the losses in the Soviet Union. The failed attempt to take Stalingrad was dressed up as an imminent victory. Hitler himself was shielded from the harsher truths of the operation, and continued to issue orders that did little to alleviate the suffering of his troops, and often only weakened their situation. On 19 November 1942, the Red Army launched Operation Uranus, a counter-attack in the form of a pincer movement against the rear of German forces in Stalingrad. Russian tanks and troops moved behind the German forces from both the north and the south and after four days successfully encircled the entire German Sixth Army. A quarter of a million German men were cut off from their comrades.[83]

Hitler refused to contemplate a withdrawal, and instead ordered General Friedrich Paulus to fight on. Food and ammunition deliveries by the Luftwaffe proved inadequate, as did attempts to airlift casualties to safety. As temperatures plunged below minus thirty degrees centigrade, the already inadequate food rations were further reduced. Starving German soldiers were forced to slaughter their horses for food, and later to dig up the frozen carcasses to eat the bones.[84] Thousands of Paulus's men starved and froze to death, and the area of Stalingrad that was controlled by the Germans dwindled. Hitler gave strict instructions that news of the encirclement was to be kept from the German people.

Eventually, on 2 February 1943 – and against Hitler's orders – the last of the 91,000 remaining troops surrendered. The Soviets counted 250,000 German and Romanian corpses in and around Stalingrad, and it is estimated that the total Axis losses in the campaign for Stalingrad were 800,000. More than a million men were lost on the Soviet side.[85]

The infantry regiment that Gustav should have joined was mostly wiped out as it retreated from the Red Army across the River Don, near Stalingrad.[86] The events bear a strange similarity to those that saved Adolf Mahr's life during World War I, when his arm injury prevented him from joining a regiment that was mostly drowned in battle along the Danube.

The tide of World War II had changed. The Red Army, despite its previous losses, had survived the worst the Germans could throw at it, and was getting stronger. For the first time, it began an advance towards the Reich, and there would be little mercy shown to anyone who stood in its way. Despite the best efforts of the Nazi authorities to boost morale, many German people realised that the war was as good as lost.

6

THE TIDE OF WAR TURNS, 1943–45

The Mahrs had still not felt the full impact of the war. They had seen none of the effects of war in Bad Ischl, and in Berlin there was rationing, but seldom air raids. They were aware of losses on the Russian front, and felt sorry for their schoolmates who had lost brothers there, but personally they had suffered little so far. By sending letters through Oswald Müller-Dubrow, a former member of the Dublin German colony who now lived in Switzerland, Maria Mahr was able to stay in touch with her good friends Else Brase and Nadja Winkelmann in Dublin. In a letter dated 26 January 1943, she mentioned that Hilde had been invited to Mona Brase's birthday party, and had to stay overnight because of 'visitors from the air' [an air raid].[1]

Mona Brase, only daughter of Colonel Fritz and Else Brase, had been sent from her Dublin home to boarding school in Germany in 1937. She was just thirteen years of age. While at boarding school, she was in contact with the Baczkowskis, an elderly couple who had no children of their own. Mrs Baczkowski and Mrs Brase had been in finishing school together many years before. When war broke out, the Baczkowskis officially became guardians of Mona, and she went to live in their home at Lichterfelde Ost, in Berlin's southern suburbs. This allowed her to stay in regular contact with the Mahrs, whom she had known from Christmas parties and the Hitler Youth in Dublin.

Maria Mahr continued:

> We had a lovely Christmas as the six of us were all together and well. We even had visitors for the youngsters to celebrate New Year's Eve with.
>
> I'm feeling very down today as Gustav is leaving us this evening. He is going south and the pain of parting is going to be very heavy. Thank

God he is well. The homeliness of the last half year has done him the power of good.

Adolf is travelling a lot lately between Berlin and Bonn as he is lecturing the winter term at the University of Bonn. [Mahr was a guest lecturer in archaeology for three or four days every second week during the 1942/43 winter semester.][2]

Unfortunately in the last few months I do not feel up to the mark. In autumn I got such bad stomach pains, like those of five years ago before I had my gall bladder taken out. I had to have myself well and truly checked out in the Robert Koch hospital and there they found traces of an ulcer of the duodenum. Now I have to follow a diet which is very difficult. All the work in the last year has been exhausting but it's now getting better. Hilde is thank God relatively healthy, the inflammation under her arm is gone.

The news about Herr Budina surprised us. How is he supposed to support his family? He gets only a small army wage. When the news arrived that Kilmaccurra [sic] was lost for them, Budina was just staying with us and we felt how heavily the blow struck him and how he suffered because of the separation from his family, and worrying about them. It was such bad luck for the whole family that he didn't stay in Kilmaccurra. Now he is going to get into agriculture in the East and he's happy about that. Hopefully it will work out better for him financially. Herr Mecking is busy with his branch in the East and Herr Krause will follow shortly to work with him. Frau Mecking is expecting her fifth child.[3]

Charles Budina had leased Kilmacurragh Park Hotel in County Wicklow, but left Ireland to join the German cause in September 1939. Shortly afterwards, the hotel was destroyed by fire, a blow that was compounded by his absence from family. The agricultural project in the east that Maria Mahr mentioned was old-fashioned colonialism: the Germans, having conquered vast farmlands in Romania and Ukraine, needed the likes of Budina and Krause to farm them and secure food supplies for the Reich, while people such as Mecking provided turf.

In February 1943, Goebbels called for the '*Fabrikaktion*' (Factory Action), a multi-day round-up sweep of Berlin to remove the *Mischlinge*, the intermarried Jews, Jews who worked in armaments factories, Jews who were in hiding, and any others who had so far avoided detention. Some five thousand Berlin Jews were taken from their workplaces and homes for deportation to Auschwitz.⁴ The journalist Ruth Andreas-Friedrich described the scene:

> Since six o'clock this morning trucks have been driving through Berlin, escorted by armed SS men. They stop at factory gates, in front of private houses; they load in human cargo – men, women, children. Distracted faces are crowded together under the gray canvas covers. Figures of misery, penned in and jostled about like cattle going to the stockyards. More and more new ones arrive and are thrust into the overcrowded trucks, with blows of gun butts. In six weeks Germany is to be 'Jew-free'.⁵

Berlin was declared 'Jew-free' on 19 May 1943.⁶

One night, Hilde witnessed a ferocious row between her parents. She listened from the next room as a furious Maria Mahr told her husband: 'No SS man will ever enter this house again.'⁷ She had just found out about the mass murder of Jews in the East. The news she had received might have come from one of two sources. The first possibility was Charles Budina, who stayed with the Mahrs occasionally around the time he worked in agriculture near Kiev in the Ukraine. The Jews of the Ukraine had been annihilated in 1942. The head of the SS, Heinrich Himmler, reported to Hitler in December that, in the previous four months alone, some 363,211 Jews had been killed in Bialystok, the Caucasus and the Ukraine.⁸ Because the killings were mostly by gunshot and by *Einsatzgruppen*, who performed their tasks without the privacy of an extermination camp, news of the murders spread quickly. Budina might have told Mahr about what was happening in Banoviche, Ukraine, in 1942 or 1943.⁹

The other likely source of information about the genocide of the Jews was Adolf Mahr's own experiences in the Baltic States. Germany took Latvia, Lithuania and Estonia from the Soviet Union in mid-1941, and mobile killing units rushed to the advancing front line to trap Jews and partisans. The resulting massacres, which were often carried out with extensive help from local police and civilians, resulted in the deaths of tens of thousands of Jews, including 46,692 in Lithuania alone in the three months up to September 1941.¹⁰

During the 1942/43 period, Adolf Mahr was invited to the University of Riga to give a lecture, and at that time he made a study tour of the

Baltic States. 'He must have seen or heard something that was going on,' says Gustav. 'He either witnessed atrocities by Polish and Lithuanians against Jews, or was somehow otherwise aware of it.'

Hilde raises another reason for the row between her parents – one that suggests that her mother's desire to keep SS men out of the family home was less a moral stand than to do with protecting her children. In early 1943, the Mahrs were visited by Dr Koslowski, a Polish archaeologist, who had been captured by the Germans, put in a concentration camp, and eventually released, on condition that he never discuss what he had seen in the camps. He was told that, if he discussed the camps with anyone, he would be killed. 'Mother didn't want him back in the house because there were three girls [there] and she was afraid that one of us would overhear something and repeat it in school. Then we'd all get into trouble,' she says.

At about this time, the marriage of Maria and Adolf broke down, although they continued to live together. Maria railed against Adolf and blamed him for the disaster the family was facing. Ingrid says that she often heard Maria shout at him: 'Why do you mix in politics? Why don't you stick to your old pottery?' 'And Father always said, "I can't fight, because of my arm. I want to be of some use to my country."'

The air raids on Berlin were relatively light until the early part of 1943. Then, the Allies stepped up their bombings, and brought home to Berliners the full effects of the war that was being waged from their city. Francis Stuart's girlfriend, Madeleine Meissner, who was a student in Berlin at the time, described the period:

> In the new year of 1943 everything became worse. The air attacks at night were regular and heavier, the food situation became more desperate, and, on top of that, a Siberian-like winter had set in. Perhaps that winter may have only felt colder, as we had little heat and almost no nourishing food. It snowed in huge white drifts which were not cleared away, but just piled up on the edge of the pavement. Children loved it as they could play hide-and-seek there. Everywhere heating became a major problem. We sat through lectures in our boots and coats with gloves on .... There seemed to be little point in earning money, as you couldn't buy anything with it, except at very high prices on the black market.[11]

Since Hilde was now a senior pupil in her school, she was placed on air-raid duty one night a week, where she was responsible for getting civilians into the safety of the shelters, and also for putting out fires. This latter task in particular called for bravery. Standing on the roofs of buildings, she had to extinguish the fire if a firebomb had already exploded; if it hadn't, she had to grab the firebomb and throw it onto the street below, where it could do little harm.

On Hilde's second night on duty, one of her classmates was killed:

> It was the worst air raid. I had no chance to do anything. Six big bombs fell on the opposite side of the street, and the houses were wrecked, right to the ground. There was such an explosion that one of the iron doors of my attic flew back and I was caught between the wall and the iron door. I could do nothing for myself until the others helped me out .... It was the first time I saw dead bodies, one of our schoolmates was amongst them. It was like the war films, but I could only think: try to survive for yourself. You can't help that killed girl. The cellar was full with injured people and we would try to help them and have them bandaged and put on stretchers.

She did not see many dead bodies because they were mostly buried under destroyed buildings. The city quickly adopted a routine: 'Immediately after an air raid, the next morning they would dig out the corpses and remove them. I didn't see many corpses. I didn't realise that the digging out was done mostly by people of the concentration camps,' Hilde says.

There was no time to mourn. 'Everyone was too busy,' she says. 'The next night it would start again. We were under a constant strain of fear. ... I only had the feeling that I didn't understand why this was happening. I wanted to get away from it .... You fear it would hit you or your people, but I didn't feel like I belonged to Berlin, so it was just a personal experience.'

The historian Patricia Meehan describes one of the tactics of the bombers:

> High-explosive bombs were dropped first, which drove people into their shelters. These were followed by incendiary bombs. When people emerged to fight the fires, more high explosives were dropped, people fled again to the cellars, and the fire could rage unchecked. The most

successful incendiaries in these raids were the thirty-pound bombs, which contained phosphorus and could not be put out by water. Everyone, including the fire guards, was afraid to go near them. Fire passed from one burning human being to another if they touched. In Hamburg those who leaped into the canals found the inextinguishable fire floating on the surface.[12]

Hilde's Berlin schooldays were ended that spring when her school was destroyed during an air raid. The other children in the school were sent to the relative safety of Cottbus, south-east of Berlin, near the Polish border. Maria Mahr, instead, took the girls back to Bad Ischl. Adolf Mahr stayed in Berlin and continued his work with the Foreign Office. Meanwhile, Gustav's luck continued to hold. In late March, just as the bombings intensified in Berlin, he was sent to Tunisia, where his work included deciphering British codes from the North African conflict. But soon afterwards, he says, 'I was caught with my pants down.'

The unit he joined had already retreated, and within six weeks the Germans had capitulated. They hoped for a plane to come by to pick them up, but none came. Likewise, a German ship was expected to evacuate him to Sicily, but that did not come either. With no other hope, he and up to 130,000 other Germans and Italians could only abandon their weapons and wait to be taken as prisoners of war. Everyone wanted to avoid capture by the French because they had a reputation for taking revenge on their German captives. The Americans were regarded as being more benign, as were the British, but the latter were likely to ask Gustav awkward questions about his nationality, so he hoped to avoid them too. Even though he had been born in Austria, his accent suggested that he was Irish. Since Ireland was then still part of the British Commonwealth, he could have been mistaken for a British subject, and potentially shot as a traitor.

On 4 May 1943, the Australians took him into custody. They handed him over to the British, who in turn presented him to the Americans.[13] Along the way, he altered his troop identification number, so his captors believed him to be an infantryman. If they realised he was in a reconnaissance division, he would have been subjected to interrogation.

Gustav was eventually placed on an American troop ship and sent to a prisoner-of-war camp in the United States for the duration of the war. For the Mahr family, there could scarcely have been better news: for a young German in uniform, it was the safest place to be.

This news was tempered that summer when Adolf Mahr phoned his wife in Bad Ischl to say that their Berlin apartment had been destroyed in a firebomb raid. With the help of some locals, he had tried to put out the fire, but they were mostly old people and succeeded only in slowing the progress of the blaze. Mahr received burns while trying to rescue his books from the burning building. 'Books were the most important part of his life, and he tried to save them by bringing them to the back of the house from his study room at the front, which was on fire,' says Hilde. 'He had to stop because the wooden ceiling fell through. He had a lot of burns on his head, back and shoulders.' As a result of the blaze, the Mahr family's possessions were reduced to little more than a few suitcases of clothes.

The Irland-Redaktion service continued to broadcast despite the bombings, and in April and May 1943 Francis Stuart advised Irish people to vote against Fine Gael in the general election of 22 June. The government felt that this was an unwarranted interference in its domestic affairs and lodged a formal complaint with the Foreign Office in Berlin. Undersecretary of State Hencke, who received the protest from the Irish chargé d'affaires, William Warnock, noted that the Irish government had no objections to the radio service generally, except that it criticised an opposition party.[14] The protest by the Irish government would have been raised with the director of the radio service, Adolf Mahr, who was still officially a civil servant in the Irish government.

It is interesting to note that it was not the service itself that was a bone of contention, but its occasional content. The service tried to avoid antagonising the Irish government. There was some – but very little – anti-Jewish material on the Irish service. The historian David O'Donoghue has noted that Hartmann took the view that 'minimal use of anti-Jewish material would keep the SS radio bosses off his back'. Exceptions to this rule included the 'Patrick Cadogan' talks, which began in May 1943. In a typical talk, Cadogan (real name P. J. Dillon) lectured the Irish on the 'evils of Jewry and Bolshevism', saying: 'These two terrible evils, Judaism and Bolshevism, are so real that I must bring home to you, my fellow Irishmen, the great danger to our country, to our holy faith, that lies in the Jewish plans . . . . Be on your guard for the protection of our holy Catholic faith and for the salvation of Ireland.'[15]

In July, the bombing of Berlin was so intense that the *Rundfunkhaus* staff had to leave the city, and settle in the relative safety of Luxembourg, seven hundred kilometres to the south-west. Irland-Redaktion went off the air for nearly two months until mid-September. By the end of 1943, programme output had been reduced to one talk per night, although it rose to three talks per night in 1944. Mahr stayed in the Foreign Office in Berlin but was a regular visitor to the studion in Luxembourg. By now, he was going to work with all his belongings in a briefcase. That way, if his latest home got destroyed in a bombing, he could easily move to another.

Elizabeth Clissmann, who met Mahr during this period in Berlin, felt that he was a lonely man, separated from his family, and with not enough to do: 'He was at a loose end because, in wartime, the people are interested in those men who can go out and fight; those who are active. But Mahr was an elderly man already.'

At one party, Mahr asked her if she would darn two holes that had appeared in his overcoat. Clissmann went to work with a needle and thread and found that the holes were both the size and shape of coins. 'These are burns,' she said. Mahr told her how, on his way home one night, he came across two or three women desperately trying to pull furniture and other belongings out of a burning house. He went to help them but did not notice that, with the heat of the fire, the lead was melting off the roof, dripping down and burning holes in his overcoat. Clissmann says:

> One of the sad things about bombing the German cities was that it was all women and children who suffered. There weren't many men around; they were at war. . . . But that's typical of Mahr; he would go into a burning house to help people he hadn't met before; he was only passing on the street. He was a good and kind man, with a social conscience.[16]

Maria Mahr wrote to her friends Frau Winkelmann and Frau Brase from Bad Ischl again in November 1943. She said: 'My thoughts are still with Ireland every day, and my homesickness is still as big as before.' She said that Adolf had attended a gathering of the German-Irish group in Berlin at Karl Kuenstler's house, and that she would go to Berlin in December for fourteen days to help him fix up the burned house. Hilde would stay in Austria to mind her sisters.[17]

On Christmas Eve 1943, Hans Hartmann's broadcast reminded

listeners of the time he had spent in Ireland, and especially the party that had been held in the Gresham Hotel for the German children, at which he had played the part of Father Christmas.[18] Even though that had been just five years before, it was already a different age for everyone who had attended the party.

In January 1944, Maria Mahr wrote again to Mrs Brase and Mrs Winkelmann, from her home in Bad Ischl:

> Adolf arrived [from Berlin] on the 23rd December in good form, and that was a relief after these fearful weeks. As a lovely Christmas present he brought two letters from Gustav from the lake in Tonkawa, Oklahoma dated the 26th and 27th of September. Now at last we can write to him, and we are delighted to know that he's well.
>
> And knowing that you will definitely write to him, thank you in advance for everything I know you will do for our boy. He really wants Chemistry and Physics study books and we will naturally try and send him these but we are unsure whether or not we will be able to. Perhaps you could help us from Dublin. He wants to study eagerly and make use of the time. He writes so contentedly, so we are really relaxed.[19]

Tonkawa was Gustav's first prisoner-of-war camp in the USA. The POWs went from America's East Coast deep into the South by sealed Pullman train, which Gustav recalls as being 'quite luxurious'. They spent their time in the camp trying to school themselves: Gustav wanted to learn physics and chemistry, and he built himself a table so that he could study while sitting on his bed. One American officer brought in a gramophone and classical-music records for the prisoners.[20]

Maria Mahr continued:

> Unfortunately my husband returned to Berlin on the 3rd January. He wants to make arrangements over the phone to meet up with Baczkowskis and Mona, as we haven't heard from Mona*kind* ['*kind*' means 'child'] in so long, even though Herr Baczkowski had given us news from Mona via letter. We're sorry we haven't seen them in so long. [Mona Brase was no longer living with the Baczkowskis. She was working as a Red Cross nurse in different camps in the Berlin area.]
>
> Have you had another ex-pat Christmas party? On Advent Sunday last I was thinking about you in Dublin a lot as I assumed you would have another party just like in the years before the war. As we had had news from Gustav, we were able to celebrate Christmas in gratefulness

and happy with the girls, and we celebrated Christmas Eve in a traditional way.[21]

By 1944, Mahr was head of Ru IX, a section that dealt with political broadcasting to the USA, Britain and Ireland.[22] He was also head of Ru II, which covered Britain, Ireland and English-language programmes for the British Empire, and Ru XI, which dealt with special information matters, believed to relate to the Foreign Office's secret transmitters.[23]

As a presidential election loomed in the United States, Germany hoped that Roosevelt would not win a fourth term in the White House, and that in his place a new leader might seek an early end to the war, and so help Germany retain its pre-war borders.[24] Hitler's coup d'état specialist Dr Edmund Veesenmayer, of the Foreign Office, was given the responsibility of carrying out an anti-Roosevelt campaign, and trying to persuade the Irish, Polish and Italian minorities in America that the US should withdraw from the war in Europe. The station, broadcasting from Germany, would be made to sound as if it was actually in Ireland, and staffed by Irish people. It would follow a similar model to Free India Radio, which was broadcast into India, from Holland, while purporting to come from Burma.[25]

Using short-wave radio, the Germans were reaching between three and seven million American listeners by January 1941. Mahr, in a report to von Ribbentrop at that time, called for the targeting of Irish-Americans, initially to swing public opinion against US entry into the war.[26] After Pearl Harbor, he modified his plan and called for an effort to hinder the Democratic Party's 1942 congressional-elections bid. In 1944, it was amended again in an effort to hamper Roosevelt's fourth bid for the White House. Mahr felt that, if he could reach a sizable slice of the Irish-American population, which he estimated to be between five and six million, he could swing their votes against Roosevelt.[27]

In August 1943, the Foreign Office's North American committee met and was told that a suitable person had been found to broadcast to the Irish in the USA, in a twice-weekly service. O'Donoghue has suggested that that person might have been Frank Ryan, the senior IRA figure then resident in Berlin. Veesenmayer urged Ryan to relocate to Luxembourg, where he could work with Hartmann and Mahr, but the plan fell apart in the spring of 1944, when Ryan became ill with pneumonia.

Elizabeth Clissmann was asked to prepare a report for the Foreign Office on the feasibility of broadcasting anti-Roosevelt propaganda to Irish-Americans. She was sent to Luxembourg to learn how Irland-Redaktion operated. There she found a team working in difficult conditions: it did not even have a map of Ireland to use as a reference. Despite morale being low, everyone was very protective of their job. Clissmann said: 'It was terribly important not to lose your job because without a job you could be drafted. You could be put in munitions, or sent to the front, so it was not just a job; it might be a question of losing your life.'[28]

Clissmann noticed that Hans Hartmann had a free hand in running the station, and that Mahr was simply an overseer. 'He just looked in and said "How're ye getting on, lads?" That's my impression,' she says. 'He was more the schools-inspector type than the school-principal type . . . . Mahr was hands-on in terms of being a shield; Hartmann would have looked upon him as a shield against the Ministry [the Foreign Office].'[29]

Mahr, Clissmann felt, 'seemed happy enough, but a little lonely'. Unable to practise his primary profession for several years, he could not resist the opportunity to take Clissmann and others from the Irland-Redaktion team on an archaeological field trip in the area. It was the middle of winter, yet, despite the cold weather, he brought the group to see the Igel column, the tallest Roman column north of the Alps, dating from 250 AD.[30] 'We went into some place and got boiling water,' says Clissmann. 'Mahr had cubes of dried tea (like a teabag) and he made a hot mug of tea for everybody. We were delighted. Typical of Mahr to look after everyone, and also lecture us on the monument.'[31]

Clissmann noticed that Mahr was in a quandary over the proposed service, and shared his doubts about its feasibility. Although he had originated the idea of the station, he felt that the form it was about to take was not workable. For example, the Foreign Office had a policy of supporting its ally Japan, so in its coverage it would have to celebrate Japanese victories over the Americans. This, they both knew, would be counterproductive among the Irish, who had a high regard for all things American. Mahr wanted to scrap the plan, or secure from his superiors special conditions for the new station.[32]

Clissmann felt that Mahr had little to do with the anti-Roosevelt plan, and that he was not being kept informed of more sensitive plans. 'Veesenmayer was very political – on the illegal political side of the Irish question [using the IRA to attack Britain, and perhaps Ireland]. I don't think they would have trusted Mahr. If they were working on the illegal side, they were very worried about talk getting back to Warnock, the Irish representative [in Berlin].' Aware that Mahr had attended these gatherings, Veesenmayer and Helmut Clissmann were worried that he might say something that could alert the Irish government to their group's 'illegal' activities.

With regard to her husband, Clissmann says:

> Helmut was on the illegal side. He wouldn't have been against Mahr, but wouldn't have wanted him on the political side. Not that he wouldn't trust him, or thought he was a spy, but he might let things slip. He hadn't much experience of Mahr and didn't know how he would react in certain situations. Helmut would only deal with people who were the same kind of people, the same ilk.

The plan failed to hatch for three reasons: neither Elizabeth Clissmann nor Mahr wanted it to work; Frank Ryan died in a Dresden hospital on 10 June 1944; and Veesenmayer had far bigger issues on his mind. He had been moved to Budapest in March, where he was named Reich Minister, which effectively put him in control of occupied Hungary. By the time Budapest was overrun by the Red Army less than a year later, some 570,000 of Hungary's Jews had perished, on Veesenmayer's orders.[33]

As more government departments moved out of an increasingly dangerous Berlin, Mahr's work regularly took him to the nearby town of Krummhübel, in the Silesian area of present-day Poland. Maria and the girls then moved to Krummhübel: apart from Gustav, the family was united once more. With hindsight, it seems to have made little sense to take the children out of school yet again, and to remove them from the relative safety of Bad Ischl into an area that was directly in the path of the advancing Red Army. It seems that nobody expected the Russian troops to arrive as quickly as they did.

There were just six weeks left in the school term before the summer break, during which Hilde went to summer camp. She had now reached the age for compulsory National Labour Service, and in October she joined a camp slightly north of Berlin. *Arbeitsdienst*, or 'working duty', served many functions, but at this stage of the war its primary function was to keep up factory and farm production levels by replacing the men who had been sent to the army with female labour. In her first camp, she sewed army uniforms, and later worked in a munitions factory. Labour Service had a similar status to military service, and Hilde was furnished with a military uniform and papers. The women lived in camps, and although they had freedom of movement, they were allowed just one free day per month. Hilde used her free day to visit her father in Berlin.

Adolf Mahr remained busy with his radio service and other projects. On the third and fourth of April 1944, he attended a joint SS, Foreign Office and Propaganda Office meeting in Krummhübel on the subject of the 'Jewish Question'. The purpose was to devise an effective strategy for disseminating anti-Semitic material overseas. Mahr's role was to 'handle the foreign anti-Jewish action on the radio'.[34]

The conference was told that, since Jews were so successful in other countries, such as the Soviet Union, the USA and Britain, the entire international community had to act against them. Eberhard von Thadden, the German Foreign Office official in charge of Jewish affairs and liaison with the SS, asked delegates to adhere to the following principles in their respective countries:

1. Suppression of any Semitic propaganda that could interfere with the German measures.
2. Preparation of foreign peoples so they understand the German measures against the Jews.
3. Ongoing reporting of possible diplomatic ways of working against the Jews in other countries.
4. Reporting of possible counterproductive reactions from the Jews in order to facilitate a quick response.

Mahr made a speech in which he reported on anti-Jewish propaganda on foreign radio services. He asked for a foreign German station that could deliver anti-Jewish material. He wanted to see a greater German impact on the airwaves of other countries, although he stressed that the sovereignty of these countries had to be protected. Within Germany, he said, the standard of broadcasting should be kept high.

Later in the conference, Mahr suggested lists to be drawn up of pro-Jewish freemasons, journalists, writers and economists. He encouraged the publication of a diplomatic handbook of Jewish world politics, which also could be published in English and French.³⁵ The minutes of the meeting were circulated, although some of the proposals were so secret that they could not be written down.³⁶ Each delegate was required to work on the proposals and meet a year later to report on progress. This did not happen, because of Germany's impending defeat.

As is often the case with Mahr, it is difficult to understand his motivations at this conference. He comes across as an ardent anti-Semite in calling for anti-Jewish propaganda in foreign radio services, yet in the service, where he had control, there was little such material. Perhaps it was a career-enhancing move, and he was deliberately taking a tough line to impress his superiors. Gustav Mahr says that his father was not involved in Jewish persecution, although he concedes that his participation in such meetings might lead some to describe him as a 'desktop war criminal'.³⁷

The historian Mark Hull believes that Mahr's participation at such a meeting is incriminating: 'While it doesn't place Mahr as an architect of the Holocaust, it makes his sympathies clear. In law, abetting a crime often gets you the same penalty as those who actually carry it out.'³⁸ The D-Day landings in Normandy on 6 June 1944 for many observers marked the beginning of the end for Nazi Germany. Two weeks later, the Red Army opened its spring offensive, and a month after that, several German army officers tried to assassinate Hitler in the famous July Plot. Had this plot succeeded, millions of lives might have been saved, because Hitler's successor would probably have tried to sue for peace. Instead, by surviving the July assassination attempt, the Führer was further convinced that God was on his side, and that his mission must continue.

For Irland-Redaktion, the end was clearly in sight. Irish public opinion mattered little any more, because, in the absence of a German invasion of Britain, Ireland had lost her strategic importance. The BBC ceased monitoring the service in July 1944, and although the Irish army continued to tune into Hans Hartmann's talks, transcripts were rarely typed up.³⁹

On 25 August, Paris was liberated, and American troops began to close in on Luxembourg in early September. The Irland-Redaktion team, along with the other European services, evaded capture by moving north to the village of Apen, near Oldenburg, and set up studios in Bremers Hotel. Mahr's team – Hans Hartmann, a secretary and a translator – moved there too, but Mahr stayed in Berlin.

Fearful of being overrun by the Red Army, the SS started to evacuate the concentration camp at Auschwitz on 18 January 1945. They destroyed the gas chambers, burned incriminating documents and forced the stronger prisoners on a march to other camps closer to the Reich. Wearing light prison clothes, in a Polish winter when temperatures reached minus thirty-five degrees centigrade, most did not survive this death-march. About 3,000 prisoners who were deemed too weak to walk were left behind to die at the camp. By the time the Soviet 107th Rifle Division emerged from the snow-laden woods on 27 January and stumbled across the camp, many of these prisoners had died, and the rest were found wandering about the camp.[40]

The scenes at Auschwitz, and other information of Nazi atrocities, further convinced Russian troops that they were fighting an evil enemy that deserved no mercy. The Red Army took revenge upon German civilians and troops alike. Anyone who was believed to have helped the Germans was either shot or sent to the rear of the advancing Red Army, for transportation to the gulags. News of the retributions leaked out from the reconquered territories to the areas that were still occupied by German forces. It sparked the largest panic migration in history: almost 8.5 million Germans fled their homes in the eastern provinces of the Reich.[41]

Millions of refugees were now on the move over vast swathes of Poland, Ukraine and Belarus. By mid-February, close to 7 million people were heading from the 'evacuated areas' to the Reich, where they expected some kind of protection. Already more than 40,000 refugees were arriving in Berlin each day. The capital, whose resources were already stretched by continuous air raids and severe rationing, could not cope with its existing population, never mind the recently arrived hordes of sick and hungry refugees. The authorities, fearful of an outbreak of typhus or some other contagious disease, tried to make the trains from the east go around the city, or drop off passengers elsewhere.[42]

The historian Antony Beevor described one typical trek, from the regions along the Baltic coast, heading for Berlin:

> The vast majority of the refugees were women and children since almost all the remaining men had been drafted into the *Volkssturm* [local defence militia]. The variety of transport ranged from handcarts and

prams for those on foot to every sort of farm cart, pony trap and even the odd *landau* [four-wheeled, horse-drawn carriage], exhumed from the stables of some *schloss* [country house]. There were hardly any motor vehicles because the Wehrmacht and the Nazi Party had requisitioned them already, as well as all fuel. Progress was pitifully slow, and not just because of the snow and ice. Columns kept halting because carts were overloaded and axles broke. Hay carts, filled with household objects, hams, kegs and jars of food, were turned into covered wagons with a crude superstructure and carpets draped over the outside. Mattresses inside provided some relief to heavily pregnant women and nursing mothers. On icy surfaces, undernourished horses found it hard work. Some carts were hauled by oxen whose unshod hooves were worn raw by the roads, leaving bloodstains in the snow. And when an animal died, as was often the case, there was seldom time to butcher it for food. Fear of the enemy drove the refugees on.[43]

The fear related to the murder of civilians, and the rapes. The Russian war correspondent Vasily Grossman noted 'the horror in the eyes of women and girls. . . . Terrible things were happening to German women. A cultivated German man explains with expressive gestures and broken Russian words that his wife has been raped by ten men that day . . . . Soviet girls who have been liberated from camps are suffering greatly too.'[44] Grossman also told of a young mother who was being raped continuously in a farm shed. Her relatives came to the shed and asked the soldiers to allow her a break to breast-feed her baby because it would not stop crying. Even non-German women were not safe. Rapes were reported of Ukrainian, Russian and Belorussian women, and of girls released from slave labour in Germany.[45]

Mahr, still living in Berlin, could not have failed to notice the catastrophe unfolding all around him, but Irland-Redaktion continued to broadcast right up to the final week of the war. The air raids were so severe that each time Hilde travelled to visit her father, she found him living in a different apartment, the previous one having been destroyed. In all, Mahr was bombed out twelve times in Berlin.[46]

In January 1945, more than four million Russian troops were massed in Poland, preparing to invade the Reich. It was no longer safe for Maria, Ingrid and Brigit to stay in Silesia, and Adolf felt that they should return to Bad Ischl. Ingrid helped her father burn his documents relating to the

Krummhübel Conference and other matters, but Maria made no preparations to leave. She was depressed and exhausted, and fed up with leaving a place once she had made it home. 'I'm not packing,' she said; 'I don't care if the Russians come. We came to Germany with only some clothes. Then Berlin, where we had a nice flat, but that got bombed. So we only had a suitcase of clothes again. Then we were in Bad Ischl, but Father suggested we come to Silesia. Now the Russians are coming. I'm tired of packing and running. I'm fed up. I can't run any more.'[47]

Despite Maria's pleas, her daughters put her on a train with her luggage, and they travelled to Berlin to catch a train south the following day. There they met up with Hilde, who had special leave from her labour camp that day. The family spent that evening in a house Adolf Mahr was staying in at Dahlem in the western suburbs of Berlin. Ingrid wandered into the garden and watched as planes flew over the city's jagged skyline, and dropped bombs. Soon after the raid ended, Adolf brought Ingrid into the city to retrieve bags and suitcases, belonging to the family, which he had stored in one of the museums. They walked through the burning city together, until they came to the museum, which was also on fire. Adolf told Ingrid to wait while he went inside the building to retrieve their property, but she stopped him just as the building collapsed. Later they found out that Mahr's efforts would have been in vain: the museum director had already saved the luggage and taken it away.[48]

In the chaos of a Berlin train station the following day, as thousands of refugees arrived from the east to the perceived safety of the Reich, and thousands of well-connected Berliners fled the city for the safety of the countryside, Adolf and Hilde Mahr waved off Maria, Ingrid and Brigit. It had been a difficult morning trying to get them to the train station, and then on to a train. Adolf Mahr, because of his damaged arm, was unable to carry much. Maria Mahr, who had been lame all her life, was now physically and emotionally exhausted, and also incapable of carrying suitcases, and Brigit, aged twelve, could not carry much either. So it fell to Ingrid and Hilde to bear most of the load. They got their mother and sister on to the crowded train, then pushed their luggage to them through a window.

As they said their goodbyes, each family member knew that they might not see each other again. They expected Bad Ischl to be safe: it was of no strategic importance and was not lying between the Soviet forces and Berlin. Adolf's life was in constant danger as the Allies stepped up the frequency and ferocity of the air raids on the German capital. Hilde was in less danger from the air raids, but in more danger of being captured by Russian troops. She was now living in a camp in Gransee, on the Polish border, north of Berlin.

In March, Adolf Mahr finally left Berlin, and joined Hans Hartmann and the Irland-Redaktion team in Oldenburg, near the Dutch border. Hilde came into the city to say goodbye to him. A despondent Adolf told her that Hitler was a sick man and really belonged in a lunatic asylum. He said: 'This war is lost. There is nothing to be done about it. We just have to see how we can survive.'[49]

As they parted, both of them knew that they might not see each other again. As a parent, Adolf's emotional pain was, perhaps, stronger. While he departed for the relative safety of north-west Germany, he knew that his eighteen-year-old daughter was going towards the Eastern Front, to an area that was about to be overrun by the Red Army. It should have been the other way around. The Red Army now had 6.7 million men bearing down on Germany – twice the strength of the German army when it had invaded the Soviet Union in 1941.[50] It was not a question of 'if', but rather 'when' they would overrun Hilde's area. He knew the fate that awaited her if she was caught by Russian soldiers, but there was little choice: although her chances of survival were slim, she might also be shot if she failed to return to her camp.

Showing remarkable foresight, Adolf thrust a railway map of Germany into Hilde's hand, and said: 'Save this map for yourself because you have no knowledge of German geography. You will never find your way if you don't have a railway map.' It turned out to be a most useful piece of advice.

Adolf moved to a cluster of villages which included Apen, Augustfehn and Westerstede, about twenty kilometres from Oldenburg, and fifty kilometres from the Dutch border. The many members of the broadcasting teams, which included Poles, Arabs and Indians working on their respective stations, were billeted with landladies in the villages. Mahr took a room with the Schroeder family in Augustfehn; William Joyce and his wife stayed with Frau Kruse in Apen.[51]

Mahr's team held out until the beginning of May 1945, less than a week before the formal German surrender. Even as the Red Army began its final Berlin offensive, the programmes continued to go out on air, with a mixed bag of war communiqués, music and news. Hans Hartman presented a final ten-minute bulletin in Irish on 2 May, before fleeing to stay with relatives on a farm at Westerstede. The final piece of music broadcast to Ireland was John McCormack singing 'Come Back to Erin'. Mahr and the rest of the team then went on the run.[52] So did Hilde, but in a different way.

7

Hilde's Journey, 1945

Less than three weeks after saying goodbye to her father, and shortly before Soviet forces overran the area, Hilde Mahr's *Reichsarbeitsdienst* camp at Mecklenburg was disbanded. The 180 girls were ordered back to Berlin by train on 16 April 1945. Hilde had her lunch, and in the afternoon packed her bags and caught the 5.45 PM train for Berlin. Along the way they stopped in Kremmen and Velten, and then waited until the air raids over Berlin ended that night.

Tuesday, 17 April 1945

The group arrived into Berlin's Stettiner Bahnhof (now called Nord-Bahnhof) Station at 2.30 AM. For the other girls, there was some comfort in being reunited with friends and family, albeit in a city that was being bombed day and night. For Hilde, it was a more frightening prospect. The eighteen-year-old was now alone, and, apart from Gustav, who was in a prisoner-of-war camp in the United States, she had no way of knowing if the rest of her family was alive or dead.

To stay in Berlin was unthinkable. Even if she survived the air raids and the shelling, she stood little chance of surviving the imminent downfall of the city, and the aftermath of a Red Army victory. She was aware of the widespread attacks on German women that had take place in east Prussia, Pomerania and Silesia, where the number of rape victims was later estimated to be 1.4 million. There was every reason to believe that the women of Berlin would suffer the same fate, and studies after the war confirmed that this was indeed what happened. Within weeks of Hilde arriving in Berlin, the Red Army took the city, and raped more than a hundred thousand women, mostly in gangs. Doctors in the city estimated that ten thousand women died as a result of the attacks, mostly through suicide.[1]

Hilde thought about trying to join her father near Oldenburg, but that area had been overrun by the British, so she would have to pass through the fighting of the Western Front in order to look for him. It would be foolish to even try to do this. Her best prospects seemed to lie in joining her mother and sisters in Bad Ischl, but how? The village was 600 kilometres away to the south. She would have to get out of Berlin and its hinterland, then travel through the Protectorate of Bohemia (formerly part of Czechoslovakia) and into the former Austria – always close to the ever-advancing Russian front.

Apart from having no money, food or transport, she could be executed by the Nazi government for trying to leave the city. Goebbels had declared that leaving Berlin without permission was tantamount to desertion.[2] The following week, more than two thousand passes were issued to allow senior Nazi Party officials to leave the city,[3] but ordinary citizens who tried to leave without permits were hanged.[4] Hilde's chances of survival seemed poor whether she stayed in Berlin or not. As she stepped over dead bodies and the carcasses of horses, and the rubble of Berlin's once-magnificent buildings, she saw a people weakened by daily and nightly bombing raids, and inadequate food and water supplies. She decided to head for the south of the city by U-Bahn and descended into either the Oranienburger Tor or the Zinnowitzer Street Station. Immediately, several people tried to stop her from entering the station and warned her against looking inside. She ignored their advice and continued down the stairs – and was shocked by what she saw there. It was a 'sea of bodies' – hundreds of dead women, children and old people floating in the underground station.

The continuous bombing raids had weakened the subterranean structures that prevented water from the canals and rivers from entering the underground tunnels. The air raid of the night before had caused flooding in the tunnels where tens of thousands of civilians had taken shelter. Many of the old and sick, and others, drowned; nobody will ever know how many.

As she returned to street level, Hilde decided to try to leave Berlin on foot, but she stood little hope of getting by the *Feldgendarmerie* who patrolled the exit routes, ready to execute 'defeatists'. She walked south across the ruined city, past the ruins of Humbolt University, where Marx and Engels, and also Albert Einstein, had studied. Across the street was the Babelplatz, site of the first big official Nazi book-burning in May 1933. She crossed Unter den Linden, the street 'beneath the lime trees', the great showpiece boulevard that leads to the Brandenburg Gate. The Nazis had cut down the original trees to make way for their flagpoles. Beyond the Brandenburg Gate was the Reichstag, regarded by the Soviet armies as a symbol of the Third Reich. She also passed near Hitler's bunker, where the man whose political movement had dominated her life since she was seven years of age would commit suicide thirteen days later.

After walking about five kilometres through the ruined city, she reached the Anhalter Bahnhof, and came across a group of soldiers boarding a train to the south. She approached the sergeant and asked if she could join the group. 'I have military papers. I am on leave. I'm allowed to go with military transport. Can I try to get down south with you?' she asked.

It was true that, as a member of the National Labour Service, she was allowed to use military transportation, but not without good reason. If the sergeant allowed her to board the train, she could at least escape Berlin. If not, she risked being arrested by the *Feldgendarmerie* for trying to escape, and then would probably be put into an army section in the city.

The sergeant was taking about a hundred men in uniform to a position to the south of Prague to meet an advancing unit of the Red Army. Technically, they were soldiers, but Hilde realised that they were just old men, badly trained and poorly armed, drafted in a last desperate attempt to save Nazi Germany. It was, in all probability, a suicide mission. Perhaps in earlier times the sergeant would have stuck by the rules, and maybe even turned her over to the authorities. But, surrounded by the smouldering ruins of the Third Reich, he offered Hilde a new lease of life and let her board the train.

Hilde was the only female on board as the train left for Dresden at 7 AM. Berliners could already hear the approach of the Red Army's guns as its final push for the city intensified. In the two weeks that followed, 100,000 Russians would die in the battle for Berlin.[5] There are no figures for the number who died on the German side.

Hilde kept a diary during this time. She recorded that progress was slow owing to two air raids in the area, and in Zossen, a company of train-based anti-aircraft soldiers got on board. Shortly before noon, they passed through the charred city of Dresden. It had been two months since British and American bombers had made a smouldering ruin of the once-beautiful capital of Saxony, killing between 35,000 and 50,000 people.[6] Suddenly the planes were back and Hilde's train was the target. The city's air-raid sirens no longer worked, so the train stopped only when the driver realised that it was under attack.

'There was no siren; just suddenly bombs starting coming down all around the train,' she says. 'There was a whistle and the train stopped, and someone shouted: "Get off the train, get off the train, and run!"'

Most of the soldiers ran into a railway yard near the Neustädter Station, and took cover among machinery and parts of old trains there. She got about fifty metres from the train before diving behind some scrap metal. 'Bombs were falling on the train and all around it,' she remembers. 'A bomb dropped beside me and metal started flying around everywhere. I had a rucksack and in that there was a blanket. I just crawled under some metal and put the rucksack in front of me, and hoped I wouldn't be hit.'

The raid lasted a full hour, during which time the train was destroyed, along with the Hauptbahnhof (Dresden's main railway station), the Neustädter Station, and all the nearby tracks and embankments. Six of the soldiers were also killed.

There was no time to grieve or dwell on what had happened. As ambulances arrived, the army group were called together and marched down the tracks through Dresden and onwards to Strehlen, twenty-four kilometres away. Hilde remained with them as they completed the four-hour march. During this time, they witnessed further attacks by low-flying bombers, but since they were on foot, they were not the targets.

They reached Strehlen in the early evening, and Hilde had a 'cat's-lick' (a quick clean) before departing at about 8 PM for Pirna. From there they took another train at 11 PM for Bodenbach (renamed 'Podmokly–Tchech') and passed the remainder of the night peacefully. It had been a long and violent day: thousands of people all around Hilde had lost their lives. She must have wondered how long her own luck would last.

WEDNESDAY, 18 APRIL

In the early hours, the group reached Bodenbach, and they slept on the stone floor of the station until 5.30 AM. They contacted the local police sergeant to ask for food: her diary does not record whether this was successful or not. The group left for Aussig (now named Usti) at 8 AM; shortly before reaching the town, they were attacked again by planes. Hilde spent much of the day sheltering from air raids by the entrance to a mining tunnel. In the early evening, they left for Lobositz (now named Lovosice, in the Czech Republic), where they arrived at 6.30 PM. Following unsuccessful attempts to get field rations, they sat outside for three hours in the wind and rain until 9.30 PM, when they departed for Prague in 'second-class seats, upholstered!'

THURSDAY, 19 APRIL

On reaching Prague at 1 AM, the group finally got food rations. While sheltering from an air raid in a medical centre, Hilde and her companions ate pea soup. She then slept for a few hours on a stone step with her head resting on the company's typewriter. She eventually woke because of the discomfort she was in: her body and limbs were aching. Prague's location deep in the heart of Europe had protected it from the air assaults that had destroyed several of the cities in the Reich. Unlike Berlin and Dresden, there was a relative air of calm and normality there.[7] Hilde spent the morning walking around the city with Hanisch, one of the officers from the company, while waiting for an engine to arrive. At about 1 PM, their train left for Budweis – the original home of the famous American beer. Hilde noticed that it was 'Most beautiful weather, so the trip was relatively nice.'

The group was now close to the Sudetenland. Hilde's paternal grandparents were from this region, and her relative, Maier von Weinertsgruen, had been involved in 'Germanising' it in 1939. For centuries, the so-called *Volksdeutsche*, or ethnic Germans, had lived and farmed the lands in this, the former Kingdom of Bohemia. But their presence would soon come to a bloody end when all German-speaking inhabitants of the Sudetenland were expelled as the Third Reich crumbled. Columns of refugees headed for the German border while vengeful Czech partisans, newly liberated after seven years of German rule, subjected them to robbery, beatings, rapes and murder.[8] The area was to be resettled by Czechs from other parts of Czechoslovakia, and Czech names restored to streets and towns. It was a reversal of Maier von Weinertsgruen's project.

Friday, 20 April

It took the party twelve hours to get to Budweis, where the train rested on a siding until 6 AM, before departing again in the direction of Portschitsch. Hilde woke at 7 AM. She had been so tired that she hadn't noticed the train start moving. Later that morning, when the train stopped again, the group walked to the grounds of a nearby mansion and slept for most of the day. It was 10 PM before they left for Krummau.

Saturday, 21 April

Tired and hungry, the group arrived in Krummau shortly after midnight. Hilde and Wehnert, another army officer, went to the military supply office in search of rations, but were unsuccessful. In the morning they returned, this time with food. They wandered around the town until midday, and then endured yet another air raid. At 2.30 PM they got soup, and then went to a meadow, where they fell asleep. At 8 PM, their train left, and they travelled from the present-day Czech Republic back into Germany.

Sunday, 22 April

Around midnight, their train broke down and the group got stuck in Fischhaus, thirteen kilometres outside the town of Passau. It was pouring with rain, and there were no trains for many hours, so the troops found shelter in three big barns in Ruderting, where they slept that night in hay, 'drenched wet to the skin', as Hilde put it.

Monday, 23 April

In the morning, at 7.30, Hilde and the group's sergeant got a lift to Passau from the farmer who owned the barn, and there they picked up rations and made enquiries. They returned at midday with soup for the group, but at this point Hilde had decided to leave her companions.

Passau marks the point where the Rivers Inn and Ilz run into the mighty Danube. The beautiful baroque town straddles the river as it leaves Germany and enters Austria. Napoleon Bonaparte, upon seeing the town for the first time, is said to have remarked: 'In all of Germany I never saw a town more beautiful.' In order to slow the Soviet advance, the retreating German forces had blown up all the bridges in Passau except the biggest one – and that one was already loaded with explosives. Hilde realised that this bridge was her last chance to get across the Danube into Austria.

She fetched her luggage, said goodbye to Company Commander Nagel, her friend Harms, and the rest of the company who had fed and looked after her. She knew that, without their help, she might have been stranded in Berlin. She returned to Passau with the company sergeant, said goodbye to him, and ventured towards the town's last remaining bridge. She did not know where the men would end up, but she felt that they would meet the Red Army at some point and that, when that happened, it was unlikely they would survive.

A German soldier stood guard at the bridge with strict instructions to keep people off it. This was partially for their own safety: a call could come at any moment with an order to blow up the bridge. The Germans would also have been concerned about someone getting onto the bridge and defusing the charges. The soldier stopped Hilde from stepping on to the bridge, but she couldn't afford not to cross there: 'I've got to get to my family in the south, and I'm not going to swim through the river,' she said. 'I've got to get over there somehow. There's no other bridge than this one.'

Just like the sergeant in the Berlin train station, the guard disobeyed orders and told Hilde that he would look the other way. If anyone asked, he hadn't seen her. The span of the bridge was so long that it took twenty minutes to cross! Below her were powerful explosives ready to blow at a moment's notice. Above her was the possibility of another air offensive. She cut a lonely figure on the deserted bridge high above the Danube, but kept walking, in the knowledge that, by getting across, she was entering Austria, the country of her birth – where, she hoped, her mother and sisters were living.

Hilde was not the only lone female walking through the countryside at that time. She came across many others wandering around looking for loved ones. But there were no young men: they had all been sent to war. She used the map her father had given her, and followed the railway tracks as he had instructed. Even though she was now far away from the intense bombings that were occurring in northern Germany, she had the unfortunate status of being in the middle of a world war where every side was a threat to her. If she was captured by Soviet troops, she would probably be raped and maybe murdered. If she was caught in uniform by the

British or the Americans, she would be imprisoned and interrogated for information about escaping Nazis. Encountering a German unit would have been dangerous too: she was a deserter – an offence that carried the death penalty.

'You stopped being afraid,' she says. 'You just have one aim; you want to do something, you think that's the right decision, you do that. Don't get yourself into danger unnecessarily. That bridge was necessary. I had to get over the bridge; there's no other bridge. But you don't take unnecessary dangers.'

What about the fear of rape? 'I was not really afraid that a German soldier would do anything to me. They had much sympathy for all these young girls, hanging around lost, trying to find people, to get home to their families. . . . It would have been more likely that I was raped by the Russians. But you wouldn't be afraid of your own . . . . And you could be sure that the Americans or the British would not rape. Because we were sure that if it was found out, they would be punished or even shot for that.'

That evening, she missed the 4 PM train to Attnang, but caught the 8 PM Linzer train to Schärding. She slept that night in the station building.

TUESDAY, 24 APRIL

The following day, Hilde walked an exhausting sixty kilometres to the town of Wels. She was now in the Salzkammergut, the picturesque holiday region of mountains and lakes near Salzburg where her father had excavated salt mines the year she was born. The area was familiar to her: she had gone to school in nearby Gmunden. Bad Ischl, the geographical centre of the region, lay another eighty kilometres away.

WEDNESDAY, 25 APRIL

Hilde slept the night in a railway station. She tried to make an early start the next morning, but the train she was due to board had been destroyed by Allied aircraft. Instead, she set off on a train for Attnang at 11 AM; when it came to a halt two hours later, she continued on foot, through the ruins of the town. That day, she came across the horror of the concentration camps for the first time. She omitted this episode from her diary in case she was arrested by German forces and it was used against her.

In the days before, the railway junction at Attnang-Puchheim had been destroyed in an Allied air raid. The embankments had been damaged and then washed away in heavy rains, so that the train tracks now ran through thin air. A group of uniformed men were working in the deep mud trying to repair the tracks; as Hilde walked closer, she realised that they were concentration-camp prisoners, working under armed guard.

There was nothing she could do for them. She could neither turn back, nor turn away, so she walked through the group. 'There for the first time I saw these awfully starved people,' says Hilde. 'These were all Jewish men, about a hundred of them.' As she passed, she noticed that some of the men were picking white objects out of the mud and eating them. Hilde realised that the derailed train had been carrying raw white beans and had spilled its cargo on to the ground. She knew that uncooked white beans are poisonous; perhaps the men knew this too, but in their hunger they ate the beans as they worked.

She continued through the ruins of Attnang as far as Wankham, six kilometres away. It was now 4 PM, and the next train was not due to depart for six hours. It was too long a wait for someone who had no food and was very tired. But at the same station she saw a stationary train with a driver inside. She approached, and asked the driver if he might be going to Bad Ischl. He replied that he would be leaving in an hour or two but that he was not allowed to take passengers. With the same urgency she had employed in the days before, she pleaded: 'I can't walk all the way to Bad Ischl. I am nearly starved; I have no food any more. I need to get to my family tonight.'

The driver was reluctant, but agreed to hide her in the engine of the train. She climbed inside the outer panelling of the engine, and hid under her blanket. She was then locked inside, and told to remain silent. She could not see the driver from her hiding place. She was there for two hours – so long that she thought the driver had forgotten her.

Suddenly the train started to move. It went to and fro, as it gathered other carriages, and then started to move off. But there was a problem. Hilde crawled out of her hiding place to look out through the engine's ventilation slits. She could see that the train was going back in the direction she had come from! A terrible feeling came over her: she was on board a locked train engine heading away from the only place where she could hope to find her family. Soon she realised why the driver had been reluctant to bring her onto the train: it was being used to transport the workers she had seen on the broken train tracks, to and from the concentration camp at Ebensee. The train slowed and stopped, and she looked out to see the same workers who had been eating the poisonous beans getting on to the train. Soon the driver knocked on the panelling of the engine to see if she was all right.

'Yes, I am,' she said quietly.

'OK, we will continue now,' he said, and the train began to move in the other direction.

When the train got to the concentration camp, the workers walked through the gates, probably for the last time. Hilde did not look out, for fear of being seen by a camp guard. 'If they had found me there, the driver would have been shot. And probably the same for me too,' she says. 'So I was like a little kitten, hiding in that corner. I said to myself: "God bless me, let's hope that this works out properly." I didn't have any other choice.'

At that point, the driver whispered to Hilde that he was getting off the train there but that another driver would soon come along and that he would tell him she was there. Divested of its prisoners, the train now shunted backwards and forwards as it took on a cargo of oil. Eventually the train got going again, and after a while the new driver knocked and asked: 'Is there anyone in there?'

Hilde replied that there was, and that she wanted to get off at Bad Ischl. The driver told her that he would make a stop at the main station but that she couldn't get off there, or she would be seen. After that, there was an industrial zone: he would stop there for a moment, and she could jump off.

As they reached the industrial zone of Bad Ischl at around 8.30 PM, the driver gave her notice and let her out of her hiding place. He stopped for a moment, and she threw her bag off the train and then jumped off. It was dark, but she knew where she was. She had regularly swum in the nearby river. It was a short walk from the industrial zone over a bridge to the house where she hoped to find her mother and sisters. She was exhausted and hungry, and had no alternative plan if they weren't there.

She went to the door and rang the bell, but then 'got a blow, a disappointment,' she says. 'My younger sister Brigit opened the window upstairs and looked down. And she gave a cry: "Mum, mum, come!" And my mum shouted: "Adolf, Adolf, is it you?" And of course I was disappointed. She wasn't expecting me.'

Maria, Ingrid and Brigit Mahr had been sharing the house with Hilde's uncle Franz Hoernisch, her aunt Auguste, their two grown-up daughters (their husbands were in military service) and their children. They brought Hilde upstairs, and she noticed that everyone was crying. Brigit took off Hilde's boots, and everyone recoiled from the smell. She hadn't taken off her boots in five days because she had been afraid that, once they were off, the leather would shrink and the boots would not go back on her feet. When Brigit took off the boots, the socks came off with them, and the boots fell apart.

Soon afterwards, Hilde collapsed. She had inflammation of the lung and a high fever brought on by the strain and by being wet for days and nights. Brigit remembers her older sister sleeping for 'nearly a week without saying a word to anyone'. The eighteen-year-old had travelled 600 kilometres in eight days through one of history's most dangerous war zones.

Hilde was not out of danger yet, though. Her leave had long expired – which meant that her rationing cards had expired too. And without ration cards, she couldn't buy food. By law, she should have gone to the municipal office in Linz or Wels to enrol for service again, but her uncle told her that she was not to leave the house: 'You stay up there and we'll feed you. There were nine, but we can also feed ten. But please hide,' he said.

The war seemed to drag on and on, and nobody could get reliable information about it. They did not believe what they heard on the radio – and that part of Austria was isolated from the war. Hitler committed suicide on 30 April. On 4 May, American troops moved into Bad Ischl, marking the end of the war for the Mahrs, although not the end of their struggle.

'We saw the Americans come through in their jeeps and their tanks,' says Hilde. 'We all had our white sheets hanging out of the windows. We were happy to see them. We didn't cheer them, because in this region there had been hardly any fighting. Further west, where the war was bad, the people partly welcomed the Americans because they knew there was going to be an end of the bombing and shooting. It was a very silent takeover here.'

The Americans carried on as far as Linz, where they met up with Soviet forces. Since November 1942, the Red Army had pushed the Germans from the edge of Stalingrad back through southern Russia, Ukraine, Moldova, Romania and Hungary, and from parts of Czechoslovakia and Austria. They stopped at Linz, just a hundred kilometres from the Mahr home.

With the war over, the victorious Allies set about fixing the perimeters of the new Europe. The principles upon which the occupation of defeated Germany was to be carried out were laid down at the Big Three Conference (of the United States, Britain and the Soviet Union) at Potsdam in July 1945. What was later called East Germany was taken by Russia, while the US took control of the southern regions, France the western parts, and Britain the northern parts. It was said at the time that the Americans got the scenery, the French got the wine, and the British got the ruins.[9] Although the Mahrs were in some ways fortunate to find themselves in the scenic part, the American zone, there were no obvious benefits in the immediate term. There was no mail service, little transportation, and little industry. Furthermore, civilians were not allowed to move between zones. This meant that his family had no way of finding out whether Adolf Mahr, whose last known whereabouts was in the British zone, was alive or dead. Even Gustav couldn't find out whether his family had perished at the end of the war.

As the weeks wore on, the first signs of a post-war society appeared. Food and fuel were still rationed, but the Mahrs had a small garden where they planted onions, cabbages and other vegetables. Hilde got work in the kitchen of a nearby military hospital. Apart from the payment she received, she was allowed to take soup and bread for her family every day. Ingrid and Hilde also went into the hills to cut firewood. During that summer of 1945, six years after first arriving in Bad Ischl on holiday from Dublin, the family had enough to survive, although little else.

Like millions of families all over Europe, the males were missing. Late that summer, Dr Hoernisch was imprisoned for his previous Nazi activities. There was no word from Gustav to indicate when he might be allowed home. Nothing had been heard of Adolf for five months, and Maria Mahr had given up hope that they would ever get back together as a family. 'She kept saying "What are we going to do?"' says Hilde. 'Her money was running out. She was so downhearted. She had three children:

I was just nineteen, Ingrid sixteen and Brigit thirteen, and she said "I don't know how we are going to survive; I don't know if Dad is alive." We had not heard from him yet.'

Like many families in similar situations, even if the news were bad, they preferred to know if their loved one was dead or alive. Hilde, being the oldest remaining child in the family, felt a responsibility to find her father: 'I said to my mother, I am going up to Germany, and I will make my way somehow to north Germany and try to find where Dad is, so that we can make arrangements; if he would come down to us, or we would go up to him.'

Those over the age of eighteen who did not have a profession were required to work in the local municipality to help register civilians and give them identity cards. Hilde, who had turned nineteen in July, worked there, and through her job she became friendly with several German soldiers who had been wounded during the war. Now recovered, they wanted to return to Germany. Even though movement between the zones was illegal and dangerous, they were determined to cross into Germany. They invited Hilde to come along. Hilde went home and presented her mother with a most difficult dilemma: keep her safely in Bad Ischl, which meant that she would never find out the fate of her husband, or allow her to leave, with the many dangers that entailed – but also with the possibility that she may reunite the family. Maria gave permission for her daughter to leave.

Hilde failed to report for work on 26 September 1945. The night before, she and six former German soldiers had set off from Bad Ischl westwards over the mountains. They walked through the night and for most of the following day until they crossed the border and reached the spa town of Bad Reichenhall, in Germany.

With little public transport in operation, thousands of displaced people soon realised that the best way to travel in Germany was on the trains that brought coal from the Ruhrgebiet region in the north down to southern Germany. The large coal wagons were laden with coal on their southbound journey, and were supposed to be empty on their return north, but instead they usually carried a cargo of people. Hilde and her companions jumped aboard one of the trains as it left Bad Reichenhall and headed north.

Although the coal wagons were cold and dirty, Hilde was in a stronger position than she had been during her previous trip. She now had a rucksack of food, and some money, although there was still very few places that had anything to sell. Once again she donned her uniform, so that if she was stopped she could claim that she had been dismissed from some camp and was looking for her family. The train's cargo must have looked a strange sight. Even though the wagons had been emptied of their coal, they were still lined with coal dust, and everyone who sat in the wagons became covered in soot. Hilde's uniform soon became black, as did her blanket and the canvas cover she used at night. Thick chains hung like clotheslines from one side of each wagon to the other. The lucky ones got to sit on the chains and rock to the motion of the train, while the less fortunate had to sit in the dirt on the floor. Sitting on the chain one day looking at the scores of dirty faces in the wagons ahead and behind, Hilde noted that the train 'was full of refugees. Everybody was going somewhere else. All of Germany was on its way on the coal trains.'

Riding the rails in this fashion was not allowed, so just as the train stopped at a station, the illegal cargo jumped off, in case of a police raid. Then, as soon as the train started to move again, they climbed aboard; usually, the stronger ones got on first, and pulled everyone else up.[10] There was a sense of companionship on the trains, a shared experience of having come through the war – of having been displaced, and to be looking for family members. They passed the hours talking about their experiences and sharing intimate details, as strangers often do.

'Since we were all involved in this situation, you didn't have the feeling that it was a hardship for you personally. It was a hardship for everybody,' Hilde says. 'And I was happy and healthy, and solid, and capable of trying to find a new way. Others were nearly wrecked – killed or lost. I knew I had a family and I knew that if we got together again, we would manage somehow.'

For three days and three nights, she travelled through the heart of Germany. Leaving the border areas, she went through Rosenheim, via the south of Munich, through Memmingen and Tuttlingen, up to Stuttgart, and to Frankfurt, where she parted from her companions. Looking at the destroyed towns of Germany, she 'got the feeling there wasn't a single place left that had one stone on top of another'.

The poet Stephen Spender, who travelled through Germany in the same year, wrote: 'In the destroyed German towns one often feels haunted by the ghost of a tremendous noise. It is impossible not to imagine the rocking explosions, the hammering of the sky upon the earth, which must have caused all this.'[11]

Even though war was over, the extent of the poverty in Germany meant that it remained a dangerous place. Large numbers of former slave labourers – people who had been taken from conquered territories in the east to work in the Reich – had remained in Germany. Many had neither the means nor the inclination to return to their native countries, and instead roamed about in gangs, hungry and angry. The historian Patricia Meehan noted: 'Throughout the summer Russians and Poles with little means of reaching home, and many not wanting to go, roamed the countryside in marauding gangs, murdering, raping and pillaging, driven by hunger and by vengeance.'[12]

The thought of such attacks caused Maria Mahr great pain. For a long time, there was no news from Hilde. It seemed that she had simply disappeared. To make matters worse, her brother-in-law was released from prison shortly after Hilde's departure, and he chastised Maria severely for allowing her to leave. 'How could you let that girl of nineteen years go? It is irresponsible of you,' he said repeatedly.

At last, a letter arrived, but it wasn't from Hilde; it was from Adolf. He was alive and living in Oldenburg, but was desperately worried about Hilde, for whom he had searched for months. He had no idea that she had made it to Austria, and was now back in Germany looking for *him*. While the news that Adolf was alive was greeted with relief, it meant that Hilde's journey was unnecessary – which only increased Maria Mahr's distress.

Hilde had six addresses in Germany where her father might be. They were all in northern Germany: in Bielefeld, Hamburg, Bremen and Oldenburg. She decided to try Oldenburg first since that was where he had been headed when she had last seen him, six months previously. After bidding goodbye to her companions, she carried on north through Dortmund, Bielefeld and Osnabruck, en route to Oldenburg. She still slept in the open wagons; fortunately for her, it did not rain.

On 30 September, Hilde reached Oldenburg, and found her way to the first address on her list: the home of Hans Hartmann's mother. Hartmann had been working with Adolf Mahr until the demise of Irland-

Redaktion, so she hoped that Mrs Hartmann might be able to help find her father. She announced herself to a surprised Mrs Hartmann, who could not believe that she had travelled all the way from Austria. She showed Hilde to a one-room flat just around the corner, where her father was living. She told Hilde that her father had spent months looking for her, and had feared the worst when he had failed to find her. Mrs Hartmann said: 'Adolf will get the fright of his life when he sees you.'

Adolf Mahr could only have imagined that Hilde was among the large number of his friends and family who had died during the war. In a letter to Dr Michael Quane of the National Museum of Ireland that year, he said: 'The house of my wife's parents in The Hague was destroyed by one of the many stray V-1 bombs. Her mother died soon afterwards from semi-starvation.' He also explained: 'My distant brother-in-law, the Director of the Vienna Zoo, committed suicide (with his wife) when the Russians entered Vienna.'[13]

Mahr also mentioned to Quane the fate of Jozien van Bemmelen's daughters in Vienna: 'Mrs Mahr's sister (who lives in Vienna), her girls had terrible experiences (unspeakable), but they are now recovering. They are all ill.' What Mahr did not want to put in writing was that at least one, and maybe both, of Jozien van Bemmelen's daughters had been raped by Russian soldiers when Vienna was invaded.

Jozien herself was interned by the Austrian authorities, even though her alleged crimes had been committed in Holland. She was imprisoned alone in the dark in a tiny cell for three months, on near-starvation rations.[14] Mahr also said: 'Other members of the family are scattered beyond reach (or locked up in Italy, Czechoslovakia, etc.).'[15]

Among Mahr's friends who were 'scattered beyond reach' was Heinz Mecking, the former adviser to the Turf Development Board in Ireland, who had replaced Mahr as local leader in Dublin. He was taken prisoner by the Red Army and starved to death in a camp in Moldova;[16] Karl Kuenstler, a bachelor who had befriended the Mahrs while studying in Ireland, was called up to the *Volkssturm* (People's Army) and was last seen defending a Berlin suburb during a Red Army attack; his body was never recovered. The former ambassador to Britain and friend of Mahr, Joachim von Ribbentrop, was hanged following his trial at Nuremberg in 1946. The most infamous of them all, the Irishman William Joyce (Lord Haw-Haw), who had been on the run with Mahr at the end of the war, was hanged for treason by the British in January 1946.

Later, Dr Hoernisch of Bad Ischl died. He had 'lost his job and fortune' by the time of his release from prison, and then simply gave up the will to live.[17] More innocent victims of the war included Mr and Mrs Baczkowski, who had become Mona Brase's guardians after the teenager was stranded in Germany at the outbreak of war. Since defeat by the Soviet Union looked inevitable, the Baczkowskis often told Mona to have sleeping tablets ready. For many Germans, death was preferable to living under Communist rule: an overdose of sleeping pills was the method of choice for the aged couple. In spring 1945, Mrs Baczkowski called Mona aside and returned her Irish passport to her. It was a sign to Mona that, after six years of being her foster-mother, they might not see one another again.

Mr Baczkowski had learned Russian during the Great War, and as the first Russian soldiers appeared in the southern suburbs of Berlin, he felt that he might be able to use his Russian to reason with them. However, during his first exchange with Red Army personnel, he was told to 'get the women'. They did not want to talk; they only wanted to round up the women of the locality. This told Mr Baczkowski all he and his wife needed to know. They sat on their sofa and took sleeping pills that day. There were so many dead, and so few people to bury them, that neighbours buried the Baczkowskis in their garden. A year later, the same neighbours had the grisly task of exhuming the bodies for reburial in a proper graveyard. Mrs Baczkowski's sister, Martha Hannay, who had also befriended Mona, took sleeping pills as Red Army soldiers entered the cellar where she and others were hiding in Berlin. She passed out immediately, but it took her three days to die.[18]

Mona Brase, who was a Red Cross nurse in the north of Berlin, was not with the Baczkowskis at the time. She returned to Dublin after the war and worked as a radiologist in Mercer's Hospital. Would she have taken the pills? She still can't say.[19]

Adolf Mahr had searched for Hilde from May until September that year. He had placed notices pleading for information about her in transport stations, police stations, local registration offices, internment camps, and newspapers, and on street walls. He had contacted all his friends in western Germany, but nobody had heard or seen anything of her. He knew that she had been in the most dangerous part of Germany, and that the Russians had attacked many young women in the area. When Hilde failed to turn up, he assumed that she had not got away. He thought she could not have gone south to Austria; it was too far. He had given up hope of seeing her again. Mrs Hartmann was correct: he nearly fainted when he saw Hilde standing at his apartment door.

Despite his worries, Mahr was living in relative comfort in Oldenburg. After the war, he had moved there in order to establish contact with the Natural History Museum in the city, and to use its library. He still had many friends in the area from his radio-service days, and, most importantly, he also had money left over from a large payment that had been made to him by the broadcasting authorities towards the end of the war.[20] He was even in touch with the British army's Monuments and Fine Arts team – civilian officers in charge of collections and museums in the occupied areas. He was not in hiding, but had to report to the British military authorities regularly.

Yet Mahr was hardly a free man. He knew that he would be arrested and interned if he returned to Austria. It had been illegal for Austrians to join the Nazi Party before 1938, and the new Austrian government would enjoy making an example of Mahr. This meant that Maria and her daughters would have to leave Austria if the family were to be reunited.

Hilde stayed with her father from September until December 1945, and during that time they arranged to rent two rooms with the Schroeder family, again in Augustfehn. The Schroeders were not so pleased at the prospect of five Mahrs showing up in their home, but the occupying powers had ruled that anyone with spare rooms was obliged to take in people who had no homes. The next step would be for Hilde to make the illegal and dangerous journey back to her mother and sisters in Austria, and then to put in place arrangements to get them out of there, and to take another il-legal and dangerous journey to northern Germany.

The mild autumn weather gave way to a bitter north-German winter as Hilde prepared for her return journey. This time the trains would be full of coal and she would have to lie on top of the cargo, where she would be exposed to the wind, as well as snow and rain. To protect her from the elements, a dressmaker friend of Adolf gathered some old plastic covers from English military vans and made them into a raincoat for her. As before, there were hundreds of people travelling illegally on each train. Sometimes she was lucky enough to get on board a train that had been used for transporting animals. The closed wagons and hay offered warmth, but invariably they were crawling with fleas and other insects. Mostly, however, she travelled on coal wagons, and learned from the others quickly to dig a hole in the coal and sit in this hole for protection from the elements. She marvelled at the sight of hundreds of people, buried in coal, with only their heads showing: 'We dug with our hands like moles and sat into the coal. Me and hundreds of others, like mice and rats travelling together.'

Crossing from British-controlled Germany to American-controlled Germany and into American-controlled Austria, Hilde tried to pass through borders on overnight trains to lessen the chance that she would encounter guards. The plan mostly worked, but her return south was more eventful than her journey north had been: she was arrested twice. The first time, she was detained at Eichenberg, on the border between the British- and American-occupied zones of Germany. While being questioned in a police station, she asked to go to the toilet, and before leaving she placed her rucksack on a windowsill in the station. She then got out through the toilet window, retrieved her bag at the windowsill, and fled. Getting through the main gate of the barracks was simply a confidence trick. She walked out through the gate as though she had permission to leave, and said hello to the guards. 'They were so surprised to hear the English language, they didn't stop me,' she says.

Her second arrest was at Reichenhall on the Austria-Germany border. She was on a bus when she was arrested for not having the proper papers to cross the border. During questioning, an officer interrupted and asked if her father was Adolf Mahr, the archaeologist. He had known her father before the war, and so let her through. That officer, like so many others in his position, was a native of the area who had emigrated to the United States, and had then been recruited into the fledgling CIA. He was also, according to Hilde, Jewish.

After three months away, and a five-day return journey, Hilde once again returned to her family. They had not heard from her during this time, and a letter from her father saying that they had met in Oldenburg had not yet reached Austria. They had once again assumed the worst – which made the reunion as dramatic as the one the previous summer. She brought news of her father, and the possibilities of reuniting the family in northern Germany. Now they had the difficult task of crossing from Austria to Germany.

8

The Dust Settles, 1946–47

At least 9.3 million Germans died, mostly of starvation, between 1945 and 1950: in other words, almost as many Germans died in the aftermath of the war as had died during it. These deaths happened in a famine that was deliberately caused by the victorious Allies. The Russians and Poles, with the help of the US and Britain, seized a quarter of Germany, which included the best farmland, and expelled some sixteen million civilians to the cities. This was the largest and most brutal ethnic cleansing in human history. Millions of people, nearly all of them women and children, died in the trek. The four occupying powers then prevented Germany from making fertilizer and destroyed its manufacturing capacity, thereby bringing about a famine.

These are the findings of the Canadian academic James Bacque, whose book *Crimes and Mercies* (1997) cited archives that were opened in Moscow soon after the collapse of the Soviet Union. If Bacque's claims are true, it is a dreadful indictment of the Allied forces. It means that they not only engaged in genocide, but did so on a scale comparable to that practised by the Nazis.

The widespread hunger, the abuse of prisoners, and destruction of German industry was well documented during the 1940s. The common perception that Germany began to prosper after the introduction of the American Marshall Plan in 1948 is certainly true, but before that, and for the first two years of the plan, Bacque alleges that there was a deliberate policy of starving the German populace by blocking food aid, tying up its fishing fleet, stripping its factories of machinery and tools, and keeping prisoners of war in concentration camps on rations that were well below subsistence levels. Bacque compares conditions in some of the prisons to those at Belsen during the Nazi era.

Such depths of poverty among a predominantly female population, while the males of the occupying armies had plentiful supplies of tradable commodities such as chocolate and cigarettes, inevitably led to widespread prostitution. One police chief commented: 'Even nice girls of good families, good education and fine background have discovered their bodies afford the only real living.' By December 1946, nearly half a million girls in Berlin were exchanging sex for western goods. In the British zone, 80 percent of orphaned girls suffered from VD.[1]

Concerned that Germany might once again grow strong and rearm, the Allies began work in September 1945 on a formula that would set the German standard of living at 74 percent of the European average of the years from 1930 to 1938.[2] Factories and other infrastructure that might raise development beyond that level were destroyed. As late as 1949, thousands of German workers in the British zone protested as factories were dismantled and shipped to Britain. Members of the new German police service stood guard while explosives were placed inside intact factory buildings and detonated. This happened while millions of Germans were still living in ruins.

The Mahr parents could not see any future for their family in Germany. Adolf understood that opportunities to resume his career there were, and would remain, slim. A country living in such poverty would have little interest in archaeology. This posed a particular difficulty if the family were to reunite. There was little point in the Mahr women coming to Germany, and he could not join them in Austria, so Ireland offered the best chance for them to prosper again. Writing to her father in Holland from Bad Ischl in January 1946, Maria Mahr said: 'We hope that we may be able to return to Ireland this year. That would be our only possibility to recover from this horrible war.'[3]

In order to get an exit permit from Germany, Mahr needed a declaration from Ireland that she was willing to accept him and his family. During the summer of 1945, Mahr sent a letter, via a British officer in the High Commissioner's Office in London, to the Department of Education in Dublin requesting it to facilitate his family's return to Ireland. He asked that it negotiate with the British and American military authorities in

Germany and Austria 'for the granting of transit visas, decision about the travelling route, etc.'

Acting on this, Colonel Dan Bryan, the head of Irish Military Intelligence, who had tracked Mahr's Nazi activities since the late 1930s, drew up a report for Éamon de Valera in August 1945, in which he urged the government not to come to Mahr's aid:

> Dr Mahr was the most active and fanatical National-Socialist in the German colony here. During the war, he worked for the German Foreign Office. Ostensibly he was concerned with cultural propaganda, but there is some slight evidence that he knew of, and was connected with, some of the attempts of German secret service activity in this country, particularly the dropping of the parachutist [John Francis] O'Reilly. Herr Hempel [Minister at the German Legation in Dublin] had always a strong dislike and distrust of him. He told me once that he blamed Mahr's influence for the fact that the German Foreign Office failed on occasion to act on the counsels of prudence he constantly gave them as regards this country.[4]

Bryan could hardly have made a more damning claim against Mahr than to say that he had worked against the development of a peaceful relationship between Germany and Ireland. No evidence has yet emerged to support the claim, and there is ample evidence to suggest otherwise. Saying that he helped land spies into Ireland has a degree of truth, but not in the way that Bryan intended.

The 'spy' was John Francis O'Reilly, a colourful character from County Clare who was a casual worker in Jersey when Germany occupied the island in 1940. He accepted work with the Luftwaffe at an airfield in Jersey but soon moved to Berlin, where he presented programmes for Irland-Redaktion; he got along well with Mahr.[5] As Germany's fortunes in the war turned, O'Reilly came up with a clever plan to get back to Ireland: he volunteered for a spying mission to his native land and received training in parachuting, code transmission and other necessary skills.[6] Knowing that O'Reilly's intention was only to get home, Mahr used his influence to have him dropped in Ireland.[7] In December 1943, O'Reilly landed by parachute close to his family cottage near Kilkee. Soon, before he had transmitted a single message, his father turned him in to the police – and collected a £500 reward for his efforts. O'Reilly was interned until the end of the war, and on his release was given the reward money by his father. O'Reilly junior used the money to buy a pub in Dublin, and for decades afterwards regaled customers with tales of how he had tricked the SS into flying him to Ireland during the war.[8]

This version of events was not relayed in Bryan's report on Mahr. It continued:

> It is difficult to see how we could very well make a special request to the Allied authorities on Dr Mahr's behalf at the present stage, having regard to his character and his previous political activities as National-Socialist leader of the German colony in Dublin . . . . Our inclination would be to say that, in your view, it would be inopportune to take any action on Dr Mahr's request at the present time.

Sensing the potential difficulty of de Valera's position with regard to Mahr, Bryan suggested that he not commit his views to paper. 'Perhaps you may prefer, in the circumstances, that the matter should not be dealt with by way of official minute, but to give the papers to the Minister for Education and have a word with him on the matter yourself,' he said.

If Mahr had known about the moves against him, he could perhaps have found a way to challenge them. But de Valera followed Byran's advice, and no discussion on the affair was committed to paper. That autumn Mahr wrote a personal letter to Dr Quane in the National Museum, in which he said it would be most desirable 'if I and the members of my family could obtain Irish nationality. In any case, the two youngsters are born in Dublin and I should have regularised my position long ago.'[9] He asked Quane to pass along greetings to all the Museum staff, and to the many other people he knew in Dublin. This amounted to a public signal of his intention to return to Ireland. For the Irish government, this meant that Mahr would not go away quietly, and that it would eventually have to confront the difficult issue of accepting a Nazi back into its civil service.

In December 1945, James Dillon, the former deputy leader of the Fine Gael party, which was then in opposition, seized the opportunity to embarrass the de Valera government by raising the Mahr issue in the Dáil:

> Am I to understand that this gentleman returned to Nazi Germany in time to take part in the nefarious activities of the Nazis in that country

and now, having backed the wrong horse, he is sitting there waiting to come back and land here as soon as the opportunity offers?[10]

The Minister for Education, Thomas Derrig, had sought approval for Mahr's promotion to the top job at the National Museum in 1934, even though Mahr had been a leading Nazi for more than a year at the time. Now, he had to admit that the government had granted him leave of absence for the duration of the war. It was clear that there was no legal impediment to prevent him from returning:

> Dr Mahr was appointed the official Irish representative to the Sixth International Congress of Archaeology to be held in Berlin in August, 1939, and he left Ireland in the preceding month to attend that congress, bringing his family with him to spend a holiday in his native home in Austria. When war became imminent he tried to return to Dublin but was unable to do so, owing to the delay in bringing his family from Austria. He then reported to the Irish Chargé d'Affaires, with a view to getting a 'safe conduct' to return to Ireland, but it was not possible to have this done and he was granted leave of absence without pay until circumstances permitted him to resume his position. I am not in a position to say anything further at the moment, nor can I say when Dr Mahr will be in a position to resume.[11]

This was not good enough for Dillon, who sensed the government's discomfort on the issue. 'If this gentleman turns up tomorrow with the battle-stained flag of Nazi Germany wrapped around him, will he be reinstalled in this position?' he asked. 'Will we go on retaining a gentleman seated in Germany for the last six years so long as the going was good?'

The issue was not resolved in the Dáil debate, but Dillon's intervention had successfully brought into the public domain Mahr's intention to return to Ireland, and in the process had embarrassed the government that had previously promoted Mahr. In the weeks that followed, Dan Bryan drew up another report on the Mahr affair, in which he stated: 'Mahr was born in 1887 and would, therefore, be sixty and attain the minimum limit for retiring in 1947.' This was a veiled suggestion that the government did not need to resolve the issue. It could hold on for a couple of years and then pension off Mahr.

Bryan further damaged Mahr's prospects of returning by stating:

Mahr while resident in Ireland was an open and blatant Nazi and made many efforts to convert Irish graduates, and other persons with whom he had associations, to Nazi doctrines and beliefs.

Apart from his pre-war and war activities, which brand him as a Nazi of some importance in relation to Ireland and make, in my opinion, any question of his immediate return unwise, there is no guarantee that further discoveries may not establish that his activities in connection with Ireland went further than propaganda.

In the circumstances I recommend that no consideration be given to his return until the situation in regard to Germany and German nationals is much clearer.[12]

Despite Bryan's assertions, there was still no evidence that Mahr had broken a law or acted against the interests of Ireland. However unpalatable it may have been for the government, Mahr was legally entitled to resume his position.

The dilemma facing the Irish government was eased by the intercession of the British government a month after the Dillon/Derrig debate in the Dáil. In January 1946, Mahr was arrested by British troops in Oldenburg. He was imprisoned in the former Nazi concentration camp at Fallingbostel, a village on the moors of northern Germany.

Mahr had lived openly and freely for seven months after the end of the war, so why the British should suddenly arrest him remains unclear. Could the arrest have been a favour to de Valera, to prevent any further embarrassment to his administration? This scenario appears likely, but for the fact that London seemed to be unaware that Mahr had been arrested as late as two months after the event. On 2 March 1946, R. W. Selby of the Foreign Office wrote to Major W. S. Mars at MI5 saying that 'an Irish acquaintance of a member of the Foreign Office' had said that Adolf Mahr would soon be 'invited to return to Éire and resume his post'. The acquaintance said that Mahr had been a 'prominent member of the Nazi Intelligence Service in Dublin before the war, and the acquaintance considers that steps should be taken to prevent him from leaving Austria [*sic*].'[13]

Major Mars replied to say that MI5 had 'a certain amount of information about this gentleman, and are always glad to have advance information of the proposed movements of people of this sort.'[14] It seems, therefore, that the arrest was ordered by the authorities in Germany.

Nevertheless, it can be claimed with some justification that the British tried to kill Mahr, quietly. Apart from interrogation about his Nazi activities, the Mahr family says that the fifty-eight-year-old was starved and forced to sleep outside in freezing conditions, on open ground and without any kind of bedding.[15] He may also have been beaten.[16] Mahr's health deteriorated quickly, and two months after his arrest he was close to death. He was eventually allowed to sleep indoors, but this did little to ease his condition.

This account is consistent with a report on Allied prison camps by the Bishop of Chichester, George Bell, who found that interrogations were often brutal. Men who had not yet been found guilty of anything were 'terribly beaten, kicked and so mishandled that traces could be seen weeks afterwards. The notorious Third Degree methods of using searchlights on victims and exposing them to high temperatures were also applied.'[17]

In the same month that Mahr was detained, a British army conference recorded: 'reports are being received that we are allowing internees to exist under conditions which were little better than those in German concentration camps'. It said that the majority of inmates were emaciated, many with their bellies swollen from lack of food. The death rate among ageing men in poor physical health would be very high and would, if it got out of hand, 'reproduce some of the more sensational features of the Nazi concentration camps'.[18] Around the same time, an MP told the British House of Commons that prisoners were beaten unconscious by British officers and NCOs, and that the concentration-camp system of 'roll-call' was maintained, with men standing outside for hours in all weathers. If they dropped, they were left where they fell.[19]

Eight hundred kilometres away in Bad Ischl, Maria, Hilde, Ingrid and Brigit made plans to join Adolf Mahr, whom they believed to be still a free man. They would have to get out of Austria and move through American-controlled Germany into the British-controlled zone. The journey would be illegal and dangerous. Maria Mahr despaired once again at having to gather all her belongings and her daughters, and flee to a new home. It was her sixth move in as many years, and each occasion marked a further reduction in her circumstances. This time, she was destined for an area that was unfamiliar to her, to resume a difficult marriage to a husband whom she had not seen for a year. If the trip was successful, there was a faint hope that they could leave there as soon as possible and get back to Ireland. If it was unsuccessful, she might end up in prison for leaving Austria illegally. It was probably a blessing that she did not yet know that, while she was packing her few meagre possessions, Adolf was close to death in a British prison camp.

An elderly couple in the Bad Ischl area had been granted permission to leave Austria and resettle in Germany. They teamed up with two other couples who had received similar permission, and together they acquired a lorry to carry them and their belongings over the border. They offered the remaining space on the back of the lorry to the Mahr women if they could pay their way; instead of money, fuel for the truck would suffice. The only possible source of petrol for the lorry was at the nearby American-army base, where Ingrid had already ingratiated herself with some American soldiers. They turned a blind eye when she and Hilde entered the snow-covered base during evening prayer service, pulling a sleigh with the thirteen-year-old Brigit on board. On the base, the Mahr girls found three canisters of petrol, placed them on the sleigh under the blanket, and put Brigit sitting on top to conceal the theft. They waited until the evening prayer service was over, and when crowds started to emerge from the army church, nobody took any notice of the two teenage girls pulling their younger sister on a sleigh up the snow-covered street.[20]

With the price of their passage having been raised, the Mahrs still faced the difficult task of getting through a military-police checkpoint at the Austria-Germany border. Hilde, now experienced at travelling by unconventional means, forged exit permits for her family and then got them 'officially' stamped, with the help of a friend working in the local municipality.[21]

Ten people were on the lorry as it departed from Bad Ischl for the German border in February 1946. The temperature was minus seventeen degrees, so everyone was covered in layers of clothes to protect them from the cold. The principal family, the Shreys, did not know the Mahrs well and were not aware that they had false papers. Maria Mahr was both depressed and terrified of being arrested, and was no longer able to make clear decisions. Hilde became the leader of the Mahr group.

At the border, the military police checked everyone's papers and waved the lorry through, but barely 500 metres from the checkpoint, and not quite out of Austria, the lorry broke down. Its human cargo sat in the cold and dark while its driver worked on the engine. Back at the checkpoint, the alarm was raised when someone realised that the Mahrs could not have obtained permission to leave Austria. Military police drove after the Mahrs, but they had no powers beyond the Austrian border. Thinking that the Mahrs had already entered Germany, they gave up their chase soon after it had started, never realising that the fugitives were in a broken-down lorry just beyond view. After about half an hour, the engine started again and the Mahrs left Austria. It was many years before they found out from friends in Bad Ischl just how close they had come to being arrested.

In Germany, the Mahrs bade goodbye to their travelling companions. They proceeded to Frankfurt, where they stayed with the Strasburgers, the family that had known Maria Mahr's family for two generations, and whose son Gerhard had been Gustav's superior in the German army. After a couple of days there, they boarded a train for Oldenburg, and an expected rendezvous with Adolf. It was only when they reached the city that they learned that Adolf was in a prison camp. Apart from being shocked by the news, the Mahr women had to face the prospect that their family had lost its primary income earner, and that they had moved from the relative comfort of Austria to a region that was in ruins and where they were strangers.

Leaving the others in the city to rest, Hilde travelled to Augustfehn to prepare the two rooms that she and her father had booked some months before. Once again, however, her hopes were dashed: the lady of the house, Mrs Schroeder, reneged on their deal and refused to take in the Mahrs. Hilde was shocked. The implications of Mrs Schroeder's decision went far beyond what the old lady could imagine. It meant that the Mahrs had no home, and little chance of finding one. Hilde tried to figure out a future for a family where the father was dying in a prison camp for Nazis, the mother was too depressed to think coherently, the brother was in a prison camp in the United Sates, and the two youngest sisters were too young to work. They couldn't return to Austria, because they had left there illegally. What was the nineteen-year-old to do?

She walked the thirteen kilometres from Augustfehn to Hans Hartmann's house, where she relayed the events, through floods of tears. Hartmann, the tall academic who had played tennis with Hilde's mother during better times in Dublin, and who had been the subject of Hilde's own teenage crush, returned to Augustfehn and successfully 'twisted Mrs

Schroeder's arm'. The law at the time said that anyone with a spare room in their house must make it available to people who needed it. Hartmann explained to Mrs Schroeder that, if she refused to accommodate the Mahrs, she might be forced to take in strangers. At least she knew the Mahrs, and that they were good people, he reasoned.[22]

The Mahrs' new home was made up of just two rooms with a kitchenette, in a place that Gustav later described as a 'forlorn village miles out in the bogs [where there was] no chance of finding work or decent quarters'. Hilde soon found work in a local farm, where she was paid with potatoes and vegetables. They had the bare essentials but little else.

During Easter 1946, Gerhard Strasburger came north from Frankfurt to visit the Mahrs. He had visited Gustav at the family home in Berlin in 1941, and had struck up a friendship with the fifteen-year-old Hilde. Now that she was almost twenty, he felt that the time had come to suggest marriage to her, and to have her return to Frankfurt with him. Hilde refused, saying that there were too many other things she had to attend to first. 'I have to get food for my family,' she said, 'and even if this wasn't the case, I want to do some kind of training or education before having a family of my own, so that I can always stand on my own feet.' Strasburger returned to Frankfurt alone.[23]

By his third month in captivity, Adolf Mahr had grown weak from starvation and had dysentery. Maria Mahr was allowed to visit him for two hours in the prison hospital in early April. She later wrote to her father in Holland: 'I fear that Adolf will perish by the same disease [dysentery] as poor Uncle Joe and his son Frans. Do you or Jaap know of a remedy? He badly needs good food, but as our rations are so small, we can supply him with very little. Would it be possible to send us a parcel from Holland?'[24]

Rather than risk letting Mahr die in the camp, the British authorities sent him home, where his death would draw less attention. On 10 April, a day after one of his wife's visits, he was released, but nobody was notified to come and pick him up. Despite being barely able to walk, he had to make his way to Augustfehn alone. He was so skinny that his bones were protruding through his skin, and the slightest touch from anyone caused him severe pain. When Hilde arrived home from work that evening, she was met at the door by her mother, who warned her: 'Don't be surprised, and don't show your horror. Father looks awfully bad.'

There was barely enough food to feed the five Mahrs, but in the circumstances this was a blessing: there was no opportunity to overfeed him. A starved person is barely able to digest food for a considerable period after feeding resumes. Another starved man in that area was released at the same time as Mahr, but he returned to a family that was able to feed him well. He died soon afterwards, and the Mahrs think that it was because of overfeeding.

Despite his joy of seeing his wife and daughters again, Adolf was very depressed, Hilde remembers: 'When he got out of prison, he was absolutely physically wrecked for a couple of months. We couldn't speak about the war; it was all too depressing. Our lives were simply too depressing. We hardly knew how to manage to stay alive and to feed ourselves.'

Mahr's heart, already weakened by his collapse a decade earlier in Ireland, and further damaged by a lifetime of smoking and heavy coffee-drinking, was slow to recover from his period of starvation, but with the help of a doctor friend, his condition improved and he began walking from one farm to another, receiving free potatoes, carrots and other foods. The locals were largely sympathetic towards him: it had been a pro-Nazi area, and after the war several Dutch SS men had hidden there from Allied forces.

Unknown to Mahr, further moves were being made to prevent his return to Dublin. He and another former Dublin Nazi, Otto Reinhard, had made official requests to get their government jobs back, and once again Colonel Dan Bryan was asked for his advice. In May 1946, he wrote a letter marked 'Secret' to F. H. Boland, a top official in the Department of Foreign Affairs, saying that new information had come to hand that should make the departments concerned 'still more hesitant about any proposal to re-employ these people in the immediate future.'[25] The new information, Bryan explained, was that, '[in 1940] Mahr approached one of the German intelligence sections which dealt with matters concerning a landing in Ireland, with a long report, and was, as a result, employed in that section for a year or two'. Bryan's letter was an unfair attack on Mahr because it implied that Mahr's report had been used in the planning of an invasion of Ireland, whereas the report had called on Germany to respect Ireland's neutrality at a time when that neutrality was most under threat.

In mid-1946, the first relief parcels arrived from friends of the Mahrs in other countries. The senders were sometimes Jews; people such as

Alfons Barb in London, whom Mahr had helped when Barb was fleeing the Nazis in 1938.[26] The Mahrs' parcels of tea and sugar were traded locally for butter and eggs, which at the time were luxury items.

In June 1946, the family received a further boost when Gustav was released from captivity and returned to Germany. He stayed first with the Strasburgers in Frankfurt, and after a few days boarded a converted goods train and headed north to Augustfehn. It had been three years since the Mahr family had lived together in an attractive apartment in an intact Berlin. In the meantime, all of them had been close to death, and they must have wondered if the day would ever come when they would be reunited. There was an emotional scene when Gustav stepped off the train in Augustfehn to be greeted by his family. 'It was like being born anew,' he says. He noticed that his whole family looked hungry, but in particular his father was still 'very shaky', even though it was now two months since his release from prison. He was able to walk on his own, but was still weak.

Gustav reported to the military government in the British zone. They allowed him to stay, and furthermore gave him a job as an interpreter, a position he would hold for five years. The job paid relatively well – which was very important for the otherwise impoverished Mahrs. They rented an acre of land and sowed vegetables. Gustav also cut turf in a bog near the village. For the first time in many years, the family had the basic necessities as they headed into the winter: food, shelter, heat – and each other.

The family survived this time also because, according to Gustav, Adolf Mahr was a 'great organiser'. As his strength returned, most days he put on a rucksack and walked around the farms buying food cheaply from one farmer, and trading commodities with another. The walking strengthened his body, and restored his self-esteem somewhat.

The Mahrs' marriage had effectively broken up around 1941, although the children did not notice at the time. Maria Mahr had blamed Adolf for the family's unfolding tragedy, and from then on there was little love between them. Now, in the reduced circumstances in Augustfehn, they tried to get together again, 'even sexually', according to Gustav. 'Mother was a very vivid, lively and sexy person, but Adolf was much cooler in that respect,' he says. 'But he was probably too weak at the time to . . . . Their reunion wasn't a success.'

Adolf lived in a tiny attic area of the family's quarters. There was a little cubbyhole where he had a bed and a typewriter, and from there he started writing to all sorts of people once the German postal service started up again. 'He fought as best he could,' says Gustav. 'He wasn't hopeless. He had heaps of friends, and kept up a terrific correspondence.'

It was now the summer of 1946: according to Gustav, it 'was beautiful but we were starving'. Gerhard Strasburger visited, and again he suggested that Hilde join him in Frankfurt. He could help her get training as a medical assistant at the hospital in Frankfurt, and his family would allow her stay at their home nearby. Now that both Gustav and Adolf Mahr were returned to their family, Hilde's responsibilities to her mother and sisters were lessened. She agreed to Gerhard's offer and prepared to begin a new chapter in her life. There was only one problem: her father. Adolf was 'a little upset', according to Hilde: Gerhard was a Jew.

Despite all he had lived through and all that happened in Europe, he still clung to the anti-Semitic prejudice that was at the heart of the Nazi creed. Gerhard Strasburger was a Jew, so Adolf did not want his daughter to marry him.

Strasburger came from a long line of scientists — something which would normally have pleased Adolf Mahr. Gerhard's grandfather, Eduard Strasburger, was a founder of the modern study of biology.[27] He had been a colleague and friend of Maria Mahr's father, who was also a leading scientist: the families had known each other for three generations. Gerhard's father had been a physician at the University of Frankfurt but, following the introduction of the Nuremberg Laws in 1935, was dismissed from his position because his grandmother was Jewish. He was so upset at losing his job that he suffered a heart attack, and died three weeks later at the age of sixty-four.

Gerhard Strasburger was deemed to be 12.5 percent Jewish (he was the great-grandson of a Jew), so he was eligible to serve in the German army, but only in the lower ranks: he was not Jewish enough to avoid military service, but too Jewish to be allowed into the higher ranks. For Adolf Mahr, he was a suitable friend for Gustav, but too Jewish to be allowed to marry into the family.

Adolf took Hilde aside to point out that the man she intended to marry was from a family 'where there is Jewish blood', and to let her know that he did not approve of the match. Mahr had always been a dominant figure, both at his work and in the home — and was even now, in his weakened state. But Hilde had come of age and was not going to yield on this issue. For the first time, she confronted her father, and demanded: 'What do I care what you think? It is so senseless, this whole discussion about Aryan and Jewish blood.' She said: 'Daddy, I'm sure I am going to marry that man, and I'm sure that all your racial ideas do not apply to this family. There is no sense thinking about his racial background. And if you remain caught up on this point, then I cannot speak to you about it. Because I am quite sure that that is the man I want to be engaged to.' The old Nazi had met his match and backed down. Hilde went to Frankfurt that autumn with Gerhard.

Life in Frankfurt was not much better than it had been in Augustfehn. Like most families, the Strasburgers were hungry, and Hilde and Gerhard often spent the weekends cycling through the countryside swapping items from their home, such as a typewriter or carpets, for food. They survived on just one loaf of bread a week during this time. Still, Gerhard's promise was kept, and Hilde began her medical studies. After three months, her grades were sufficiently high to merit a scholarship. They arrived back in Augustfehn in December to celebrate Christmas and announce their engagement. Hilde and Gerhard married in August 1947 and Adolf gave away his daughter. The seeds of a new Germany were being sown, and old prejudices put aside.

Hilde's medical studies came to an end in early 1948 with the arrival of their first child, Hans. Despite the couple's obvious joy, it marked the beginning of another difficult time for Hilde. Gerhard, who had been malnourished for more than three years, was severely underweight, and contracted TB soon after Hans's birth. He spent most of the next two years in hospital, and Hilde had to raise Hans on health-insurance payments – the equivalent of 55 percent of her husband's salary.

In order to gain employment in the public sector – and there was little else in post-war Germany – Adolf Mahr had to submit to the denazification procedure. This involved a questionnaire consisting of 130 items relating to military service, membership of political parties before 1933, religious affiliation or lack thereof, publications written, compiled or edited since 1923, speeches, a record of employment, and journeys abroad since 1933.[28] Applicants also had to present affidavits that vouched for their good qualities. Mahr collected twenty-five such statements from friends and fellow archaeologists in Ireland, Britain, Germany and other countries. If Mahr had ever been tried, these statements would have made convincing arguments for his defence.

Alfons Barb, the Austrian Jew whom Mahr had tried to help escape from the Nazis in 1938, wrote from his new home in Leeds in January 1947:

> I became acquainted with Dr Adolf Mahr in Austria in 1925 or 1926 shortly before he left for Eire, when I was starting on some archaeological research for which I needed his help. Although he was fully aware of my Jewish race, he gave me his unreserved assistance and throughout all the following years showed me much kindness and friendship. When in 1938 I lost my position through the annexation of Austria he was one of the very few friends who not only showed me his sympathy, but tried everything in his power and went to considerable trouble in his effort to find a new position for me.
>
> In spring 1939 I succeeded in coming to London with my wife and two children. Here he called on me when he came over to England to give some lectures. He seemed somehow startled and disgusted when I told him about some features of the Gestapo in Austria; took first my children to the cinema and for tea, next day my wife and me for dinner and to the theatre; introduced me to an American and some English archaeologists, and showed me in every way his eagerness to do something for me. From our conversations I gathered that he felt rather strongly about the injustices done to me and others of my race, but that he expected these things to stop gradually. He seemed fully convinced – I was not and we had an argument about it – that there would be no war.
>
> For some of the above statements my wife and children can witness, for others I still possess Dr Mahr's letters written to me 1938–1939 which show his untiring efforts to do something for me. I also understand that I am not the only Jewish refugee to whom he showed his sympathy and helpfulness.
>
> May I add one more word: through National Socialism I lost my position, my home, many friends and relatives. My sister, her husband and her two sons were cruelly murdered by the Nazis in 1941–1942. I would not have written the above statement if I was not sincerely convinced, on the grounds of an intimate acquaintance of many years' standing, that Dr Mahr had nothing to do with the racial and national hatred, the criminal and inhuman sides of National Socialism.[29]

Sir Cyril Fox, Director of the National Museum of Wales, and, like Mahr, a past-President of the British Prehistoric Society, was also supportive, although in a more muted way. He wrote in December 1946:

> I know your published scientific work emanating from Dublin; while you were there I saw you rarely, but have talked to you on scientific matters. I know of nothing to indicate that you abused your position in the archaeological world to further political ends.[30]

Professor Paul Jacobsthal, a Jew and a well-known Classical scholar in Christ Church, Oxford, wrote:

> Though being a member of the party he [Mahr] held politics and research scrupulously apart; he never defiled history by projecting racial or other doctrines of Nazism into the past: the atmosphere in his books and papers written since 1933 is absolutely clean.
>
> When the Nuernberg laws came into force and a good many non-Aryan scholars sought refuge in this country Dr Mahr helped them wherever he could. I myself in 1937 enjoyed his hospitality in Dublin: I seldom found a friendlier and kinder reception in a museum. I was fully informed of his political attitude but felt no inhibitions to accept his services and kindness: we did of course not discuss these delicate matters but I had the feeling to have met a man of high moral standards who had joined the Hitler movement guided by pure motives not by ambition or other base instincts; at the same time I did not doubt that one day he would be terribly disappointed and feel deceived . . . .
>
> My own work and interests give me perhaps the right to say a word on Dr Mahr as a scholar. I see in him one of the ten or less leading prehistorians in Europe and America. His long and thorough familiarity with continental archaeology of many countries and periods enabled him to see the problems of Irish archaeology in a European light and to do more for their understanding than anyone else before him.
>
> British archaeologists, with whom Mahr was on most friendly terms, would thoroughly welcome his return to his post in Dublin, and it would be for the good of international archaeology if the authorities concerned would give him the opportunity.[31]

The Scottish archaeologist Howard Kilbride-Jones revealed a deep affinity for Mahr and his family in his testimonial:

Remembering how often you extended the helping hand to deserving Britons during the many years that you held the position of Director of the National Museum it comes as something of a shock to me that anyone should suspect you of harbouring anti-British feelings. I can say truthfully that I never saw any evidence of your possessing such feelings. Perhaps the best evidence that I can adduce in regard to your outlook on the racial question is the way that you had your son educated. On the many occasions on which I travelled with him, no-one to whom he was introduced ever suspected for a moment that he was other than a good Irishman!

Were I asked, I should say that your whole outlook upon life was thoroughly cosmopolitan. On the many occasions upon which I was a guest at your house, I think that I sat down to table with almost every European nationality, and with people of almost every shade of political opinion. And I remember how some of the young men who came about the house were helped on by you, some to obtain jobs, others to acquire academic honours.

And there was the case of Obermaier. I remember how, after he had to flee from Franco Spain, he found himself a penniless refugee in Switzerland, without his famous library, and too poor to start another, you put yourself to a good deal of trouble collecting odd books and scientific papers from various people, including myself, in order to start him off with another library.

Some people seem to think that the German Society in Dublin was an anti-British affair. To me it was a place where one could go and spend a pleasant social evening, exchange stories, and drink German beer. There used to be there about as many non-Germans as Germans, and I can truthfully say that never once did anyone try any political stuff with me.

To this, Kilbride-Jones added a personal letter that was longer, and perhaps more telling, than his affidavit:

You ask 'who amongst the old friends and colleagues are still friends?' The answer is none. I think that one of the most miserable people I ever met was [H. G.] Leask, who was never out of your house eating your food and then, when you can no longer be made use of, can write unpleasant things . . . .

My wife has been wondering if any of her clothes would be of use to any of the female members of your family. I believe we are permitted to send old clothes to Germany. My wife is slim, height 5 ft 4 ins, waist 23 ins, shoes 4 1/2. She has a light tweed suit, and a brown wool cardigan suit. She has also a loose-fitting 'swagger' coat that might fit Mrs Mahr. I have a Harris sports jacket and a pair of white flannel trousers, which I used to use for playing badminton in, and which I could have dyed for you, if you would care to accept them. Let me know the colour you prefer. I could also let you have two pairs of underpants. A white sleeveless pullover would suit Gustav . . . .

Apart from the letter, Mrs Kilbride-Jones had sent a parcel containing 1 lb of sugar, 1/2 lb of tea, a 1 lb tin of syrup, 2 lbs of porridge oats, and a tin of Irish stew.[32] For the Mahrs, this was a bounty.

J. M. de Navarro, a lecturer in archaeology and anthropology at Cambridge University, paid tribute to Mahr's 'power of synthesis, deep learning and breadth of outlook', and added that his denazification 'would be a very real service to archaeology and a step that would not be fraught with danger in my belief owing to his utter disillusionment with the Nazi philosophy.'[33]

T. D. Kendrick, Keeper of British Antiquities in the British Museum, wrote that he had known Mahr for twenty years: he had stayed in Mahr's house in Dublin, and Mahr had stayed with him in London. Kendrick said:

> Dr Mahr never made the slightest secret of his Nazi sympathies, but in my experience and among my friends he did not make any attempt to advocate Nazi doctrines by means of propaganda of an objectionable, religious, racial, or political kind. On the last occasion that I met him, he brought to me a Jewish colleague from Vienna, Dr Barb, and asked me to help his old friend. Dr Mahr also welcomed to an official excavation in Ireland, at which I was present, a Jewish colleague of mine, Dr Kitzinger, who was a refugee, and another refugee, Dr Freyhahn. This excavation was planned and arranged by Dr Mahr, and I can testify that he raised no objection whatever to the presence of an extremely anti-Nazi team of excavators. On the contrary, he did his best to help us in every possible way.

Monsignor John Hynes, a professor of Celtic archaeology, former President of University College Galway, and former Vice-Chancellor of the National University of Ireland, said in his affidavit that he knew Mahr 'intimately' from 1927 to 1939 in his roles at the National Museum and

the National Monuments Council, and through archaeological congresses:

> I have never known him, in any of the foregoing capacities, to do anything towards spreading Anti-Semitism, or to show any hostility to the Catholic Church (to which I belong) or to any other Christian Church. In my opinion, he faithfully fulfilled the obligations he undertook when he became an Irish Civil Servant. As far as I know, he never interfered in Irish politics. During the years he spent in Ireland, he was always on excellent terms with the Christian Clergy of the country. They and I feel a deep debt of gratitude to him for his work on 'Christian Art in Ireland'.[34]

Joseph O'Neill, the former Secretary of the Department of Education, said that he could not furnish Mahr with an affidavit, because 'a retired officer is debarred by the rules of our Service from making any statement, oral or written, in connection with matters of which he had cognisance in his official capacity.' However, he offered the following 'unofficial' opinions:

> The fact that they [the Irish government] have kept your position open for you, in case you may return, is of course pretty clear evidence that they have no information either from their own or the British Intelligence Services that you abused your residence or your position here in the interests of a power hostile to Great Britain. If there had been any evidence of such activities on your part while you were here, either from Irish or British Intelligence sources, not alone would the Government not be willing to keep your position open, but they would have dismissed you at once from your post in the Museum and deported you for misuse of it.[35]

M. S. Dudley Westropp, the former Keeper of the Art Division at the National Museum of Ireland, said that he had known Mahr since 1927 and that their families were on friendly terms:

> I always found Dr Mahr a thoroughly honest man and as far as I know he never abused his official position and scientific reputation for the dissemination of Nazi propaganda; also I do not think he took any part in Irish politics or inculcated anti-semitism, nor did he go in for propaganda hostile to the Church or racial doctrines.[36]

J. H. Delargy, the great collector of Irish folklore, and Director of the Irish Folklore Commission, wrote a personal note saying: 'You know, in spite of wars and politics and such, some of your old friends like to remember how kind Mr and Mrs Mahr were to them long ago. I always liked you, even although I often disagreed with you! And I don't forget kindness.'[37] In an affidavit sent later, Delargy (also known as Séamus Delargy and Séamus Ó Duilearga) said that he had known Mahr almost from the time of his arrival in Ireland, and in particular during the 1931–39 period:

> I have profited on numerous occasions by his sound advice and his profound erudition, especially during the formative years of our Commission, of which he was a founding member.
>
> ... I can testify that, to my knowledge, he allowed no ideological views to influence the conduct of his work on behalf of the Museum in Dublin or in the country.
>
> During the late War, while my sympathies were on the side of Britain, I could only think with kindness of my old friend, Dr Mahr, and wish him and his family the best of good fortune.[38]

Similarly worded affidavits came from C. W. V. Sydnow, a professor at Lund University; Dr O. Tschumi, Professor and Deputy Director of the Historical Museum of Berne City; Professor Knud Jessen of the University of Copenhagen, who had come to Ireland in 1934 to work on the Quaternary Research Committee with Mahr; and Professor A. Staffe of the University of Berne. Staffe said that Mahr had always refused to allow Nazism to cloud his archaeological judgement.

Frieda Hayek, wife of the former Managing Director of the Irish Sugar Company, also penned an affidavit for Mahr. She was a Czech-born Jew who had been incarcerated in an Austrian concentration camp during the war. The Mahr family contends that Adolf Mahr played a leading role in securing her release, although Hayek (née Loewenthal) does not mention this in her affidavit. The Mahr family also contends that, despite her religious background, she was a supporter of National Socialism; this also is not mentioned in her affidavit. Mrs Hayek first gave a brief description of her status: 'Since the end of 1939 registered as a full-blood Jewess married to a Gentile; in February 1945, in the course of an anti-Jewish drive of the German government, arrested, jailed and afterwards assigned to a so-called "Labour Camp"; later released on account of chaotic conditions of the transport system.' She added:

> When during the war years my husband on repeated occasions approached Dr Mahr, then working at Berlin, for his advice and help in my husband's attempts to get me out of Germany, Dr Mahr did his very best in our interest, but obviously he had very little, if any, influence.
>
> It is in a spirit of genuine gratitude that I testify herewith that Dr and Mrs Mahr have in all those years of anti-Jewish discrimination, in Dublin as well as here, shown themselves to be my friends, that they visited me frequently and that they and their children, by their intimate contact with me, have ostentatiously ignored and counteracted the policy and the slogans of the party which ostracised the Jews.[39]

Frieda Hayek's statement was accompanied by a certificate from the Jewish Central Committee for the American Zone of Austria, Subcommittee Gmunden, which said: 'We hereby certify that Mrs Frieda Hayek, of Gmunden, Feuersteinstrasse No. 3, is registered at our local Information Centre as a Jewess and that she is recognised as a victim of political persecution during the Nazi era.'[40]

The most obvious sources from whom Mahr should have received affidavits were his former colleagues at the National Museum of Ireland. It was there that he had performed his best work: a letter on headed notepaper from the museum would, presumably, have helped his case greatly. Yet none of his references came from serving members of staff there. It is unknown whether or not any of them refused Mahr's request for an affidavit. Perhaps Mahr already sensed that he would receive little help from that quarter.

It may seem surprising that several Jews were among those trying to help Mahr resume his professional life. This may be attributable to the general confusion that surrounded the genocide of the Jews in the aftermath of the war. At the time, the word 'Holocaust' was not widely used. It was a nineteenth-century word meaning 'great slaughter' that was not applied to the murder of Jews by the Nazis until the mid-1950s.[41] The fact that the number of Jews killed was as high as six million would have seemed an exaggeration to many people in the immediate aftermath of the war. This figure was not generally accepted until the detailed planning of the genocide was revealed during Adolf Eichmann's trial in Israel in

1961. Even in Israel, many Holocaust survivors complained that they were not believed when they spoke about Jews walking into the gas chambers without a fight. One relation of the Mahr family, a historian, told Gustav that the number of dead Jews totalled two million. In Ireland, when the first newsreels of the liberated Auschwitz and Belsen camps were shown in cinemas, many believed that they were looking at Allied propaganda. A newspaper reader in Kilkenny wrote that the British had faked the images of Belsen by using 'starving Indians'.[42]

Following 'denazification', a former Nazi could expect to be given one of four classifications, with Category I reserved for the most virulent Nazis. Mahr was designated a Category II Nazi,[43] a category reserved for activists, militarists or profiteers. This was a positive development for him in that it meant that he would not be brought to trial, did not have to pay fines, and would later be eligible for downgrading to Category III status. The bad news was that he was debarred from public office, from voting, from the teaching, legal, and journalistic professions, and from employment in civil administration. There were also restrictions on his residence in, and his movement within, Germany.[44] In effect, he was not allowed to work: there was no way out of his poverty.

In November 1946, Mahr's name was raised again in a bitter row in the Dáil. This happened while the Minister for Finance, Frank Aiken, was discussing a supplementary payment of £1,000 to enable the Royal Irish Academy to defray the costs of temporary professorships. James Dillon became suspicious that the money might be used to bring Mahr back to Ireland. Although it is unlikely that this was Aiken's intention, Dillon was not going to let the opportunity pass: 'I have no grudge against him [Mahr] but he took his hook out of this country on the eve of the war and thought that he would come back with a Brown Shirt and a Swastika.'

Aiken matched fire with fire, retorting: 'I'll say this for that gentleman [Mahr], that he went *towards* the fighting, unlike Deputy Dillon.' Nothing came of the dispute except that the government was reminded that it would not be able to bring Mahr back to Ireland without a struggle.

The winter of 1946/47 in Germany was the coldest for a hundred years. The Rhine was clogged by ice for fifty-five days.[45] Blizzards halted supplies, and 111 factories were closed – which left nine thousand workers idle.[46] Most of the buildings in the big cities were still in ruins, so cardboard was used to replace the broken windows. Coal was still very scarce for civilians.

Adolf Mahr reached sixty years of age in May 1947, but there was little to celebrate. While other men of his age were thinking of retiring, he was wondering how he would ever be able to work again. It was a decade since he had been elected President of the British Prehistoric Society, and had delivered the address that had assured him of a place among the world's leading prehistorians. At the time, he enjoyed a comfortable middle-class life and had opportunities to travel all over Europe. Now he was trapped in a country where he was not allowed to work, and he was prevented from returning to the only country in which he could expect to make a living. He felt that the treatment he had suffered was particularly unfair considering that no charge had been brought against him: he had, in his view, simply belonged to a much-maligned group.

In November 1947, Mahr sought help again in Ireland, this time by sending a personal letter to his former friend Éamon de Valera. Because Mahr was never tried or even formally interviewed about his work in relation to Ireland, this letter is the closest we can come to hearing his defence against the many charges that were made against him:

> I beg leave to turn to you in my desperate situation with a personal appeal for your help.... It is now well over two years since the cessation of hostilities, half the duration of the shooting war, and I am still here. I have ever since frantically tried to enlist the support of the Dublin authorities in my endeavours to get back to my unfinished work which I consider to be the vocation of my life.
>
> So far I have met with no success. I can, naturally, understand that my past political sympathies and the general situation render my case somewhat delicate, but I beg Your Excellency to consider also the extenuating factors....
>
> I hereby declare most solemnly that I have never done anything against the security of either Eire or Britain. Nor was I ever, officially or unofficially, asked to undertake anything of the kind. Had I ever been asked to do anything in violation of the letter and spirit of my oath of allegiance as a Civil Servant, I would immediately have drawn the consequences. If there was espionage in Ireland I knew nothing of it. Nor was I a Fifth Columnist. I had nothing to do with German parachutists and knew nothing about them until I read recently in the 'Daily Mail' about their deportation. All their names were quite unknown to me, also the

name Goertz [the best-known parachutist]. I have never, either in public orations or by any other means, made Nazi propaganda amongst the Irish or contacted any IRA man or organisation or interfered in Irish politics. My whole civic and professional existence depended upon the maintenance of peace. I would have been a madman had I ever wished for, let alone helped in the preparation of, Anglo-German war.

My conscience in all these matters is absolutely clear and I am willing, nay anxious, to face any accusant [*sic*]. The activities of our small Dublin party group were strictly limited to internal German affairs and there was nothing sinister about them. The late Colonel Brase and I as his successor merely wanted, in the interest of German reputation abroad, the mixed crowd of Germans to behave well and unimpeachably. Since the Party desired to have some level-headed man of good public reputation in charge of the Dublin group, I was persuaded to become 'Ortsgruppenleiter' in May 1937, and I duly informed the Department of this, in case it might object. I informed it again when I resigned, out of my own free will and without outside pressure, on December 31 1938, after the Sudeten crisis and the anti-Jewish riots in Germany, on reasons of principle and because I felt that it might embarrass my employers if I remained local leader of an increasingly unpopular movement. Thus I was not, according to the findings of the Nuremberg Tribunal, a member of a criminal organisation.

Finally I emphatically declare that I had nothing whatsoever to do with the dismissal of the late Herr von Dehn. In fact, no Eire German had.

Our correspondence with headquarters was conducted by ordinary post as we had nothing to conceal . . . . It stands to reason then that the British and Irish security authorities knew all about our doings and obviously they never saw any reason to intervene.

I do not and I cannot deny that I thought it my patriotic duty to join the party and that I honestly believed that it stood for the common good of all Europe. This was an error of judgement but it was not in contradiction to the loyalty and love which I felt equally for your country which had given me hospitality and an honoured scientific position.

It was from similar motives that, during the latter part of the war, I consented, under some moral pressure, to take a minor part, in a purely advisory capacity, in the supervision of the German broadcasts to Eire. It was a part time job which I did intermittently, but I was vitally interested that these transmissions would contain nothing that might offend Irish susceptibilities and thereby impair Irish neutrality, which was my only hope for eventual return. I did not write talks or speak myself and saw the texts of the transmissions only after they had been sent.

There is evidence to suggest that Mahr took far more than a 'minor part, in a purely advisory capacity' in Irland-Redaktion. Although de Valera might not have known this, he would have been aware from Military Intelligence reports that there was some doubt surrounding Mahr's resignation as local party leader in 1938. There can be little doubt, however, over the sincerity of Mahr's personal plea when he explained the hardships he currently faced:

> We have now been homeless for eight years and the last years were unmitigated hardship. All our earthly possessions are in Dublin. I live here as a pauper under miserable conditions in a place where I simply cannot do any learned work, let alone earn a living (I am not talented for the black market). I have a family to support. If I am pensioned my pension will be very small, barely enough for one person, and it will be paid out at a most unfavourable official rate of exchange. Without furniture, clothes, etc., without money, I cannot move away to a more suitable place in Germany, even if I had any chance of getting another job at my age in a starving and ruined country which is terribly overpopulated and has lost more than half its housing accommodation. My library is in Dublin, the books I had here are burned or I had to leave them behind on our flights.
>
> In short, if I cannot return I face premature physical and mental ruin. In my deep despair I beg to appeal to Your Excellency to help me out of this threatening breakdown of my and my family's existence. I hold 24 testimonials by eminent people in seven different countries who speak in my favour as a man and scholar. I could easily get many more, but there would be no point in multiplying them. Five out of these twenty-four testimonials are from Jews and emigrants whom I have helped in the past.
>
> Once more I beg to say I feel personally innocent and that I had nothing to do with, and knew nothing of, the criminal aspects of National Socialism, though I am aware of the implications of what is called collective responsibility. During the months I spent in prison and camp I had ample opportunity to think matters over and search my conscience and I do not feel guilty.
>
> From humanitarian considerations, for the sake of clemency and scientific interests . . . I implore Your Excellency to save us from our

inevitable ruin either by personally intervening on our behalf, so that I can leave our exile, or by whatever other ways and means may be at your disposal. I may add that I became technically eligible for Irish citizenship in September 1937.

Please forgive me for bothering you personally, all other ways seem to be barred to me. Mise, le meas mór, Adolf Mahr.[47]

Mahr's efforts were in vain: he did not receive a reply. A general election loomed in 1948, and de Valera was unlikely to consider taking risks for Mahr, considering the ammunition that such a move would give James Dillon and others. It is probable that the British government was also opposed to Mahr's return to Ireland, as were Irish Military Intelligence. But even if he had had support from those quarters, he would have faced further problems at the National Museum, where senior officers had a vested interest in keeping Mahr out. Pat Wallace has noted: 'Mahr had produced a generation of people who wanted his job, and they wouldn't have wanted him back.' In addition, Dr Gerhard Bersu, who had been removed from the directorship of the Romisch-Germanische Commission in Frankfurt during the Nazi era, had arrived in the Royal Irish Academy as a professor.[48] Mahr was sure Bersu was campaigning against him.

Mahr must have rued the day that he converted from his parents' Catholicism to Protestantism. For Catholic ex-Nazis, a secret 'subterranean railway' network opened that helped them to escape Europe and begin new lives in Argentina. The Vatican was usually the starting point, with a false passport and exit visa being obtained there. Hundreds escaped in this way, including the notorious 'Butcher of Riga' Eduard Roschmann; Klaus Barbie, the Gestapo chief who was better known as the 'Butcher of Lyon'; Adolf Eichmann, who attended the Wannsee Conference and later oversaw the destruction of millions of Jews; and the infamous Josef Mengele, who used his position as camp doctor in the Auschwitz extermination camp to perform medical experiments on inmates, particularly twins. Mengele sought ways of artificially increasing the incidence of twins as a means of multiplying the German population. He escaped to Argentina in 1949 and managed to bring his Auschwitz notes and blood specimens with him.[49] It seems that he later made a living as a genetics expert, claiming that he could improve the efficiency of cattle herds by making the cows give birth to twins.[50]

Mahr's old friend Osveld Menghin, a leading archaeologist in Austria and a Nazi, also escaped using Vatican contacts. Mahr later wrote bitterly: 'Menghin had everything for his passage to Argentina prepared for him in Italy. There he had someone who helped him, no one has helped me. Naturally I would go.'[51] Mahr's Protestantism meant that this route was not open to him.

Mahr would have been further galled to know that Catholic ex-Nazis and Nazi collaborators were streaming into Ireland. Around a dozen members of the Breton separatist group Bezen Perrot made their way to Ireland after the war. This eighty-strong paramilitary unit had collaborated with the occupying Germans in France as a means to winning independence for Brittany. They had worn SS uniforms, had taken orders from the Germans, and had been involved in anti-resistance activity, which included the arrest of Jews. It appears that, around D-Day, the group had participated in the interrogation and mass shootings by the SS of 'anti-German elements'. The eventual defeat of Germany meant that members of the group were no longer welcome in their native Brittany, and several came to Ireland, aided by a network of Welsh patriots.

Bezen Perrot's founder and leader, Celestin Lainé, arrived in Ireland under the name Neven Hénaff. A chemical engineer by training, he began working in Galway as an engineer in 1948. He was sentenced to death *in absentia* by the French, but because no extradition treaty existed between the two countries, he did not return there. He died in Ireland in 1983.[52]

Alan Heusaff, the Commander of the Bezen Perrot, arrived in Ireland on a coal-boat from Wales in 1950. He married a Donegal woman, had six children, and became prominent in Celtic academic circles. He was also tried *in absentia* by the French authorities for collaboration with the Germans, and sentenced to death. He could not be extradited either, however, and died in Galway in 1999.[53]

Yann Goulet, who was to become one of Ireland's best-known sculptors, had also been associated with the Bezen Perrot and other Breton separatist movements. Condemned by the French as a collabarator, he was forced to leave France in 1947,[54] and subsequently set up home in Bray, County Wicklow. He created many notable public sculptures in Ireland, including the Dublin Brigade Memorial at the Custom House in Dublin, the Christy Ring Memorial at Cloyne GAA grounds in Cork, and the Ballyseedy Memorial in Tralee, County Kerry, in memory of the eight men killed in March 1923 by Free State forces.[55] During the 1970s, Goulet helped Libyan leader Muammar al-Gaddafi make contact with the IRA; this led to the imporation of shipments of arms to Ireland from Libya.[56] Goulet became a Professor of Sculpture at the Royal Hibernian Academy,[57] and in 1982 was honoured with membership of the arts organisation Aosdána, which is funded by the Irish government.

Another notable refugee who came to Ireland after the war was Albert Folens, a former De La Salle seminarian and member of the Flemish nationalist organisation the Flemish Legion, which formed part of the Waffen SS.[58] He was injured on the Eastern Front in 1942, and was treated in a dedicated SS hospital in Karlsbad. He was arrested by the British in 1944 and sentenced to ten years' imprisonment. He escaped after two and a half years and was smuggled out of Belgium by Trappist monks; he arrived in Ireland in 1948 on a false passport.[59]

Folens qualified as a teacher from University College Dublin in 1951 and held teaching positions in Fairview CBS, Clonliffe College and Colaiste Mhuire, where he taught through Irish. In 1957, Albert and his wife, Juliette, established the Folens Group to publish and print French textbooks. They soon diversified into a wide range of educational books, and the company is now the largest publishing group in Ireland. He died in 2002.[60]

During the Arms Trials of 1970, when Charles Haughey and Military Intelligence Officer Captain James Kelly faced charges of conspiracy to import arms for the IRA, their co-accused included Albert Luykx, a Belgian businessman resident in Ireland. Luykx, a Flemish nationalist and war-profiteer, had escaped to Ireland after the war, having been sentenced to death in Belgium for denouncing people to the SD (secret police).[61]

One of the most notorious war criminals to come to Ireland after the war was Andrija Artukovic, who arrived in spring 1947 under the assumed name of Alois Anich. Known as the 'Yugoslav Himmler', he was named Interior Minister of the Independent State of Croatia after the Nazi invasion of Yugoslavia in April 1941. This regime, which lasted for four years, pursued a 'racially pure' and 100 percent Catholic state, and directed its fury primarily against Orthodox Serbs, but also against Jews and Gypsies.[62]

In May 1941, Artukovic ordered the extermination of four thousand Serbs in his native Siroki Brijeg, and that September he approved the construction of a system of concentration camps, including Jasenovac, where 700,000 people perished.[63] As the war ended, he fled to Austria, then Switzerland, and then to Ireland, where he stayed for more than a year. In July 1948, Artukovic became the highest-ranking war criminal to find safe haven in the United States, after going there on a tourist visa that he obtained with a forged Irish identity certificate. Artukovic lived in California until the 1980s, when pressure from Jewish organisations forced his extradition on war crimes to Yugoslavia. He was sentenced to death by firing squad, but the sentence was put off on account of his ill health, and he died in a prison hospital two years later.[64]

Even Auschwitz's 'Angel of Death', Josef Mengele, was rumoured to have passed through Ireland after the war. In 1985, researchers at BBC's *Panorama* and ITV's *World in Action* programmes found evidence that suggested that Mengele may have spent six weeks in Ireland en route to South America, and that he was 'almost certainly put up by a religious order'.[65] The evidence indicated that he had been 'brought to Ireland – probably, ironically, under an assumed Jewish name – at the behest of Nazi sympathisers in the Vatican', although it seems that his Irish hosts were unaware of his true identity. G2's Colonel Dan Bryan, who had retired in 1952, was quoted at the time as saying: 'there was every possibility that Nazi war criminals found refuge with Irish religious orders' and that he had 'a general belief that people were being smuggled here on their way to South America'.[66]

Another prominent Nazi who lived in Ireland after the war, albeit much later, was Dutchman Pieter Menten, who, as an SS officer in eastern Poland, had murdered dozens of Jews. He had been made a 'custodian of Jewish antique dealerships' in Poland, a position that allowed him to amass a large collection of plundered art. On his trip back to Holland from Poland in 1943, he travelled in a private train carrying four carloads of his personal art works.[67] He later became a multi-millionaire dealer in art, and bought an estate in County Waterford in 1964. He spent much of his retirement in Ireland, until knowledge of his dark past emerged, and the government prevented him from re-entering the country in 1985.[68]

Otto Skorzeny also bought a country estate in Ireland – in County Kildare, in 1959 – and he lived there during the summer months. Skorzeny had been Hitler's bodyguard, and had carried out such daring operations as the rescue of Mussolini from his mountaintop prison in

1943. He was not considered a war criminal, although after the war he founded a secret organisation, *Die Spinne* (the Spider), which helped some 500 former SS members escape from Germany.[69]

One Nazi who, like Mahr, had great difficulty getting back to Ireland after the war was Helmut Clissmann. American intelligence files show that Clissmann may have been recruited by the Abwehr (German counter-intelligence) as early as 1930, when he was just nineteen years of age. He arrived in Ireland in 1933 as an exchange student in Trinity College Dublin, and is believed to have reported back to the Abwehr and a Nazi Party intelligence service known as 'Buro J.', through the German Legation in Dublin, on matters relating to Irish politics and English relations in Ireland.[70] He became a lecturer at Trinity College in 1934, but lost his position three years later when the authorities there became concerned about his involvement with the University Republican Club, which was associated with the IRA.[71]

During the war, Clissmann served in the German military, and was involved in the plan to invade Britain. He was sent to Wales, where he was expected to establish contact with the Welsh Nationalist Movement and enlist personnel to help German forces in the intended invasion. Should this mission fail, his orders were to contact IRA elements in England for a similar purpose.[72] Clissmann set sail for Wales on 5 September 1940, but his ship developed engine trouble and turned back: the mission was aborted.

Back in Germany, Clissmann was given the job of monitoring press and radio reports dealing with Ireland and supplying information for Mahr's radio service. He was involved in recruiting Irish prisoners of war as potential agents to be landed in Ireland.[73] He also looked after Frank Ryan in Berlin, in the hope of landing him in Ireland to raise an IRA force to help a possible German invasion.

Clissmann was arrested by the British in the aftermath of the war and suffered horrendous conditions for thirteen months at the notorious Bad Nenndorf camp in Germany.[74] As late as June 1948, the British still regarded him as a danger. A secret Foreign Office report stated: 'It would seem highly undesirable that Clissmann should be allowed to return to Eire'.[75] Another British report that month described Clissmann's history as being 'so bad that it is quite clear that he should not be allowed to leave Germany'.[76]

Nevertheless, Clissmann made it back to Ireland. Upon his release from prison, he hiked through the Alps into Italy, where he sold his camera and some other valuables. He then made his way to Rome, where one of his former students was working at the Irish embassy. The two men went to the Vatican, where Clissmann was granted a passport. Although, initially, Clissmann was not permitted to return to Ireland, he eventually flew from Rome to Shannon in 1948.[77] Clissmann enjoyed considerable success in post-war Ireland. He established a successful chemical company, became a founding member of Amnesty in Ireland, and was one of those who founded St Kilian's German School in Dublin.

Television producer Keith Farrell, who has done extensive research on the subject, believes that as many as a hundred Nazis escaped to Ireland after the war. He says that very few were German; they were mostly Flemish and Breton nationalists, and Ukranians, and were mainly low-level officials, collaborators, profiteers and members of minority political groups who had sided with the occupying Nazis, and were now unwelcome in their own countries. But, he says, as many as twenty-five of these people may have been war criminals. In most cases, the Catholic link appears to have been strong.[78]

As Ingrid Mahr neared her eighteenth birthday in 1949, she applied for an Irish passport, and got ready to return to the country of her childhood. It was a major blow for the Mahr parents to have to split the family again. In the absence of Gustav and Hilde during the war years, Ingrid had become the 'eldest child' and was her father's favourite. Adolf Mahr later described the pain of the separation from Ingrid as being 'incalculable'.[79]

Before Ingrid departed, her father typed up a list of those in Ireland who, he felt, might be able to provide assistance to Ingrid in her new life away from the family. The list contained forty-three names under the heading 'Some dependable friends in order of importance'. A number of them had an asterisk beside their name to denote 'reliable'. The names, in the order given by Mahr, were: Grete Spiegelfeld,* the family's former housekeeper; Frau Brase,* the wife of the late Colonel Fritz Brase; Mrs I. O'Sullivan,* the wife to the schools inspector and a family friend; Professor Friedrich Herkner* of the National College of Art, a former Nazi who had been allowed to resume his State job in Ireland; Karl

Budina,* son of Charles, who had run the Kilmacurragh Park Hotel in County Wicklow; Miss Maureen O'Brien,* married to Austin Macdonald of Dundrum, County Dublin; Mrs Winkelmann and Mrs Müller-Dubrow, who had been good friends of Mrs Mahr; the Hayeks, who might soon return; Dr Eduard Hempel, the former Minister at the German Legation; the leading Dublin solicitor Arthur Cox;* Mimi Crinion, formerly of Herbert Street, Dublin; Mrs Joanna Broekhoven, the wife of Henri Broekhoven, who was now Managing Director of Siemens-Schuckert; Frau E. Wenzel of Morehampton Road; Gustav's school pals Eric Ashman and Arthur Forster, and Arthur's father; Marguerit Greiner, whose husband, Harry, worked at the Solus factory in Bray; Dr Dorothy Price, who treated Mahr when he was sick, and wife of a Dublin judge, Liam Price; Elizabeth Clissmann,* the wife of Helmut Clissmann, who had been a contact person between the IRA and German counter-intelligence during the war.

In a separate category marked 'Scientific people', Mahr directed Ingrid towards L. Mongey* of Dungarvan, County Waterford; Dr Westropp* of Clonskeagh, County Dublin; Joseph O'Neill,* formerly head of the Department of Education; Dr Quane of the Museum, now living in Santry; Joe Raftery of the Museum, also living in Santry; Prof. S. P. O'Riordain of University College Dublin; Professor J. H. Delargy in Rathgar; Liam Gogan in the Museum; the photographer Thomas Mason; F. T. Riley* of Ballymore Eustace, County Kildare; M. Farrington, Secretary of the Royal Irish Academy; J. Wallace, a jeweller in Limerick; H. G. Leask of Terenure; Rev. Monsignor Hynes* of Galway; Miss Gertrude Conry; and Mrs Richards-Orpen of the Monksgrange estate, where Gustav spent the memorable summer of 1933.

Mahr also suggested people in Britain who might be helpful, including Mrs Daukes* of Bognor Regis; Dr Alfons Barb* in Leeds; Professor Paul Jacobsthal* of Oxford; Howard Kilbride-Jones* in Scotland; T. D. Kendrick* of the British Museum, and J. M. de Navarro* of Cambridge. He also asked her to check his two life-assurance policies at the Guardian Insurance Company.

The list shows that Mahr regarded Barb and Jacobsthal, his two Jewish contacts in London, as being 'reliable', but there is no mention of his former colleagues still working in the National Museum in Dublin.

Ingrid's return to Ireland was a most uncomfortable experience.

While once her father's popularity and dynamism had commanded respect for both himself and his family, now she felt that his past made life difficult for her. During an interview for a housekeeping job, she realised that the host family was Jewish, and felt obliged to tell them that she was Adolf Mahr's daughter. She did not get the job. One of Mahr's former colleagues laughed at Ingrid, saying: 'Who would have known Adolf Mahr would have become a prisoner of the English? And was broke?' The mighty had fallen, and she felt that people were jeering at her.

An exception to this was an experience she had at a Jewish-owned chemist's shop on Baggot Street. 'Mr Rosenthal was very friendly to me. I hadn't much money, and no health insurance. I needed penicillin and Rosenthal said you pay whenever you can. He never said an unfriendly word about Father. I can't understand that.'

There was unfinished business to attend to regarding the family property in Dublin. Most of the family's furniture and clothing had been sold or given away, but the fate of Mahr's notes and library remained uncertain. Adolf Mahr's books and papers had been stored in the cellars beneath the National Museum during the war. Both the British and American intelligence people had tried to gain access to his files, and there was also pressure from their Irish counterparts, who, it was feared, might have unearthed something that could embarrass the government.

Dr Quane, the Administrator of the Museum, came to an arrangement with Ingrid whereby she could remove her father's personal items and leave anything that belonged to the Museum, but she must burn everything else. Over a period of weeks, in the evenings, Ingrid went through her father's material, saving some of it, leaving some, and burning a great deal.

Ingrid first got work in the Gold Flake tobacco factory in Dublin. Later, Grete Spiegelfeld, who had been the Mahr housekeeper during Ingrid's youth, told her of a servant job at the home in which Spiegelfeld herself was working. The owner, a Mr Whitcroft, did not like the idea of having Adolf Mahr's daughter working in his home, but Grete persuaded him to take her on. 'I know this girl from birth,' she said to him. 'She is reliable and able to work. She will be a great help for me. And I want to help this child, because she is partly my child that I've raised from birth.' Ingrid got the job, and with the money she earned she began to take evening courses in clothes design. Later, this led to a job at the Arnotts department store on Henry Street.

The general election of February 1948 saw de Valera lose the grip on Irish politics that he had held for sixteen years, and John A. Costello of Fine Gael replace him as Taoiseach. Although James Dillon was now in the Cabinet, Mahr saw the possibility of salvation in the new government and wrote to Costello in May.[80] He gave an account of the previous letters he had sent to de Valera, and mentioned that he had never received an official reply. He recounted that he had been officially on leave when the war broke out and could not return to Ireland; that he had never done anything illegal or misused his position in Ireland; and that he could not possibly constitute a threat to the safety of Britain or Éire. He accepted that his position was complicated by the question of nationality:

> I am theoretically still an Irish Civil Servant but I do not know for certain whether I am now a German or an Austrian subject. My wife is born Dutch, my four children have three different nationalities (Irish, Austrian and German) . . . . I have no other desire but to obtain Irish nationality, for which I became eligible in October, 1937.

Mahr pointed out that a charge had never been made against him, but that his denazification categorisation still prevented him from working. He said that he was living as a refugee, with no pension possibilities, and his only remaining possessions were in Dublin. Mahr noted once again that he had twenty-five testimonials written by 'eminent' people in Britain, Sweden, Denmark, Switzerland and Hungary, and by anti-fascists in Germany. Mahr concluded once more with a plea:

> But even now I refuse to believe that it can really be the intention of the powers that be to ruin me deliberately and systematically in body and mind as a punitive measure . . . . I should be forever grateful to Your Excellency for an early and favourable reply.

By now Mahr had been downgraded to a Category III Nazi, which allowed him to work. Since there was no possibility of employment for him in the village of Augustfehn, he left Maria and the children for Bonn, where he took up a job at the museum. What exactly he did there remains unclear: his curriculum vitae listed his occupation as 'private activities', which may mean low-paid temporary work.[81] There, the former President of the British Prehistory Society lived in a corner of one of the rooms of the museum. He slept on an army bed in an area behind bookshelves, separated from the working area by a little curtain.

A month after Mahr had sent his letter, the Department of Education made a submission to the Irish government on his case.[82] This submission recounted its history, acknowledged that he had been 'an archaeologist of outstanding ability, and that he had always discharged his Museum duties efficiently and satisfactorily', and suggested that the government send a letter to Mahr informing him that his position as Keeper of Irish Antiquities be made available to him as soon as he could resume it. The memo suggested that his position of museum director would not be available since 'other arrangements have been made for the discharge of the Museum administration', and that his pay would be commensurate with the lesser position.

The lesser pay would have been only a slight blow to Mahr. The opportunity to work again in Ireland, to live in a proper home, and to have enough to eat for the first time in several years, must have seemed to Mahr like a godsend. The memo to the government also stated that Mahr was now sixty-one years of age and that, if he was retired immediately, he would be entitled to a pension of £151 per annum and a lump sum of £382; this was written more as an observation than as a proposal, however.

The memo was sent to the Departments of Finance, External Affairs, Justice, and Industry and Commerce, all of which made observations. The first three were in favour of bringing Mahr back, but Daniel Morrissey, Minister for Industry and Commerce, did not 'consider that the resumption by Dr Mahr of his duties in the Museum is either necessary or desirable.' The Department of Education's proposals were subsequently reversed: instead of allowing Mahr to return as Keeper of Irish Antiquities, he was to be pensioned off.[83]

Mahr got the bad news in early January 1949, and was devastated. To him, the Irish government's decision was akin to a death sentence: he was stuck in an impoverished country, judged too important a Nazi to be allowed return to Ireland; on the other hand, he was not an important enough Nazi to be offered passage to South America.

In the days after receiving the letter from Ireland, he did what came most naturally to his academic mind: he wrote a long report on the problems he faced. He weighed up the pros and cons of his situation, tried to provide some useful analysis, and suggested and dissected ideas to rectify the situation. He presented the report in the form of a poignant letter to his wife, and made a duplicate for Gustav. But the duplicate was never presented, and Maria Mahr never divulged the contents of her letter. Her children found it among her personal items forty years later.

The letter, written in German, started simply:

Dear All,

So the decision re. Dublin has been taken, and it is bad; effective 6 November [1948] I was put into pension. I receive a small pension and a one-off payment of £382 by way of a pay-off.

... Quite clearly the letter does not contain a single word of regret or recognition of work well done. It is cold and factual, only the wording that the Finance Minister 'has now been pleased' suggests a certain sympathy for the hurt they have done me.

... It is obvious that the Irish government consulted the English and they categorically said that this man should not be let go back to Ireland. I got a very clear hint when I applied for Ingrid's passport. It was for Ingrid only, and Brigit would be eligible when she reaches 18, but no other members of the family. It doesn't matter if I am Category III, IV or V; for them it is immaterial. They probably say: 'Mahr was just too clever for us to prove anything against him'.

... The deep wounding bitterness that I feel over this new twist of fate in my life, after so many ups and downs, is not lessened by the feeling I am to some extent to blame for losing my wonderful position. First I was literally consumed with hate against this 'victorious' world, which does this to me. They are good haters. But I try hard to suppress these feelings because if this world is once more to become a place where man can live, this vicious circle of hate, injustice, brutality, revenge, revenge for the revenge, must be broken . . . .

If it is any use to you to blame me, then do so. I will take the blame and cannot excuse myself. Every person is under the influence of his character, his genes, origins, his environment, his passions and instincts, his sum of knowledge, his background; the influences from outside, his loathings, his impulses or inclinations, and that what he believes is right. Overall, it depends on his own will, and I do not need to make any excuses. All the rest is an error of judgement, and therein lies a large part of the tragedy of human life.

And if you, Maria, have no wish to share the wretchedness of my old age with me and rather move to Holland, I can't blame you. Of course it is possible to foresee an improvement in Holland's economy, but I could not live off your family's charity.

So far as I can . . . I will continue to work so that the poor Lazarus of the nations [Germany] will at least in the area of intellectual performance rise again. If I could find something abroad, naturally I would go.

Still I have to try . . . . What counts in life are not the victories on the field of battle but the defeats and the spirit in which man accepts them. It is not always the best people who survive as victors. But it is bitter that I must through the changing circumstances of my lifetime start from scratch again and again, while my years without tangible results are lost.

The pension I am to receive from Ireland, depending on the exchange rate . . . will be about 150 Marks per month . . . . For living, it is too little, and for dying it is too much.

Mahr reflected on the possibility that yet another war was looming on the horizon, this time between the Allies and the Soviet Union. He could not predict whether or not his pension would still be paid in the event of another war breaking out, but it might not matter because he felt that his family would have little chance of surviving such a war. 'In Ireland there would be some chance,' he said.

Mahr took some comfort from the fact that at last there was clarity with regard to his position. He conceded that it would have been very difficult to return to Dublin 'in view of the widespread poisoned atmosphere' there:

> The Museum also will not have not improved, so again I would have had to put all my efforts into thankless organisational museum work, with an uncooperative staff, who would wait impatiently for my departure, co-operate as little as possible, and see me as an obstacle to their advancement . . . . In any case I have made myself dispensable by setting up a sort of training programme from my main staff. Perhaps it is a blessing in disguise that I can devote my last years solely to research.
>
> . . . I will try to find some kind of work in Germany, although it seems pointless nowadays. Perhaps some museum man of importance can get me in.

But Mahr had never actually worked as an archaeologist in Germany, so he had few worthwhile connections in the country. He remarked that the German scientific establishment paid less attention to him than the Irish and the English ones: 'They did not know what to do with me. And to think that for this riff-raff, idiot that I am, I sacrificed my scientific existence!'

Mahr's greatest regret was reserved for his family, and the fact that his children's lives had been ruined by his mistakes:

> And I have not only wrecked my life, and my profession, but I have also wrecked the lives of my children . . . . And this is a bitter lump in my throat. That I will have to work until my last breath is a good idea . . . . At present it is very difficult, but that can always get better. In any case I will keep trying. Keep fighting.
> Goodbye to you all.[84]

9

Epilogue

Picking up the Pieces, 1947 onwards

As the cold war began, the United States and Britain realised that they would need the new state of West Germany to act as a buffer between the democracies of western Europe, and the Soviet bloc to the east. US President Harry Truman felt that, sooner or later, the Kremlin would make Germany 'an offer it couldn't refuse',[1] and that the best way to prevent West Germany from falling under Soviet control was to help it to become strong and affluent again. The way was cleared for the German economic miracle to begin.

The first signs of Germany's recovery came on 21 June 1948, when its new currency was launched. Every citizen in the country's western zones received forty of the new Deutschmarks, with children under eighteen received twenty each. With real money in circulation, the cigarette was no longer the main unit of currency, and the vast black market collapsed.[2] As if by magic, consumer goods that had hitherto been available only through barter suddenly appeared in shop windows.

The rising tide of Germany's economy gradually lifted the scattered members of the Mahr family. In Oldenburg, Maria Mahr and her youngest daughter, Brigit, received social-welfare payments, which eased their poverty and allowed Brigit to remain in school until she was eighteen. On leaving school in 1951, she got a job in a local doctor's office and further improved her and her mother's standard of living. For two years, Hilde's husband, Gerhard Strasburger, fought tuberculosis. Adolf Mahr often came from Bonn to stay with them. He became good friends with Hilde's mother-in-law, with whom he often sat up late chatting. Hilde noticed in her father a softening in his attitudes, and an acceptance of the mistakes he had made.

In Dublin, Ingrid progressed well. In 1949, she sold the family's furniture, which had been in storage since their departure to the Reich a decade earlier. She paid off the storage bills, and some other remaining debts. She also began the process of preparing her father's substantial library for transport to Germany. She resumed contact with other Irish people, who, like her, had spent their formative years in the horrors of a Germany at war. A photograph taken at the Arnotts Christmas ball in 1950 shows Ingrid sitting alongside Mona Brase, who had got back to Ireland in September 1945, and spent all her working life as a radiographer in Mercer's Hospital, Dublin; Carina O'Sullivan, who as a child had played on the beach in Skerries with the Mahr children in 1937, but who had been trapped in Germany with her mother for the duration of the war; and Helmut and Erika Stieber, who had grown up in Carlow, were sent to boarding school in Germany during the summer of 1939, and finally returned in 1947. Helmut Stieber had been drafted into the German army and later recounted his experiences in his memoir, *Against the Odds: Survival on the Russian Front*. He spent his working life in the Electricity Supply Board, and now lives in Dublin. His sister, Erika, married and moved to Canada.

Gustav worked for the British as a translator until 1950, and in the autumn of that year married his fiancée, Clara, and moved to Bonn, to be close to his father. Gustav noticed that, despite his setbacks, Adolf's life was improving. Adolf had not lost his ability to get other people to do him favours. Gustav recalls his father's first meeting with his fiancée, 'when the old man dropped his pants and asked her to fix a hole in them for him.'

Between them, the six Mahrs were a mixture of no fewer than ten nationalities. When Gustav was returned from captivity after the war, he filled in his nationality as 'German' on his ID-card form. He was officially German and considered himself to be German, but when he indicated his intention to marry, he had no way of proving that this was his nationality. Because he had been born in Austria, he was deemed to be Austrian, and so had to take out Austrian citizenship in order to get married. As a result of the laws at that time, his wife automatically became Austrian because she was married to an Austrian, and their daughter automatically took on the same nationality, even though she had been born in Germany. Years later, the law changed, and allowed Gustav and Clara to become German again. Hilde had similar trouble when she got married, starting with a six-month wait for her birth certificate to arrive from Klagenfurt in Austria.

As funds became available for the re-education of Germans, Adolf Mahr made a modest living from lecture fees and on research projects. He presented lectures in America House and at the British Council, on subjects as diverse as the Celts, prehistoric mining in Austria, and the recently discovered Anglo-Saxon burial site at Sutton Hoo in England, where a forty-oar ship containing a wooden tomb stuffed with gold and jewelled ornaments had recently been discovered. His other pet subject was the Kon Tiki voyage of 1947, in which the Norwegian zoologist Thor Heyerdahl travelled 3,800 miles from Peru to Polynesia in a wooden raft, to prove that the Polynesians could have come from South America.[3]

In 1950, Mahr travelled to Mainz to attend one of the first major archaeological congresses held after the war. He was joined by Ingrid, who had arrived home from Dublin for Gustav's wedding: Ingrid enjoyed spending time with her father, and many of the social activities that surrounded the congress. She could see that her father enjoyed reconnecting with many of his old friends and colleagues. Such congresses had always been highlights in his professional life, and even now, when his career barely existed, they were still important to him. After the First International Congress of Prehistoric and Protohistoric Sciences in London in August 1932, he had hardly been able to contain his delight when he wrote to Albert Bender that he 'brought twelve of the best European archaeologists to Dublin to shed light on the Stone Age in Ireland'. This coming together of 'the savants' won him an invitation to the Prehistoric Congress in Madrid in 1936, when he and Maria Mahr were almost caught in the crossfire as General Franco's troops laid siege to the capital. A year later, Mahr delivered his presidential address to the British Prehistoric Society, and not only won international recognition personally, but succeeded in 'putting Ireland on the map' of European archaeology. In 1939, he was invited to deliver a series of lectures in Scotland to honour the memory of the Scottish writer Neil Munro. Afterwards, he enjoyed a joyful trip to the Scottish Highlands with his friend and colleague Howard Kilbride-Jones. This all led to the Congress in Germany in August 1939, the main reason he had left Ireland; after this, his career as an archaeologist had ground to a halt.

Despite Mahr's high spirits, his fall from grace would have been obvious to all he met. Ingrid could see that he was not faring well. He was bitter about his former colleagues in Ireland: 'Imagine Raftery and O'Riordan wouldn't even invite you over for dinner, after all I did for their careers,' he said to her.

Mahr still had no home. He was living in the draughtsmen's studio at the Museum of Bonn. But he did not have to pay rent, which meant that the stipend he got for research work went relatively far.[4] He was now fully de-nazified, so had full legal rights to work, and was intent on relaunching his career. He had got to know some influential people in the mining industry, and during the winter of 1950/51 he delivered a lecture at a miners' annual convention in a mining college at Clausthal-Zellerfeld in the Harz Mountains. Soon afterwards, he was offered the position of director of a new institute of mining history which would be established in Bonn. It was the best news Mahr had received in many years, and he jumped at the offer. The new position would give him a steady income and enable him to win back some prestige, and he would be working in the discipline in which he had specialised before he had moved to Ireland and switched to Celtic archaeology. To top it all, Gustav was to be his assistant and librarian. Adolf would be able to provide for his son again, and pass along knowledge to him as he had done during Gustav's schooldays in Dublin. Gustav would become an archaeologist: this had been his dream from the very beginning, and despite all the calamities that had occurred since then, the dream would come true. Everything was falling into place; all Adolf needed now were his books from Dublin, which, courtesy of Ingrid, were en route.

But this happy development was too much for Mahr's ailing heart. His heart was weak, and he also had high blood pressure. The war had also taken its toll, as had years of poverty, imprisonment, starvation and subsequent illnesses. In spring 1951, he collapsed at the college in the Harz Mountains, and was rushed to hospital. Neither he nor his doctors recognised that he had suffered a heart attack, and soon Clara collected him from the hospital and brought him back to his 'home' at the Museum of Bonn. Mahr was down but not out: after twelve years away from his chosen profession, the old workaholic took little rest before getting back to work.

Mahr was energised by the possibility of a return to his former glory, and immersed himself in preparations for his new institute. His financial position was now strong enough for him to be able to pay the 1,500 Marks necessary for Gustav and Clara to rent a three-bedroom apartment in Bonn. He would share the apartment with the young couple, and so have his first real home in many years. He also hoped that Maria and Brigit would soon join him in Bonn.[5] But in May, while Gustav and Clara organised furniture for their new home, Adolf had a second heart attack. This time it was a severe one.

Mahr's colleagues at the Museum of Bonn took him from his living quarters at the museum to the local hospital in Bonn. Clara contacted Maria Mahr and Brigit in Oldenburg, and Hilde in Frankfurt. Gustav was en route to Bonn with furniture: as soon as it arrived at the new apartment, he went to the hospital, where he found Adolf unconscious, and Maria at his side. In order to reduce his blood pressure, the doctors tapped his blood, but it was of little use: Adolf had also suffered a stroke and was clearly dying. Gustav had to leave the hospital again because his furniture was being unloaded; he left his mother and father alone in the hospital. Soon afterwards, Maria Mahr phoned his apartment building to say that Adolf was dead. He was sixty-four years old.

Adolf's body was still warm when Gustav returned to the hospital. His father was wearing the watch that his first fiancée had given him, near the end of World War I – and shortly before she threw herself into the Danube when she realised she wasn't good enough to be Mrs Adolf Mahr. He had always worn the watch since that time: through his second courtship, life in Ireland, a second world war, and all that had happened in its aftermath. Gustav removed the watch from his dead father's wrist, and has always worn it since.

Adolf Mahr's funeral was large, by German standards. About thirty people assembled in Bonn to pay their last respects. Ingrid borrowed money from an old friend of her father's and flew back from Dublin. She was upset to find that she was surrounded by people she did not know – people from Bonn, and coal-mining people. Among those gathered was Mahr's old friend Otto Bene, the former leading Nazi in Britain, who witnessed, and participated in, the deportation of Jews from Holland during the war. He sobbed loudly, took Gustav aside, and said: 'We have had our chance and we mucked it up. So we have to stand back and leave the future development to your generation.'[6]

The *Irish Press* carried the news to the Irish public, albeit in a strange article that contained more fiction than fact. It said:

> Dr Mahr was offered the appointment on the retirement of Mr J. J. Buckley, he refused to accept it unless he was given the title of Director. This was agreed to and he remained in Dublin until the end of the war, when he went to Germany with his family.
>
> While in Germany he was arrested on some political charge. Although he was released later he could not return to Ireland, and he had to resign from his position in Dublin. Later he obtained an appointment in a museum in Bonn.[7]

Soon after Adolf Mahr died, his beloved library arrived from Dublin – and swamped Gustav's apartment. Despite his sadness at seeing something so precious to his father arriving after his death, Gustav found the books useful as he embarked on his new career as an archaeologist. In the winter of 1951, Gustav left his job as a secretary in the mining institute, and got a stipend to study the prehistory of mining. This allowed him literally to follow in his father's footsteps: he returned to the prehistoric salt-mines at Hallstatt, Austria, where his father had first made his name, and excavated there for ten seasons. One of the texts that helped him in his new work was the record of objects found and displayed in the area, published by his father in 1914. As recently as 1963, Mahr's register was still the only organised listing of acquisitions for that site.[8]

Gustav and Clara had a daughter in 1953, who later became a psychoanalyst; and a son in 1957, who is now a computer analyst. In 1960, the family moved to Berlin, where Gustav took a position in the Archaeological Survey of Berlin, and excavated prehistoric sites in riverbeds, wooded areas and construction areas just outside the city. In 1967, he transferred to the Museum of Pre- and Proto-history in Charlottenburg, Berlin, where he worked for the rest of his career. Gustav returned to Ireland several times, most notably when he spent six weeks digging with his father's former colleague Howard Kilbride-Jones in Falcarragh, County Donegal, in 1976.

The period immediately after her father's death was difficult for Hilde. She had become pregnant with her second child during one of Gerhard's visits home, but he had returned to the infirmary, still unable to assist her financially, or to help the rearing of Hans. It was while living in similar poverty in the Vienna of 1924 that her mother had miscarried her second child. Brigit helped prevent a similar disaster by coming to live with her older sister for the last four months of her pregnancy. As Hilde put it, the two 'hung on together' with the small income they had.[9]

After three years fighting tubercolosis, Gerhard Strasburger left hospital and resumed his career procuring and selling crop fumigators. He, Hilde and their two boys moved to Dreieich, a small town near Frankfurt, in 1952. There, their two boys had easier access to schools, and Hilde became an avid gardener. She built a pond in their back garden which is now home to frogs and watercress, and a replica figurine from Pompeii. She brought a burl of redwood tree back from a holiday in California during the 1960s: it has since grown into a twenty-six-metre pillar of wood which overshadows her house. She is a member of the German Rhododendron Society.

Hilde used to suffer nightmares because of her wartime experiences. When planes flew low over her home in Frankfurt, she often found herself once again in Berlin during an air raid. But generally, this daughter of a Nazi and the son of a Jew lived happily until Gerhard's passing in 1993. Their sons, who carry that most unusual lineage, followed in their grandfathers' scientific traditions: one became a professor of medical psychology, while the other became an anaesthetist.

The love of exercise that had helped Hilde escape the worst horrors of the war remains with her. While this book was being researched, she failed to return a phone call for some days, but eventually phoned to explain why. 'I am sorry, but I was hiking in the Alps with my grandchildren all last week,' said the seventy-eight-year-old. A year later, her excuse was a trip to Greece, where she had enrolled in a two-week course in Greek dancing.

Hilde has returned to Ireland several times. Her childhood friendship with her neighbour Terry Meagher, pulled apart by her sudden departure to Germany in 1939, was rekindled in 1952 and endures to this day.

Following the death of her father, Ingrid returned to Frankfurt and worked in a clothes factory as a cutter. The most Irish of the children, she did not intend staying long – just a year in the clothes factory, after which she hoped to bring the German technology to Ireland. But she met a young machine engineer named Otto Reusswig, got married and settled in Gelnhausen, about fifty kilometres east of Frankfurt. They have two daughters: one works with troubled teenagers, the other with older people.

Ingrid Reusswig became involved in politics at the age of forty. She joined Willy Brandt's German Socialist party (SPD), which she describes as 'the party most favoured by anti-Nazis'. She took up the cause of immigrants' rights and care for the elderly, and in December 2004 received the *Verdienstmedaille des Verdienstordens der Bundesrepublik*, a medal from the German government in recognition of her work with old people and welfare organisations for more than thirty years.

'It was ironic that Father said everyone should lose interest in politics,' she says, referring to his letter to Albert Bender in 1932. 'I often think of Mother, who said, "Why don't you stick with your archaeology, because you don't understand much of politics?" I mingled in politics and I know how difficult it is.'

After helping Hilde through her second pregnancy, Brigit Mahr returned north to her mother. Brigit worked in a local doctor's office; she earned enough to support herself and her mother, who was barely surviving on social-welfare payments alone. After five years, when Maria Mahr began receiving a widow's pension, Brigit used her newfound financial independence to study sociology at the University of Hanover. In 1958, during her first semester at the university, she met a professor, Siegfried Jenkner, who specialised in the study of totalitarianism. He had a thorough personal understanding of the subject from his years in the fledgling state of East Germany. He had been denounced by communists for ordering proscribed books, and served five years in a prison camp in Siberia, where he worked in coal mines. He has written several books about his experiences.

Brigit and Siegfried were married while Brigit was still a student, and the eldest of their three children was born in 1962. Their children were educated at a Rudolf Steiner school, which promoted the awareness to nature's cycles, daily meditation and concentration practices. Although non-religious in its outlook, the school embraced Buddhist, Christian, Muslim and other practices. Brigit became very religious and was confirmed into the Protestant faith; while Siegfried became a professor of political science at the Universities of Göttingen and Hanover, she became heavily involved with the children's school and church.[10]

Adolf Mahr's death did not provide Maria Mahr with the financial windfall that a widow can sometimes expect. The two life-assurance policies that Adolf Mahr had taken out in Ireland before the war, with the Guardian Assurance Company in Dublin, were paid out at the old Reichmark levels, which meant that they were worth just one-tenth of what they would have been worth if transferred into Deutschmarks.[11] Even then, the payments were classified by the Allied authorities as alien property and were confiscated.[12]

This time marked one of Maria Mahr's lowest points. She was fifty, a widow, living on social welfare, and with little chance of improving her position. Her age, her lack of skills and experience in the workplace, and the high unemployment rates throughout Germany made it difficult for her to get any kind of work. Being a foreigner, and new to the area where she was living, intensified her loneliness. Her family in Holland were no longer able to support her, as they had in the past, and her children were not financially strong either.

Gustav was able to send money to his mother while he was still working for the military government, but this stopped once he began his archaeology studies. Money was also tight for Hilde, who had two young children and a sick husband. Ingrid was doing well in Dublin, but not well enough to support her mother. Only Brigit's meagre income from the local doctor's office kept her head above water.

In desperation, Maria began to lobby both the Irish and German governments for a widow's pension. In August 1951, with Gustav's help, she wrote to Éamon de Valera, who was Taoiseach again:

> As the widow of the late Dr Adolf Mahr, formerly Keeper of Irish Antiquities and Director of the National Museum of Ireland, may I venture to encroach upon your valuable time with this petition for aid to the country whose Government you once again represent and which my husband served for twelve years to the best of his ability. I sincerely hope you will be kind enough to pardon this rather unusual form of approach, resulting from the fact that I do not know to what official Irish governmental agency to turn in my emergency. . . .
>
> No official agency in Germany feels responsible for the widow of a

civil servant of a foreign nation. Our savings are spent, our life-assurance policies confiscated, most of our belongings lost through bombs and fire or abandoned to the oncoming foe in Silesia. Now, at the age of fifty, I am a widow and must seek employment in an area in which unemployment is rampant. This seems next to impossible, as experience is showing me, the more so as a woman at my age and with no professional training has poor chances of finding a position even under normal circumstances. Thus, although I believe I may justly claim that it is through no fault of my own, I find myself finally reduced to the state of a pauper.

Whilst we were still residing in Dublin, I remember my husband mentioning that the widow of a civil servant was, upon the decease of her husband, usually granted a lump sum roughly equivalent to one year's salary. May I ask whether I could qualify for this benefit despite the fact that I am not an Irish citizen and no longer reside within the borders of Eire?[13]

Her petition, just like her husband's letters before, was not successful: she did not even receive a reply.

Maria Mahr then turned her attention to the German government, and began a campaign to have her husband's position as an Austrian civil servant from 1915 to 1927 recognised by the German government. Because the two countries had merged (1938–45), and he had remained a German citizen until his death, Maria argued that his pension should be the equivalent of that of a German civil servant.

Her fight took nearly six years, but this time she was successful. In 1957, Maria Mahr received a substantial lump sum, and a pension commensurate with a high civil-service grade. Suddenly, at the age of fifty-six, she was financially independent for the first time in her adult life. Like a seed that had lain dormant during a long dry spell, she burst into life when the windfall arrived. She started to travel, and returned to Ireland to visit the Clissmanns, the Rafterys, and other people she had known before the war. She moved to Göttingen to be near Brigit during her final years, and got her own apartment in the city. She went to stay with Hilde and Ingrid twice a year and generally enjoyed her new role as a grandmother. She still owned several of the gifts that Albert Bender had sent her from California during that happy period in the 1930s. A piece of Bender's Chinese brocade hung in her room, and she sometimes wore a silk robe that Bender had sent. Other Bender items, inherited by Ingrid, include a batik silk shawl, a Chinese silver ring mounted with an overturn, and a Chinese silver jewellery box with enamel painting and a carved jade lid.[14]

During 1972, Maria Mahr was diagnosed with breast cancer. She had an operation in Frankfurt, and stayed with Hilde while receiving radiation therapy and recuperating. Three years later, however, it was clear that the cancer had returned and that her condition was terminal. Brigit and Ingrid collected her from her apartment, brought her to Ingrid's house, and put her to bed in a south-facing room that looks out upon a cherry tree. She died there in October 1975, and was buried alongside her husband on the side of Poppelsdorf Hill in Bonn – near the hospital where Adolf had died, and where Gustav's daughter was born. The tombstone bears only their names, and the dates their lives began and ended.

The Augusta Bender Memorial Room of Far Eastern Art at the National Museum of Ireland was taken down to make way for a medieval exhibition in 1973. The collection that had been assembled by Ireland's leading Nazi and a kindly Irish Jew is now in storage at the National Museum's Collins Barracks campus. The current Director of the Museum, Pat Wallace, hopes to exhibit the Bender material again while he is still in office, but as yet there are no plans in place to do so. Wallace, who describes himself as 'a fan of Dr Mahr', would favour naming a section of the National Museum in Mahr's honour. No doubt such a move would provoke a lively and interesting debate.

The rest of Adolf Mahr's legacy remains a moot point. Few would dispute that he made an enormous contribution to Irish archaeology, but it is often difficult to disentangle this from his political activities. Yet Mahr's achievements in the world of archaeology are tangible, whereas the results of his political work are not. If his mission was to convert the Irish to the Nazi creed, it was an entirely unsuccessful enterprise. When war broke out, an estimated 70,000 citizens of neutral Ireland served in the British forces,[15] while only Gustav Mahr and a handful of other Irish Germans served on the other side. Although there was a small rise in anti-Semitic activity in pre-war Ireland, it seems that Mahr and his group were not responsible for it. Dermot Keogh, in *Jews in Twentieth-Century Ireland*, says: 'it is difficult to make a direct connection between the activities of

Mahr's group and the spread of anti-Semitism in Dublin.'

Mahr is sometimes called a traitor, but again this is a charge that is difficult to support. A comment made by the journalist Robert Fisk about Francis Stuart is equally applicable to Mahr: 'Since Germany had not been at war against Ireland, there was no more reason to call Stuart a collaborator than there was to make the same imputation against the Irishmen who worked and fought for the British.'[16] Mahr also strongly advocated Germany's respect for Ireland's neutrality during the war. There is no evidence that he provided maps or any other information that compromised Ireland's security.

Mahr's greater crimes lie in the realm of 'what might have been'. What would his role have been had Ireland been invaded by Germany? During the late 1930s, Mahr joked about becoming gauleiter of Ireland in the event of Germany invading. If the invasion had taken place, Mahr would probably have been the strongest candidate for that job. It is even possible to see in Mahr an insightful leader with a great interest in Irish culture and learning, and a determination to make the country run more efficiently. But, of course, there was no à la carte option for Nazi governance: one could not take the good roads and increased productivity, and leave aside the deprivation of human rights. If Germany had successfully invaded Ireland, we know from the Wannsee Conference that one of the first jobs of the new gauleiter would have been to round up Ireland's 4,000 Jews for 'deportation'. What would Mahr have done then? Would he have reverted to one of his favourite sayings: 'Where you plane, you will have shavings'?

In Irland-Redaktion, the radio station that he managed, and in the Nazi group that he ran in Ireland before the war, there is little evidence of anti-Jewish propaganda, or indeed of any other hate-filled messages. One of his broadcasters, Francis Stuart, noticed upon his return to Ireland that the station had little impact, good or bad: 'I hardly ever met anyone who heard me; I don't think anyone really listened.'[17]

Even as late as 2004, Mahr made the headlines when the anti-Nazi organisation the Simon Wiesenthal Centre called for an inquiry into the contents of the Hunt Museum in Limerick, saying that the Hunts had 'close personal ties' with Adolf Mahr, and other 'notorious dealers in art looted by the Nazis'.[18] So far, little has emerged to back up these claims. In 1938, John Hunt had tried to sell the National Museum a silver seal that had once belonged to the Ulster King Hugh O'Neill.[19] Although Mahr had given Hunt a tour of the Museum, he did not buy the object, and does not appear to have maintained contact with the Hunts after that. They were not on the 'dependable friends' list he had given to Ingrid when she left for Ireland in 1948. Neither the Wiesenthal Centre nor the Hunt Museum replied to requests for more information about this issue, for inclusion in this book.

In June 2006, the expert group that examined the claims by the Simon Wiesenthal Centre reported to the Royal Irish Academy that most of the objects under suspicion were unlikely to have a 'problematic past'. The group also complained that the Wiesenthal Centre did not reply to its questions.[20]

What could Mahr have done differently? He joined the Nazi Party in 1933, but so did millions of others, often for the most noble and idealistic of reasons. The worst excesses of Nazism would have been hidden from him while he was in Dublin, and by the time the blinkers were off, there was little he could do to disassociate himself from what was happening. He could have withdrawn from the party during the 1938/39 period, and with hindsight we can see that this single move would have been the most effective in saving his career and prolonging his life. But without the benefit of hindsight, it would have seemed a foolish move to leave the party that had restored pride and unity to Germany, brought his beloved Austria and Sudetenland into the Reich, and reversed the crippling penalties that had been imposed on the German people after the Great War. From his standpoint, it was all just too wonderful to step away from. Like an unfaithful partner, he chose to flirt with the new and exciting Germany instead of being faithful to the less attractive, but more reliable, role of running a museum.

Most of Mahr's pre-war extended family, which stretched from the Netherlands to Czechoslovakia and Austria, shared his Nazi viewpoint. Maria Mahr's sister worked as a secretary to Artur Seyss-Inquart, the Reich Commissioner for the Netherlands, who was hanged at Nuremberg for his part in the deportation and shooting of hostages. Mahr's friend Otto Bene was also involved in the deportations of Jews from the Netherlands, although, remarkably, he was never prosecuted and he worked in the new German Foreign Office until the 1950s.[21] Bene even retired on a generous diplomat's pension that took into account his years of service in Holland.[22]

Maier von Weinertsgruen, who was married to Mahr's first cousin, was a member of the SS in the Protectorate of Bohemia and Moravia. Mahr's brother-in-law Franz Hoernisch was a leading Nazi in the Bad Ischl area. Although this does not excuse Mahr's loyalty to Hitler, it shows how the latter managed to win the hearts of a large number of influential people in different countries.

Mahr left Ireland for Germany in 1939, a point that marked the beginning of the end of his career. Many people have seen his move as deliberate — that he sacrificed his career and life in Ireland, for Hitler and Nazism. It is a tempting conclusion, but the available evidence suggests that, when he left Ireland, he had every intention of returning two months later. It seems that, when war became imminent, he gambled that the outcome would present the best of both worlds: a quick German victory, and a speedy return to his job in Dublin. The odds were certainly in his favour during the summer of 1939. Britain stood alone against the mighty German war machine. Few could have imagined that a six-year war lay ahead, and that Germany would be crushed.

Even if Mahr had returned to Ireland before the outbreak of war, it probably would have made little difference. Fifty other members of the German colony left Ireland on 11 September 1939 on a specially arranged passage to the Fatherland. Faced with the prospect of internment in Ireland, or a sojourn in Germany for the duration of a short war, Mahr probably would have joined the other members of the colony. It seems that he was destined to spend the war in Germany.

Mahr was a gifted and idealistic man, but also a pragmatist during a dangerous time. He was, like hundreds of millions of others, a victim of the fact that he lived in a time of war. In another time and place, he might simply have been remembered as a great archaeologist, but in the Europe of the 1930s and 1940s, it was inevitable that his life would be ripped apart by factors that were mostly beyond his control. In such times, one can do little more than look after oneself and one's family, and then hope for the best. He and his family managed to stay alive while tens of millions did not, and that alone is some kind of achievement.

Did he feel guilty about what had happened? Hilde says probably not, because he did not feel personally responsible for it. 'He was part of an ideal, but everything moved so quickly and above his head that he had no control over it,' she says. 'But he did write once that he was quite sure he did no harm to anyone personally.'

Still, he had many regrets in the latter stages of his life – none greater than his belief that his own misjudgements had landed his children in poverty. He wrote that he had ruined not only his own life but the lives of his children as well, and that caused his greatest pain. But, as time was to show, this was not the case either. They survived, prospered, and lived lives that embraced his better characteristics: the pursuit of knowledge, while helping those around them. And they shunned the hatred and intolerance that the Nazi creed promoted.

'He had not ruined our lives,' said Hilde upon reading that poignant 1949 letter to his family. 'He had given us enough strength, and back-up, and enough brains to think about it. And to work at it.' Perhaps that is Adolf Mahr's greatest legacy.

Bibliography

Adams, Ansel, *Ansel Adams: An Autobiography* (Boston: Little, Brown and Company, 1985; 1996 edition)
Bacque, James, *Crimes and Mercies* (London: Little, Brown and Company, 1997)
Beevor, Antony, *Berlin: The Downfall, 1945* (London: Viking, 2002)
─────── *Stalingrad* (London: Penguin, 1999)
Bewley, C. H., *Memoirs of a Wild Goose* (Dublin: Lilliput Press, 1989)
Burden, Hamilton T., *The Nuremberg Party Rallies: 1923–39* (London: Pall Mall Press, 1967)
Clay Large, David, *Berlin* (New York: Basic Books, 2000)
Coerver, Chad (ed.), *SFMOMA Painting and Sculpture Highlights* (San Francisco: San Francisco Museum of Modern Art, 2002)
Cooney, Gabriel, 'Building a Future on the Past', in Margarita Diaz Andreu and Timothy Champion (eds), *Nationalism and Archaeology* (London: Routledge, 1996)
Crooke, Elizabeth, *Politics, Archaeology and the Creation of the National Museum of Ireland: An Expression of National Life* (Dublin: Irish Academic Press, 2000)
Cross, Colin, *Adolf Hitler* (New York: Berkley Publishing Corporation, 1973)
Darman, Peter (General Editor), *The Third Reich Day by Day* (London: Military Handbooks, Grange Books, 2004)
de Valera, Terry, *A Memoir* (Dublin: Currach Press, 2005)
Dorril, Stephen, *Blackshirt: Sir Oswald Mosley and British Fascism* (London: Penguin, 2006)
Duggan, Lt Col. J. P., 'The German Threat – Myth or Reality', *An Cosantoir*, September 1989, 6–12
─────── *Herr Hempel at the German Legation 1937–1945* (Dublin: Irish Academic Press, 2003)
─────── *Neutral Ireland and the Third Reich* (Dublin: Gill & Macmillan Ltd, 1985)
Evans, Emyr Estyn, *Ireland and the Atlantic Heritage: Selected Writings* (Dublin: Lilliput Press, 1996)
Fisk, Robert, *In Time of War: Ireland, Ulster and the Price of Neutrality, 1939–45* (Dublin: Gill & Macmillan, 1983)
Goni, Uki, *The Real Odessa: How Peron Brought the Nazi War Criminals to Argentina* (London: Granta Books, 2002)
Herrera, Hayden, *Frida: The Biography of Frida Kahlo* (London: Bloomsbury, 1983)

Hickey, D. J., and J. E. Doherty, *A New Dictionary of Irish History from 1800* (Dublin: Gill & Macmillan, 2003)
Hilberg, Paul, *The Destruction of the European Jews* (Chicago: Quadrangle Books, 1961)
Hull, Mark M., *Irish Secrets: German Espionage in Wartime Ireland, 1939–1945* (Dublin: Irish Academic Press, 2003)
Hutchinson, John, *The Dynamics of Cultural Nationalism* (London: Allen and Unwin, 1987)
Januszczak, Waldemar, article in the *Sunday Times* magazine, 12 June 2005, p.4; article on Frida Kahlo entitled 'Her only subject matter was herself . . . '
Joyce, James, *Ulysses* (New York: Random House, 1946 edition)
Kenny, Mary, *Germany Calling: A Personal Biography of William Joyce* (Dublin: New Island, 2003)
Keogh, Dermot, *Jews in Twentieth-century Ireland* (Cork: Cork University Press, 1998)
Keogh, Niall, *Con Cremin: Ireland's Wartime Diplomat* (Cork: Mercier Press, 2006)
Kilbride-Jones, H. E., 'Adolf Mahr', article in *Archaeology Ireland*, Vol. 7, No. 3, Autumn 1993, 29–30
Large, David Clay, *Berlin* (New York: Basic Books, 2000)
Lewis, Oscar, *To Remember Albert M. (Micky) Bender: Notes for a Biography*, 1973
Lucas, James, *Last Days of the Reich: The Collapse of Nazi Germany, May 1945* (London: Cassell Military Paperbacks, 1986)
Marcus, David, *Oughtobiography: Leaves from the Diary of a Hyphenated Jew* (Dublin: Gill & Macmillan, 2001)
Meehan, Patricia, *A Strange Enemy People: Germans under the British, 1945–50* (London: Peter Owen Publishers, 2001)
Meltzer, Milton, *Dorothea Lange: A Photographer's Life* (Toronto: McGraw-Hill Ryerson Ltd, 1978)
Mitchell, Frank, *The Way That I Followed: A Naturalist's Journey Around Ireland* (Dublin: Country House, 1990)
Mitchell, G. F., *The Royal Irish Academy: A Bicentennial History, 1785–1985* (Dublin: Royal Irish Academy, 1985)
O'Beirne, Gerald, *Siemens in Ireland 1925–2000; Seventy-five Years of Innovation* (Dublin: A&A Farmar, 2000)
O'Brien, Donough, *Fame by Chance: An A–Z of Places that Became Famous (or Infamous) by a Twist of Fate* (London: Bene Factum Publishing, 2003)
O'Broin, León, *Just Like Yesterday: An Autobiography* (Dublin: Gill & Macmillan, 1985)
Ó Dochartaigh, Pól, *Germans, Celts and Nationalism: Julius Pokorny 1887–1970* (Dublin: Four Courts Press, 2004)
O'Donoghue, David, *Hitler's Irish Voices: The Story of German Radio's Wartime Irish Service* (Belfast: Beyond the Pale Publications, 1998)
O'Halpin, Eunan, '"Toys" and "Whispers" in "16-land": SOE and Ireland 1940–42', 12–13, from *Intelligence and National Security*, Vol. 15. No. 4, Winter 2000
Poliakov, Leôn and Josef Wulf, *Das Dritte Reich und seine Diener, Dokumente* (2. Auflage), Berlin-Grunewald: avani-Verlags-GmbH 1956 (*The Third Reich and Its*

Servants) (2nd edition)

Rivera, Diego, with Gladys March, *My Art, My Life, An Autobiography* (New York: Dover Publications Inc, 1991)

Snowman, Danial et al., *The Hitler Emigres: The Cultural Impact on Britain of Refugees from Nazism* (London: Chatto & Windus, 2002)

Snyder, Louis L., *Encyclopedia of the Third Reich* (Ware, Hertfordshire: McGraw-Hill, 1976)

Stephan, Annika, 'A Bio-Bibliography of Dr Adolf Mahr: His Contribution to Archaeology in Austria, Ireland and Germany', dissertation submitted in part fulfilment of the requirements for the Bachelor of Arts Degree in Humanities (Heritage Studies) at the Galway-Mayo Institute of Technology, 2002

Stephan, Enno, *Spies in Ireland* (London: The New English Library Limited, 1965)

Stieber, John, *Against the Odds: Survival on the Russian Front, 1944–1945* (Dublin: Poolbeg Press, 1995)

Stuart, Madeleine, *Manna in the Morning: A Memoir 1940–1958* (Dublin: Raven Arts Press, 1984)

Sturmer, Michael, *The German Century* (London: Weidenfeld & Nicolson, 1999)

Wallace, Patrick F, 'Adolf Mahr and the Making of Seán P. O'Riordain', pp254–63 of a festschrift for Charles Eogan, National Museum of Ireland, 2004

Wallace, Patrick F. and Raghnall O'Floinn (eds), *Treasures of the National Museum of Ireland* (Dublin: Gill & Macmillan, 2002)

Weitz, John, Joachim von Ribbentrop, *Hitler's Diplomat* (London: Weidenfeld & Nicolson, 1992)

Whitford, Frank, *Oskar Kokoschka: A Life* (London: Weidenfeld & Nicolson, 1986)

NOTES

The primary interviews with Gustav, Hilde and Ingrid Mahr took place in their homes in Germany in June 2001. Subsequent questions were answered by them and their sister Brigit during dozens of phone calls, letters and meetings, mostly between August 2004 and December 2005.

Interviews with Dr Pat Wallace and Dr David O'Donoghue were also recorded in Dublin in the spring of 2001, and subsequent meetings and e-mails were used to clarify issues, especially during the August 2004–December 2005 period.

PROLOGUE, pp13–16

1 Antony Beevor, *Berlin: The Downfall, 1945* (Viking, 2002), 255
2 *ibid.*, 262
3 *ibid.*, 3
4 *ibid.*, 4
5 Eva Braun writing to Herta Ostermayr, as reported in Beevor, 254
6 *ibid.*, 410
7 *ibid.*, 57
8 *ibid.*, 281
9 Author's interview with Hilde Mahr

CHAPTER 1: FAMILY LIFE: THE MAHRS IN DUBLIN, pp17–29

1 Hilde Mahr's conversation with the author
2 Annika Stephan, 'A Bio-Bibliography of Dr Adolf Mahr: His Contribution to Archaeology in Austria, Ireland and Germany', 32
3 *ibid.*, 41, quoting Gustav Mahr's 1964 Curruculum Vitae for his father
4 *ibid.*, 34
5 Author's interview with Gustav Mahr
6 Letter from Thomas U. Ó Murachadha, runaí, the Irish Civil Service Commissioners, 30 May 1927, to Adolf Mahr in Vienna. Hilde Mahr's archive.
7 Letter from Adolf Mahr, Austria, to the van Bemmelens in Holland, 13 October 1927. Written in Dutch. Hilde Mahr's archive.

8 O'Beirne, 80
9 Author's interview with Hilde Mahr
10 Author's interview with Ingrid Mahr
11 Dermot Keogh, *Jews in Twentieth-century Ireland* (Cork: Cork University Press, 1998), 79
12 Author's interview with Gustav Mahr
13 Author's interview with Hilde Mahr
14 David O'Donoghue, *Hitler's Irish Voices; The Story of German Radio's Wartime Irish Service* (Belfast: Beyond the Pale Publications, 1998), 6
15 'Man of Aran', article by Vincent Browne, *Film West* magazine, issue 19, taken from *www.iol.ie/~galfilm/filmwest/bissues.html*
16 Letter from Adolf Mahr to Albert Bender, 20 July 1933
17 John O'Callaghan, 'Monksgrange: The Home of Mr and Mrs John Richards-Orpen', *Journal of the Old Wexford Society*, Vol. 1, 1968
18 *ibid.*
19 Monksgrange Stud website, *www.monksgrange.com*, and author's interview with the current owner, Jeremy Hill, 2004
20 Author's conversation with Skerries resident Joe Boylan, 2000

CHAPTER 2: OFFICIAL LIFE: AT THE NATIONAL MUSEUM, 1927–34, pp30–46

1 G. F. Mitchell, *The Royal Irish Academy: A Bicentennial History, 1785–1985* (Royal Irish Academy, Dublin, 1985)
2 Letter to the van Bemmelens from Adolf Mahr, 1927, written in Dutch, translated by Hilde Mahr, from her archive
3 Gustav Mahr's interview with the author
4 H. E. Kilbride-Jones, 'Adolf Mahr', article in *Archaeology Ireland*, Vol. 7, No. 3, Issue No. 25, Autumn 1993, 29
5 The letters are held at Mills College, Oakland, California
6 *Jewish Chronicle*, 5 April 1901. Obituary to the Reverend Philipp Bender, by A.H.M. [*sic*]
7 Oscar Lewis, *To Remember Albert M. (Micky) Bender: Notes for a Biography*, 1973
8 *San Francisco Chronicle*, 5 March 1941, 1 and 13, article entitled 'A Man Who Gave Heart to S. F. Dies'
9 Meltzer, 56
10 Oscar Lewis
11 Ansel Adams, *Ansel Adams: An Autobiography* (Boston: Little, Brown and Company, 1985; 1996 edition), 67
12 Letter from Starkie to Bender, 25 November 1930, Mills College California collection
13 Letter from Bender to Mahr, 5 December 1931, Mills College collection
14 Meltzer, 56
15 *ibid.*, 57

16 Letter from Mahr to Bender, 16 March 1932, Mills College collection
17 Letter from Mahr to Bender, 10 May 1932, Mills College collection
18 Hickey & Doherty, 142
19 Letter from Bender to Mahr, 8 August 1932
20 Letter from Bender to Mahr, 8 August 1932
21 Letter from Mahr to Bender, 21 August 1932
22 Mahr's letter to Bender, 21 August 1932
23 Pat Wallace, 'Adolf Mahr and the Making of Sean P. O'Riordain', 254
24 *ibid.*, 255
25 Kilbride-Jones, 30
26 Wallace, *op. cit.*, 256
27 Wallace's interview with the author
28 Wallace, *op. cit.*, 259
29 Author's interview with Pat Wallace
30 Author's conversation with UCD Professor of Archaeology, Barry Raftery
31 Author's interview with Joseph P. Murray at his home in Dublin, 14 September 2005
32 Elizabeth Crooke, *Politics, Archaeology and the Creation of the National Museum of Ireland: An Expression of National Life*, 137 (Dublin: Irish Academic Press, 2000)
33 Frank Mitchell, *The Way That I Followed: A Naturalist's Journey Around Ireland* (Dublin: Country House, 1990)
34 Author's conversation with Dr Michael Ryan of the Chester Beatty Library, Dublin, February 2005, and e-mail 5 October 2006
35 Author's conversations with Ned Kelly, Keeper of Irish Antiquities, the National Museum of Ireland, 2005
36 Mahr's Presidential Address of 1937 to the British Prehistoric Society
37 Patrick F. Wallace and Raghnall O'Floinn (eds), *Treasures of the National Museum of Ireland* (Dublin: Gill & Macmillan, 2002), 19
38 Crooke, 80
39 Committee of Enquiry Report 1927 in Crooke, 144
40 G. F. Mitchell, *The Royal Irish Academy*, 155
41 Author's interview with Pat Wallace
42 Mahr letter to Bender, 21 August 1932
43 Wallace and O'Floinn, 228
44 Author's interview with Pat Wallace
45 Stephan, 48
46 John Hutchinson, *The Dynamics of Cultural Nationalism* (London: Allen and Unwin, 1987), 123–7
47 Cooney in Crooke, 32
48 Mahr's Presidential Address of 1937 to the British Prehistoric Society
49 Mahr's letter to Bender, 21 August 1932
50 Author's interview with Pat Wallace

51 Bender's letter to Mahr, 29 September 1933
52 Éamon de Valera's speech, 25 June 1934, National Archives, File 80 Ed.
53 'Bender Memorial Room; Culture and Citizenship', *Irish Press*, 8, 26 June 1934
54 Files in the Director's Office, National Museum of Ireland
55 Stephan, 68
56 G. F. Mitchell, *The Royal Irish Academy*, 158
57 O'Neill to McElligott, 6 March 1933 DoF E53/3/33, Document No. 348-32F, in O'Donoghue, 5

CHAPTER 3: NAZI LIFE, 1933–37, pp47–67

1 Letter from Gustav Mahr to O'Donoghue, 28 November 1990. O'Donoghue's archive
2 Interviews with the Mahr family
3 Author's interview with Gustav Mahr
4 Louis L. Snyder, *Encyclopedia of the Third Reich* (Ware, Hertfordshire: McGraw-Hill, 1976), 339
5 Bender's letter to Mahr, 5 April 1933
6 Mahr's letter to Bender, 28 April 1933
7 Alfred de Zayas in James Bacque, *Crimes and Mercies* (London: Little, Brown and Company, 1997), xvii
8 Gogarty's letter to Bender, 11 September 1938; Bender archive, Mills College California
9 Bender's letter to Mahr, 12 May 1933
10 Mahr's letter to Bender, 4 June 1933
11 *ibid.*
12 Gustav Mahr's conversation with the author
13 Gustav Mahr's interview with the author
14 *ibid.*
15 *ibid.*
16 Author's interview with Hilde Mahr
17 Adolf Mahr's letter to van Bemmelens, 1921. Hilde Mahr's archive.
18 Author's interview with Gustav Mahr
19 Adolf Mahr's letter to the van Bemmelens, 1923. Hilde Mahr's archive.
20 Adolf Mahr's letter to the van Bemmelens, July 1923. Hilde Mahr's archive.
21 Stephan, Appendix Three
22 Gustav Mahr's interview with the author
23 *ibid.*
24 Mahr's letter to Bender, 16 June 1933
25 David O'Donoghue, *Hitler's Irish Voices: The Story of German Radio's Wartime Irish Service* (Belfast: Beyond the Pale Publications, 1998), 7
26 *ibid.*, 19

27 J. P. Duggan, *Neutral Ireland and the Third Reich*, 63 (Dublin: Gill & Macmillan Ltd, 1985) and *Herr Hempel at the German Legation 1937–1945*, 66–67 (Dublin: Irish Academic Press, 2003)
28 O'Donoghue, 8–9
29 Rudolf Muhs, lecture entitled 'Otto Bene: A Nazi Career in Britain and Elsewhere', part of the 'Personalities of the Right in Central and Eastern Europe', from a series of lectures at Royal Holloway College, University of London, 23 November 2005
30 Letter to Sir Russell Scott at the Home Office from someone at the Foreign Office who had an undecipherable signature, 13 August 1935, British Public Records Office, File HO 45/25385
31 Stephen Dorril, *Black Shirt: Sir Oswald Mosley and British Fascism* (London: Penguin, 2006), 262
32 Letter to Sir Russell Scott at the Home Office from someone at the Foreign Office who had an undecipherable signature, 13 August 1935, British Public Records Office, File HO 45/25385
33 *ibid.*
34 *ibid.*
35 O'Donoghue, 21
36 Snyder, 14
37 O'Donoghue, 21
38 *ibid.*
39 *ibid.*
40 Snyder, 336–37
41 Duggan, *Herr Hempel at the German Legation*, 21
42 Mahr's letter to de Valera, 27 November 1947, National Archives of Ireland
43 Duggan, *op. cit.*, 24–25
44 *ibid.*, 10, 26, 29
45 Ingrid Mahr's interview with the author
46 Snyder, 161
47 Snyder, 161
48 Gustav Mahr's interview with the author
49 Author's interview with Mona Brase
50 *Irish Press*, 14 April 1936
51 *Irish Times*, 21 December 1936
52 Hickey & Doherty, 448
53 *Irish Times* and *Irish Independent*, 20 December 1937
54 Cross, 264

CHAPTER 4: IMPENDING WAR, 1937–39, pp68–104

1 Mahr's letter to Bender, 19 September 1935
2 Mahr's letter to Bender, 19 June 1936

3 Maria Mahr's letter to Bender, 14 July 1936
4 Mahr's letter to Bender, 10 December 1936
5 *Irish Press*, 10 April 1937
6 *Irish Times*, 16 April 1937
7 Terry de Valera, *A Memoir* (Dublin: Currach Press, 2005), 211
8 Author's interview with Gustav Mahr
9 *Irish Times*, 10 April 1937
10 *Irish Press*, 12 April 1937
11 *ibid.*, 12 April 1937
12 *Irish Independent*, 14 April 1937
13 *Irish Press*, 16 April 1937
14 *Irish Times*, 16 April 1937
15 *ibid.*, 16 April 1937
16 *www.worldwar-2.net/timelines*
17 Author's interview with Pat Wallace
18 Mahr's letter to Bender, 7 December 1937
19 Keogh, 118
20 *The Wordsworth Dictionary of Biography* (Helicon Publishing Ltd, 1994)
21 Mahr's letter to Bender, 2 April 1938
22 Snyder, 8
23 *Irish Press*, 14 March 1938; Keogh, 118
24 Robert Fisk, *In Time of War: Ireland, Ulster and the Price of Neutrality, 1939–45* (Dublin: Gill & Macmillan, 1983), 71
25 *Archaeology Ireland*, Autumn 1993. Note, Kilbride Jones told the story saying Robert Corish was Minister, but it was in fact Seán MacEntee
26 Mahr to O'Neill, 21 July 1938. File D/Taoiseach S 6631A, National Archives, Dublin
27 O'Neill to Ó Muinhneachain, Department of the Taoiseach, 22 July 1938, and note to Murray, 23 July 1938; file D/Taoiseach S 6631 A, National Archives, Dublin
28 Mahr file, Irish Military Archives, 11 November 1938
29 O'Donoghue, 23
30 Bohle letter to Mahr, 8 February 1939
31 Keogh, 118
32 *ibid.*, 119
33 *ibid.*
34 Hickey & Doherty, 31
35 Mahr's letter to Bender, 11 November 1938
36 Danial Snowman et al., *The Hitler Émigrés: The Cultural Impact on Britain of Refugees from Nazism* (London: Chatto & Windus, 2002)
37 Irish Military Archives, May to Mahr, 20 May 1939
38 Irish Military Archives, Stadlen to Mahr, 22 May 1939

39 Irish Military Archives, Kohn to Mahr, 14 June 1939
40 Yad Vashem, The Central Database of Shoah Victims' Names
41 Snyder, 201
42 Snyder, 115
43 Gustav Mahr interview, 2001
44 Ó Dochartaigh, cover page
45 Keogh and Ó Dochartaigh
46 Pokorny to Best, 21 October 1935, Richard Irving Best papers, National Library of Ireland
47 Ó Dochartaigh, 115
48 O'Brennan letter to Bender, 27 December 1938
49 *ibid.*
50 *ibid.*
51 Maher to J.McG, 6 December 1938; Irish Military Archives, Mahr File
52 Walshe memo to de Valera, 22 February 1939, Irish Military Archives
53 Author's interview with Gustav and Hilde Mahr, based on their reading of their mother's letters to her father in early 1939
54 Author's interview with Ingrid Mahr
55 Mahr file, Irish Military Archives
56 *ibid.*
57 Minutes of meeting in the Department of Education, 23 March 1939; G2/0130, Irish Military Archives, Dublin
58 *ibid.*
59 *ibid.*
60 Paul Hilberg, *The Destruction of the European Jews* (Chicago: Quadrangle Books, 1961)
61 Frieda Hayek to the Mahr family, 19 June 1939. Irish Military Archives, Mahr file
62 Augusta Hornische to Adolf Mahr, 1 July 1939, Irish Military Archives, Mahr file
63 Postcard from Adolf Mahr to Grete Spiegelfeld, 26 July 1939. Irish Military Archives, Mahr file
64 Maria Mahr to Grete Spiegelfeld, August 1939. Irish Military Archives
65 Duggan, *Herr Hempel at the German Legation*, 46
66 Friedrich Maier von Weinertsgruen to Adolf Mahr, 11 July 1939. Irish Military Archives
67 Snyder, 281
68 Bundesarchiv, Berlin; files R2.05/G and R43II.1550
69 Snyder, 81
70 Hstuf. Schellenberg to OberführerJost, 13 September 1938, USSR-509; Hilberg, 182-83
71 Hilberg, 585

72 Personnel files of SS, in the Bundesarchiv, Berlin; files R2.05/G and R43II.1550
73 Hamilton T. Burden, *The Nuremberg Party Rallies 1923–39* (London: Pall Mall Press, 1967), 164
74 *ibid.*
75 Case of Dr A. Mahr, National Museum, 30 June 1948, File F.348/32, Irish National Archives; and letter from Seosamh O'Néill of the Department of Education to Adolf Mahr, 10 October 1939, Irish National Archives
76 O'Donoghue, 25
77 *ibid.*
78 Emyr Estyn Evans, *Ireland and the Atlantic Heritage: Selected Writings* (Dublin: Lilliput Press, 1996)
79 Duggan, *Neutral Ireland and the Third Reich*, 63
80 O'Donoghue, 30
81 O'Donoghue, 31
82 Duggan, *op. cit.*, 64
83 *ibid.*, 65
84 O'Brennan to Bender, late 1939
85 Letters to Albert Bender from Montague Bender of Hicks, Arnold and Bender Solicitors, 25 Southampton Street, The Strand, London, in 1924, 1933 and 1940; and Professor Friess
86 Hayden Herrera, *Frida: The Biography of Frida Kahlo* (London: Bloomsbury, 1983), 204–6
87 *ibid.*, 295–307
88 Diego Rivera with Gladys March, *My Art, My Life, An Autobiography* (New York: Dover Publications Inc, 1991)
89 Herrera, *op. cit.*, 297
90 Ansel Adams, *Ansel Adams: An Autobiography* (Boston: Little, Brown and Company, 1985; 1996 edition), 165
91 *ibid.*, 77

CHAPTER 5: NEW LIFE IN GERMANY, 1939–43, pp105–132

1 Author's interview with Ingrid Mahr
2 Letter to Mahr from Dr M. Quane, 22 November 1939, Irish Military Archives
3 Maria Mahr's letter to Joe and Lotti Raftery, 14 December 1939, File Dr J. J. Raftery G2/2320, Irish Military Archives
4 Letter from Gustav Mahr to David O'Donoghue, 28 November 1990
5 Letter from Mahr to Eduard Hempel, May 1940, Irish Military Archives
6 Thomsen at the German Legation to Mahr, 20 October 1940, Irish Military Archives
7 Author's interview with Mona Brase
8 Fisk, 221

9 O'Donoghue, 15
10 Irish Military Archives, File: G2/X/1403
11 *ibid.*
12 Fisk, 223
13 *ibid.*, 224
14 Horst Dinkel interview in *The Shamrock and The Swastika*, Aka Java Films, Dublin, 2002
15 Enno Stephan, *Spies in Ireland* (London: The New English Library Limited, 1965), 94
16 David Marcus, *Oughtobiography: Leaves from the Diary of a Hyphenated Jew* (Dublin: Gill & Macmillan, 2001), 2
17 León O'Broin, *Just Like Yesterday: An Autobiography* (Dublin: Gill and Macmillan, 1985), 137
18 Fisk, 225
19 Gustav Mahr's letter to David O'Donoghue, 28 November 1990, David O'Donoghue's archive
20 Gustav Mahr's interviews with author
21 Hilde Mahr's interview with author
22 O'Donoghue, 13
23 *ibid.*, 14
24 O'Broin, 132
25 O'Donoghue, 12
26 *ibid.*, 34
27 *ibid.*, 34
28 *ibid.*, 183
29 Mahr's 'Irland-Redaktion Blueprint', published in O'Donoghue, 183-93
30 *ibid.*, 60
31 *ibid.*, 60
32 O'Donoghue's interview with the author, 2001
33 Hilde Mahr's interview with the author
34 Anthony Beevor, *Stalingrad* (London: Penguin, 1999), 12–14
35 *ibid.*, 22
36 *ibid.*, 28
37 Snyder, 199
38 Gustav Mahr's interview with the author
39 Peter Darman (General Editor), *The Third Reich Day by Day* (London: Military Handbooks, Grange Books, 2004), 143
40 *ibid.*, 144
41 *ibid.*, 144-5
42 O'Donoghue, 77
43 *ibid.*, 78
44 O'Brien, 390

45 Snyder, 84
46 *ibid.*, 372
47 O'Brien, 390
48 Hilberg, 265
49 *ibid.*, 353
50 *ibid.*, 374
51 *ibid.*, 374
52 O'Brien, 20
53 Hilberg, 375
54 *ibid.*
55 *ibid.*
56 *ibid.*, 377
57 *ibid.*, 365
58 *ibid.*, 378
59 O'Brien, 20
60 Snyder, 97
61 *ibid.*, 320
62 Author's interview with Gustav Mahr
63 Author's interview with Hilde and Gustav Mahr
64 Hilde Mahr's interview with the author
65 Author's interview with Elizabeth Clissmann, Dublin, February 2005
66 Snyder, 346
67 Author's interview with Elizabeth Clissmann
68 Hilberg, 115
69 Frida Hayek's affidavit, 30 May 1947. Gustav Mahr's archive
70 Ingrid Mahr's interview with the author
71 Gustav Mahr's interview with the author
72 Gedenkbuch - Opfer der Verfolgung der Juden unter der nationalsozialistischen Gewaltherrschaft in Deutschland 1933-1945, Bundesarchiv German National Archives., Koblenz 1986
73 Yad Vashem, The Central Database of Shoah Victims' Names
74 This information is based on a list of deportations from Berlin found in the Gedenkbuch Berlins der juedischen Opfer des Nazionalsozialismus, Freie Universitaet Berlin, Zentralinstitut fuer sozialwissenschaftliche Forschung, Edition Hentrich, Berlin 1995. Supplied by Yad Vashem; The Holocaust Martyrs' and Heroes' Remembrance Authority, *www.yadvashem.org*
75 O'Donoghue, 62
76 *ibid.*, 82
77 Gustav Mahr's letter to David O'Donoghue, 28 November 1990
78 O'Donoghue, 105
79 Ingrid's interview with the author
80 Ingrid's interview with the author

81 Inge Deutschkron and J. Steinberg, *Outcast*, 123–24; David Clay Large, *Berlin* (New York: Basic Books, 2000), 339
82 Early draft of Con Cremin's 'Memoirs' compiled by Mgr Frank Cremins, from Niall Keogh, *Con Cremin: Ireland's Wartime Diplomat* (Cork: Mercier Press, 2006), 61
83 Darman, 157
84 *ibid.*
85 *ibid.*, 156
86 Gustav Mahr's interview with the author

CHAPTER 6: THE TIDE OF WAR TURNS, 1943–45, pp133–151

1 Maria Mahr's letter, 26 January 1943. Irish Military Archives.
2 Professor Jan Bemmann, University of Bonn, e-mail to the author, June 2005
3 Maria Mahr to Else Brase and Nadja Winkelmann, 26 January 1943. Irish Military Archives
4 Large, *op. cit.*, 338
5 Ruth Andreas-Friedrich, *Berlin Underground*, 90; Large, 338
6 Snyder, 184
7 Hilde's interview with the author
8 Hilberg, 250
9 Gustav and Ingrid Mahr's interview with author
10 RHSA IV-A-1, Operational Report, 19 September 1941; Hilberg, 205
11 Madeleine Stuart, *Manna in the Morning: A Memoir 1940–1958* (Dublin: Raven Arts Press, 1984), 30
12 Patricia Meehan, *A Strange Enemy People: Germans under the British, 1945–50* (London: Peter Owen Publishers, 2001) 35
13 Gustav Mahr's interview with the author
14 O'Donoghue, 117
15 *ibid.*, 124
16 Elizabeth Clissmann's interview with the author
17 Maria Mahr's letter, 23 November 1943, Irish Military Archives
18 O'Donoghue, 134
19 Maria Mahr's letter to Frau Brase and Winkelmann, 11 January 1944, Irish Military Archives
20 Gustav Mahr's interview with the author
21 Maria Mahr's letter to Frau Brase and Winkelmann, 11 January 1944, Irish Military Archives
22 O'Donoghue, 62
23 *ibid.*, 155
24 *ibid.*, 143
25 *ibid.*, 154
26 *ibid.*, 144, citing Mahr's report 'Radio Propaganda to Ireland', 18 March 1941,

9, AA 62407
27 *ibid.*, 144
28 Elizabeth Clissmann's interview with the author
29 *ibid.*
30 O'Donoghue, 150
31 Elizabeth Clissmann's interview with the author
32 *ibid.*
33 O'Donoghue, 155
34 Hilberg, 1999, 160-7; Mark M. Hull, *Irish Secrets: German Espionage in Wartime Ireland, 1939–1945* (Dublin: Irish Academic Press, 2003), 31
35 Leôn Poliakov and Josef Wulf, *Das Dritte Reich und seine Diener, Dokumente* (2. Auflage), Berlin-Grunewald: avani-Verlags-GmbH 1956 (*The Third Reich and Its Servants*) (2nd edition), 162
36 Gustav Mahr's phone conversation with the author
37 *ibid.*
38 Mark Hull's interview with the author
39 O'Donoghue, 159
40 Antony Beevor, *Berlin: The Downfall, 1945* (London: Viking, 2002), 45
41 *ibid.*, 48
42 *ibid.*, 49
43 *ibid.* 47
44 *ibid.*, 67
45 *ibid.*, 107
46 Author's interview with Brigit Mahr
47 Author's interview with Ingrid Mahr
48 Author's interview with Ingrid Mahr
49 Author's interview with Hilde Mahr
50 Beevor, *Berlin*, 11
51 Mary Kenny, *Germany Calling: A Personal Biography of William Joyce* (Dublin: New Island, 2003), 210
52 Author's interview with O'Donoghue

CHAPTER 7: HILDE'S JOURNEY, 1945, pp152–170

1 Beevor, *Berlin*, 410
2 *ibid.*, 57
3 *ibid.*, 261
4 *ibid.*, 281
5 World at War TV series, BBC
6 Beevor, *Berlin*, 83; Darman, 180
7 James Lucas, *Last Days of the Reich: The Collapse of Nazi Germany, May 1945* (London: Cassell Military Paperbacks, 1986), 73
8 *ibid.*, 82

9 Meehan, 13
10 Hilde Mahr's interview with the author
11 Meehan, 31
12 *ibid.*, 39
13 Mahr letter to Dr Quane, sent around August 1945
14 Author's interview with Gustav Mahr
15 Mahr's letter to Dr Quane, sent around August 1945
16 Author's interview with David O'Donoghue
17 Author's interview with Gustav Mahr
18 Author's interview with Mona Brase, February 2005
19 *ibid.*
20 Author's interview with Gustav Mahr

CHAPTER 8: THE DUST SETTLES, 1946–47, pp171–208

1 Michael Sturmer, *The German Century* (London: Weidenfeld & Nicolson, 1999), 214
2 Meehan, 189
3 Maria Mahr, in a letter to her father, 4 January 1946. Hilde Mahr's archive
4 Dan Bryan to de Valera, 20 August 1945, National Archives Dublin
5 O'Donoghue, 207
6 *ibid.*, 210
7 Ingrid Mahr's interview with the author
8 O'Donoghue, 215
9 Mahr to Quane, around September 1945. Ingrid Mahr's archive
10 Official Report, Dáil Éireann parliamentary debates, 6 December 1945, vol. 98, cols. 1549-51
11 *ibid.*
12 Unsigned report, presumably written by Dan Bryan on 19 December 1945. Irish Military Archives, Mahr file (MA, G2/130)
13 Letter from Selby to Mars, 2 March 1946; File FO 371 / 55279, British National Archives, Kew, London
14 *ibid.*
15 Author's interview with Hilde Mahr
16 Author's interview with Ingrid Mahr
17 Meehan, 70; FO 371/ 70846
18 Meehan, 74; FO 1005/1632
19 Meehan, 70; Hansard, 5th Series, Vol. 426, Col. 617
20 Author's interview with Hilde Mahr
21 *ibid.*
22 *ibid.*
23 *ibid.*
24 Maria Mahr to Professor van Bemmelen, 1 April 1946, written in Dutch, trans-

lated by Hilde Mahr
25 Bryan to Boland, 4 May 1946, (File G2/0245, Irish Military Archives)
26 Author's interview with Hilde Mahr
27 Hilde Mahr's conversation with author
28 Meehan, 102
29 Dr Alfons Barb's open letter, 13 January 1947. Gustav Mahr's archive.
30 Sir Cyril Fox's letter to Adolf Mahr, 17 December 1946. Gustav Mahr's archive.
31 Paul Jacobsthal's open letter, 29 October 1946, Mahr family archive.
32 Howard Kilbride-Jones's letters to Adolf Mahr, 2 March 1947. Gustav Mahr's archive.
33 J. M. de Navarro's open letter, 23 June 1947. Gustav Mahr's archive.
34 Right Reverend Monsignor John Hynes's open letter, 9 December 1946. Gustav Mahr's archive.
35 Joseph O'Neill's letter to Adolf Mahr, 17 May 1947. Gustav Mahr's archive.
36 M. S. Dudley Westropp's open letter, 29 May 1947. Gustav Mahr's archive.
37 J. H. Delargy's letter to Adolf Mahr, 18 May 1947
38 J. H. Delargy's open letter, 17 August 1947. Gustav Mahr's archive.
39 Frida Hayek's affidavit, 30 May 1947. Gustav Mahr's archive.
40 Certificate signed by Dipl. Ing. H. Colm and Dr E. Horowitz, Gmunden 14 June 1947. Gustav Mahr's archive.
41 *Twentieth-century Words: The Story of the New Word in English Over the Last Hundred Years*, John Ayto, ed. (Oxford: Oxford University Press, 1999)
42 'Hear no evil, see no evil, speak ... ' by Joe Carroll, *Irish Times*, 26 January 2005
43 Mahr's letter to John A. Costello, 10 May 1948, National Archives of Ireland
44 Meehan, 69
45 *ibid.*, 239
46 *ibid.*, 240
47 Mahr, writing from Augustfehn in Oldenburg to An Taoiseach [Éamon de Valera], 25 August 1947. File D/Taoiseach S 6631 B&C, National Archives, Dublin
48 G. F. Mitchell, *The Royal Irish Academy*, 159
49 Uki Goni, *The Real Odessa: How Peron Brought the Nazi War Criminals to Argentina* (London: Granta Books, 2002), 285
50 *ibid.*, 279
51 Mahr's letter to family, *c.* January 1949
52 Daniel Laurent and Ben Dekho, *French Volunteers and Collaborationist Forces: Bretonishe Waffenverband der SS Bezen Perrot*, www.axishistory.com
53 *The Breton Movement and German Occupation, 1940–44; Alan Heusaff and Bezen Perrot, a case study; a paper* by George Broderick of the University of Mannheim.
54 Research by Keith Farrell in 2006 for TV documentary on Nazis in post-war Ireland, by Tile Films, Dublin, for broadcast on RTÉ
55 Yann Goulet obituary in *An Phoblacht*, 9 September 1999
56 Article on the first anniversary of the death of Joe Cahill, in the 'Saoirse 32'

section of *An Phoblacht*, 22 July 2005
57 From the 'Biographies' section of the website of Whyte's Irish Art Auctioneers & Valuers, 38 Molesworth Street, Dublin 2, *www.whytes.ie/biographies*
58 'Hitler and the publisher', Senan Molony, *Irish Independent*, 3 January 2007
59 Albert Folens obituary 'Flemish patriot found home in Ireland', *Irish Times*, 20 September 2003, 12
60 Folens Group website, *www.folens.ie*
61 Research by Keith Farrell for TV documentary *Nazis in Ireland*, broadcast by RTÉ in January 2007; quoting his interview with Louis Rheims, one of those allegedly denounced by Luykx, and from a judgement against Luykx found in the CEGA/SOMA archive in Brussels
62 Goni, 200
63 *ibid.*
64 From the website of the Jasenovac Committee of the Holy Assembly of Bishops of the Serbian Orthodox Church, *www.jasenovac-info.com*, and the journal of the pavelic papers; the newsletter of contemporary neo-Ustasism and the history of the Ustase movement, *www.pavelicpapers.com*
65 *Sunday Independent*, 3 February 1985.
66 *ibid.*
67 'The Collector: Art and the SS', *Time* magazine, 20 December 1976
68 'Dutch War Criminal Is Banned by Ireland', *New York Times*, 22 March 1985
69 Snyder, 323
70 File sourced at United States National Archives, Folder 197, Loc: 190/38/21/1; Note on A.A. File 'Irland (Veesenmayer)', a translation of the contents of German Foreign Office file headed 'Irland (Veesenmayer)', obtained and copied by the State Department Foreign Office Field Team in August 1945
71 *ibid.*
72 Clissmann file (FO 940/49) in British National Archives, Kew, London
73 *ibid.*
74 Author's interview with Elizabeth Clissmann.
75 Clissmann file (FO 940/49), Kew, London
76 *ibid.*
77 Author's interview with Elizabeth Clissmann
78 Author's conversations with Keith Farrell, Dublin 2005–06
79 Adolf Mahr's letter to family, *c.* January 1949
80 Mahr to John A. Costello, 10 May 1948, National Archives of Ireland
81 Stephan, 63; Archive of the Natural History Museum, Vienna; abstracts drawn from various curricula vitae written by Adolf Mahr in 1948 and 1949, revised by Gustav Mahr in 1964
82 Department of Education, Submission to the Government 30 June 1948, Ref. F. 348/32, National Archives of Ireland

83 File F. 348/32, National Archives of Ireland. Memorandum for Government, Department of Education, Case of Dr. Adolph [sic] Mahr, Director, National Museum, 30 June 1948
84 Letter from Mahr to family, post 24/12/1948, probably early January 1949. Translated from German both verbally and in writing by Hilde Mahr. By her own admission, this is not a complete translation because of private family material in the letter. The letter remains with Hilde Mahr.

Epilogue: Picking up the Pieces, 1947 onwards, pp209–23

1 Sturmer, 238
2 Meehan, 15
3 Gustav Mahr's interview with the author.
4 *ibid.*
5 Ingrid Mahr's conversation with the author, February 2005
6 Gustav Mahr's interview with the author
7 *Irish Press*, 29 May 1951
8 Stephan, 35
9 Author's interview with Hilde Mahr
10 Brigit Mahr's phone call with author, January 2005
11 Author's interview with Hilde and Gustav Mahr
12 Maria Mahr's letter to Éamon de Valera, 25 August 1951
13 Maria Mahr's letter to Éamon de Valera, 25 August 1951
14 Ingrid Mahr's letter to author, 21 December 2000
15 Geoffrey Roberts, *War, Neutrality and Irish identities, 1939–1945*; 'The Challenge of the "Irish Volunteers" of World War II', a paper delivered by Geoffrey Roberts of University College Cork, at the UCC Conference 'Ireland & World War II', May 2001
16 Fisk, 407
17 *ibid.*
18 Arthur Beesley, 'Limerick museum at centre of looted Nazi art claims', *Irish Times*, 7 February 2004.
19 John Hunt's letters to Adolf Mahr, 16 and 19 May 1938. Archives of the National Museum of Ireland.
20 Arthur Beesley, 'Hunt Museum items unlikely to have "problematic past"', *Irish Times*, 17 June 2006
21 Hilberg, 704
22 Dr Rudolf Muhs, lecture entitled 'Otto Bene: A Nazi Career in Britain and Elsewhere', Royal Holloway College, University of London, 23 November 2005

INDEX

Emboldened page ranges refer to chapters. References are to Adolf Mahr unless otherwise specified.

Abbey Theatre 86
Abwehr (German counter-intelligence) 200
Adams, Ansel 32, 104
Adler, Alfred 73
Æ, *see* Russell, George
AEG company 56
Against the Odds: Survival on the Russian Front (Stieber) 210
Aiken, Frank 71, 72, 192
Air Raid Protection (ARP) 89, 90
air raids 136–38, 148
   on Hilde's train 155
al-Gaddafi, Muammar 198
Ancient Monuments Council of Ireland 39
Andreas-Friedrich, Ruth 135
Anich, Alois, *see* Artukovic, Andrija
Anschluss 73, 74, 124
Antiquaries of Ireland, Royal Society of 30
Antiquités Nationales, Musée des 36
anti-Semitism 51, 53, 68, 83, *see also* Jewish persecution
   in countries other than Germany 79
Aosdána 198
Archaeological Survey of Berlin 214
archaeology, Celtic and Irish 42–44
Argentina 196

Arms Trials (1970) 198
Army School of Music, Irish 56
Artukovic, Andrija (Alois Anich) 198–99
Ashman, Eric 24
Ashman, Mervyn 24
Augustfehn 179, 182
Auschwitz 98, 122, 147, 192, 196
Auslandorganisation (AO) 58–59, 78

Bacque, James 171
Bad Ischl (Austria) 92, 99, 102, 107, 138
   American army arrives 162
   safety of 148–49
Balfour Declaration (1917) 49, 51
Ballinderry (County Westmeath) excavation 39
Barb, Alphons 80–82, 127, 182, 188
   statement on behalf of Mahr's denazification 185–86
Barbie, Klaus 196
Battle of Britain 111
BBC 199
Beevor, Antony 147–48
Bell, George 177
Belsen 172, 192
Bender, Albert
   background 30–32
   Mahr discourages donations from 41
   attitude toward Nazis 48–50
   gifts to Mahr family 85–86

245

learns of Mahr's Nazi activities 102
Diego Rivera commission 103
death and funeral 104
Bender, Gertrude 102, 127, 128
Bender Memorial Room of Far Eastern Art, Augusta 45, 46, 50, 69, 219
Bene, Otto 57, 58, 91, 122, 213
and deportation of Jews 123
retirement 221–22
Bergin, Osborn 84
Berlin 13–15
air raids 136–38, 140, 148
and 'Factory Action' 134–35
Bersu, Gerhard 196
Best, Richard 84–85
Bewley, Charles 80
Bezen Perrot 197
Big Three Conference (Potsdam conference) 163
Boden, E. 65
Boden, Hans 101
Bohle, Ernst-Wilhelm 78
Boland, F.H. 181
Bonaporte, Napoleon 157
Brase, Else 107
Brase, Fritz 11, 24, 56–57, 64–66, 77, 88, 194
Brase, Mona 133, 168, 210
Braun, Eva 13
Bremer, Walther 18
Brennan, Michael J. 71
Briscoe, Robert 81
British Intelligence 89
British Museum 188
British Union of Fascists 58
Broekhoven, Henri 19, 57, 64
Brown, Bishop of Galway 87
Bryan, Dan 12, 90
opposition to Mahr's post-war return 173–75, 181
on war criminals in Ireland 199

Budina, Charles 57, 61, 71, 101, 134, 135
Burden, Hamilton 98–99
Butler, Eamonn 71

Celtic Golden Age 40
Chamberlain, Neville 55, 76, 79, 88–89
Chester Beatty Library 37
Christian Art in Ancient Ireland (Mahr) 34, 46, 189
Civil Service Commission, Irish 18
Classification of Intermarriages Act (1938) 127
Clausthal-Zellerfeld mining college 212
Clissmann, Elizabeth 116, 125–26, 140
and anti-Roosevelt propaganda 143
Clissmann, Helmut 57, 64, 65, 78, 101, 144
difficulty returning to Ireland 200–201
Cloone, Padraig 23
Coffey, George 37
cold war 209
Commissar Decree 117–18
Commons, British House of 177
Congress of Archaeology, Sixth International (Berlin) 90, 175
Costello, John A. 204
Cremins, Con 131
Cremins, Frank 79
Crimes and Mercies (Bacque) 171
Crooke, Elizabeth 38

Dáil Éireann 175, 176, 192
Dalton, Miss L. 66
D-Day 197
Delargy, J.H. (Séamus) 190
de Navarro, J.M. 188
denazification procedure 184–88, 192, 204, 212

Derrig, Thomas 32, 46, 175, 176
Deutschkron, Inge 131
de Valera, Éamon 87, 173–74, 176
  allowed Germans to leave Ireland 1939 101
  close ties with Mahr 75
  and Harvard excavations 40
  ignores Mahr's plea for assistance post-war 12, 193–96
  ignores Nazi danger 66–67
  loses election of 1948 204
  promotes Mahr to Director of National Museum 45
  rules on refugees 79
de Valera, Ruairi 66
de Valera, Terry 71
Devlin, D. 64
Dillane, Mike 26
Dillon, James 174, 175, 176, 192, 195, 204
Dillon, P.J. 139
Dinkel, Horst 110
Drimnagh excavations 24, 25
Dublin Museum of Science and Art 38
Duggan, John P. 101–2
Duignan, Michael 25, 36, 40

Education, (Irish) Department of 19, 45–46, 172, 205
Eichmann, Adolf 121, 122, 127, 191–92, 196
Einsatzgruppen 97, 117, 135
Electricity Supply Board (ESB) 66, 210
Eucharistic Congress of 1932 33–34
Evans, Emyr Estyn 100

'Factory Action' 134–35
Falcarragh, County Donegal 214

Fallingbostel concentration camp 176
famine in Germany 171–72
Farrell, Keith 201
Farrington, Tony 46
'Final Solution' 121, 122, 124
Fisk, Robert 110, 220
Flaherty, Robert 25, 26
Flemish Legion 198
Folens, Albert 198
Folklore Commission, Irish 190
Forbes, T. 64
Foreign Office (Berlin) 108, 173
Foreign Office (British) 58, 200
Forster, Arthur 24, 94
Fox, Sir Cyril 186
Frank, Anne 122–23, 124
Frankfurt 184
Freud, Sigmund 73
Friedrich, Melanie 97
Funk, Max 91–92
Furlong, George 89

G2, *see* Irish Military Intelligence
Gaelic League 84
Garda Special Branch 88
genocide by Allies 171
German Academic Exchange Service 57
German Association, Dublin 23, 61, 187
German Legation in Ireland 59, 62, 71, 94, 200
Germany
  economic recovery 209
  famine after World War II 171–72
  World War I reparations 47, 65–67, 73, 75
Gisevius, Hans Bernd 83
Gmunden (Austria) 92, 105–6
Goddard, Paulette 103
Goebbels, Josef 112, 134, 153

Gogarty, Oliver St. John 45, 50, 86
Goulet, Yann 197–98
Greiner, Harry and Margaret 101
Grossman, Vasily 148

Hahn, Wolfgang 56
Haller, Kurt 110
Hallstatt saltmine and graveyard 18, 214
Hampton Hall, Balbriggan 61, 62
Hannay, Martha 168
Hartmann, Hans 63, 101, 113, 116, 128, 140–42, 166
   assistance to Mahrs in 1946 179–80
   ran Irland-Redaktion 143
Harvard Mission 39–40, 46, 69, 100
Haughey, Charles 198
Haw-Haw, Lord 58, 112, 113, 128, 167
Hayek, Dora 61–62
Hayek, Frieda (née Loewenthal) 126, 127, 190–91
Hayek, Theo 92, 105–6, 126
Hayes, Richard 89
Heaney, Michael 35
Hempel, Eduard 59, 65–66, 88, 173
   deal with de Valera on evacuation of Germans 101
Hénaff, Neven 197
Herzog, Chaim 21
Heusaff, Alan 197
Heydrich, Reinhard 121
Heyerdahl, Thor 211
Hilberg, Paul 123
Himmler, Heinrich 135
Hitler, Adolf 36, 47, 48, 55, 59, 64
   'Germanisation' plans 91
   at Hossbach Conference 66
   opinions on youth 60
   and Stalingrad 132
   and Sudetenland 75–76
   on war against Russia 117

Hitler Youth 12, 60, 61, 62, 71, 112
Hoernisch, Auguste 92–93, 162
Hoernisch, Franz 126, 127, 162, 168, 222
Holocaust 191–92
Home Office 58
Hull, Mark 146
Hunt Museum, Limerick 220–21
Hynes, John 188–89

invasions of Britain and Ireland 108, 110, 111
Ireland 36, 41, *see also* Operation Green
   and Jewish refugees 79–80
   neutrality 114, 115, 120, 181
   opposition to Mahr's post-war return 172–76
   recruitment of Germans into Free State 11
   war criminals in 197–201
Irish Glass Bottle Manufacturers Ltd. 56, 101
Irish Independent 65, 72
Irish Military Intelligence (G2) 12, 88–93, 96, 100, 112, 173, 196
Irish National Archives 99
Irish Press 87
   on Anschluss 74
   on Hitler Youth 62
   obituary of Adolf Mahr 214
   on visit of *Schleswig-Holstein* 70
Irish Republican Army (IRA) 66, 100, 101, 114, 198
   at Trinity 200
Irish Sugar Company 92, 190
Irish Times 63–64, 65, 72
Irland-Redaktion 112–16, 128–29, 139, 173, 220
   during air raids in 1943 140
   at end of war 146–47

Mahr's position in 195
   in Oldenburg 150
ITV 199

Jacobsthal, Paul 186
Japan 143
Jasenovac concentration camp 199
Jenkner, Siegfried 216–17
Jessen, Knud 46, 190
Jewish Central Committee, Austria 191
Jewish persecution 48, 66, 83, 123–24, 135, *see also* anti-Semitism
Jews in Ireland 21, 94–95, 219–20
Joyce, James 84
Joyce, William (Lord Haw-Haw) 58, 112, 113, 128, 167
July Plot 146

Kahlo, Frida 103
Keitel, Nona 61
Keitel, Wilhelm 12, 61
Kelly, James 198
Kelly, Ned 37
Kendrick, T.D. 188
Keogh, Dermot 219–20
Kilbride-Jones, Howard 24, 25, 30, 36, 211, 214
   statement on behalf of Mahr's denazification 186–88
   on ties between de Valera and Mahr 75
Kilmacurragh Park Hotel 57, 61, 71, 134
Kirwan, P. 64
Kohn, Arthur 82, 127
Kokoschka, Oskar 23
Kon Tiki voyage 211
Krause, Karl 56, 86, 101, 134
Kristallnacht 83
Krummhübel (Poland) 144
Kuenstler, Karl 57, 86, 101, 106, 167

Lainé, Celestin (Neven Hénaff) 197
Lang, Charlotte (Lotti) 37
Lange, Dorothea 32, 33
Lavery, Sir John 45
League of German Girls 60
Leask, H.G. 187
Leningrad, siege of 119
library of Adolf Mahr 19, 139, 210, 212, 214
Lithberg, Nils 30, 38, 46
Loughcrew burial site 23
Luftwaffe 116
Luther, Martin 121, 122
Luykx, Albert 198

McCormack, John 151
McDunphy, Michael 66
McElligott, James J. 46
McGurk, Richard 71
Macken, Mary 90
Maher, T. 86
Mahler, Gustav 73
Mahr, Adolf Maria 8, 15, 94, 104
   family relations 17, 20, 25, 136
   first fiancée 54, 213
   conversion to Protestantism 52, 196
   career at National Museum of Ireland 19, **30–46**
   politics **47–67**
   resignation as leader of Nazi party 76–78
   efforts on behalf of Jewish friends 80–82
   efforts to return to Ireland at outbreak of war 99
   report on radio propaganda to Ireland 113–16, 128
   imprisonment by British 176, 180–81
   list of dependable friends in Ireland and England 201–2

final illness and death 212–13
legacy 219–23
Mahr, Brigit (daughter) 8, 162, 216–17
Mahr, Gustav Johann (Adolf's father) 8
Mahr, Gustav (son) 8
  education 21–22
  and Hitler Youth 60
  interest in archaeology 24
  liberal politics 51
  State Labour Service 111, 118–19
  translator for German army 128–29
  becomes prisoner of war 138–39
  release from prison camp 182
  marriage 210
  becomes archaeologist 212
Mahr, Hilde (daughter) 8, 12, 14–16, 215
  education 22–23
  compared to Ingrid 24–25
  air-raid duty 137
  joins National Labour Service 144
  journey in search of family, 1945 **152–70**
  journey in search of Adolf 164–67
  1946 brings family from Austria to Germany 178
  marries 183–84
Mahr, Ingrid (daughter) 8, 89, 105, 178
  on Hitler Youth 61
  marriage and political career 215–16
  returns to Ireland 1949 201–3, 210
Mahr, Maria (née van Bemmelen) 8
  background and interests 20
  early married life 53
  parents' financial assistance 52
  blamed Adolf for family tragedy 182
  widowed 217–19
Malahide Castle 28
Man of Aran 25–26

Marcus, David 110–11
Marshall Plan 171
Mars, W.S. 176
Mason, Thomas 23, 33
May, Frederick 82
Meagher, Donald and Desmond 24
Meagher, Terry 24, 55, 215
Mecking, Heinz 23, 57, 78, 86–88, 101, 134, 167
Meehan, Patricia 137–38, 166
Meissner, Madeleine 136
Mengele, Josef 196, 199
Menghin, Osveld 197
Menten, Pieter 199
Mercader, Ramón 103
Merkel, Friedrich 89
MI5 176
Military Geographical Data on Ireland 108–9, 115
Military Intelligence, Irish 78
Mitchell, Frank 37
Mitchell, G.F. 30
Monasterboice 62, 71
Monksgrange estate 27
Morrissey, Daniel 205
Moscow 119
Mosley, Sir Oswald 58
Mühlhausen, Ludwig 108, 112, 113, 115
Müller-Dubrow, Oswald 57, 63, 133
Muller, F.E. 64
Munro, Neil 211
Muntz, B. 64
Murray, Joseph 37
Museum of Irish Industry 38
Museum of Pre- and Proto-history (Berlin) 214

na gCopaleen, Myles 84
National Gallery of Ireland 32
nationalism, Irish 40

National Library of Ireland 84
National Monuments Act (1930) 46
National Museum of Ireland **30–46**, 70, 109, 167, 196, 219
Natural History and Prehistoric Museum (Vienna) 17
Natural History Museum (of Ireland) 38
Natural History Museum (Oldenburg) 169
Nazi Party, British 57
Nazi Party in Ireland 56, 68, 74, 87, 101
    secession from British Nazis 57
Neugebauer, Helene 101
neutrality, Irish 114, 115, 120, 129
    Mahr's attitude toward 194–95, 220
Newgrange 62, 71
Nuremberg Laws 68, 84, 126, 183
Nuremberg Rally 91, 98
Nuremberg Trials 59, 124

O'Brennan, Kathleen 45, 85–86, 102
O'Broin, León 111, 112
O'Cuiv, Seán 64
Ó Dochartaigh, Pól 85
O'Donoghue, David 100, 101, 114–15, 116
    on Irland-Redaktion 139, 142
    on *Military Geographical Data on Ireland* 109
Ó Duilearga, Séamus 190
Offences Against the State Act 100
O'Neill, Seosamh (Joseph) 46, 76, 88, 189
Operation Barbarossa 116
Operation Green 108, 110
Operation Sealion 108, 110, 111
Operation Typhoon 119
Operation Uranus 132
O'Reilly, John Francis 173, 174

O'Riordain, Sean P. 36, 37, 40, 70
O'Sullivan, Carina 210

Papal Nuncio 59
Passau (Austria) 157, 158
'Patrick Cadogan' talks 139
Paulus, Adriana Jacoba 8
Paulus, Friedrich 132
Pearl Harbor 120, 142
Petrie, George 37
Plass, Martin 89
Pokorny, Julius 84, 85, 112
Poland, invasion of 100
Potsdam (Big Three) conference 163
poverty, post-war 166
Praeger, Robert Lloyd 46
Prague 88–89
Prague Topographical Office 96
Prehistoric and Protohistoric Sciences, International Congress of 33, 34, 211
Prehistoric Congress, Madrid (1936) 211
Prehistoric Society, British 73, 186, 193, 211
prison camps, Allied 177
propaganda, German 112, 142–43, 145–46, 220
prostitution 172
Prussian Museum of Prehistory 107

Quane, Michael 106, 167, 174, 203
Quaternary Research Committee 46, 190

Race and Resettlement Office 96
Raftery, Barry 37, 101
Raftery, Joseph 24, 36, 40, 70, 100
    appeal for help from Maria Mahr 106–7

rape of German women 148, 152–53, 159, 168
Red army, *see* Russian army
Red Bank Restaurant 37, 57, 61
refugees 147–48
Reinhard, Otto 23, 56, 66, 101, 181
Reusswig, Otto 216
Rhineland 68
Richards-Orpen, Edward 27
Richards-Orpen, Goddard 27
Richards-Orpen, Puffet (Charmian) 27–28
Riefenstahl, Leni 61
Riga (Latvia) 128
Rivera, Diego 103
Roosevelt, Franklin D. 79, 142
Roschmann, Eduard 196
Royal Dublin Society 30
Royal Hibernian Academy 198
Royal Irish Academy 36, 38, 46, 192, 196
Ru II, IX, and XI 142
Russell, George (Æ) 33, 45, 89
Russell, Seán 101
Russian army 13, 116, 132, 144
    cause German retreat 119–20
    losses following invasion 117
    revenge on Germans 14, 147
    spring 1944 offensive 146
Ryan, Frank 115, 142, 144, 200
Ryan, Michael 37

St. James Terrace, Malahide 28
St. Kilian's German School 201
San Francisco Chronicle 104
San Francisco Museum of Art 31–32
Schleswig-Holstein (battleship) 70–72
Schmauser, Heinrich 98
Schroetter, Erich 59
Schroetter, K. 64, 71
Schroll, Maria Antonia 8

Schubert, Irmgard 61
Scott, Sir Russell 58
Selby, R.W. 176
Seyss-Inquart, Artur 124–25, 221
Shannon hydroelectric scheme 11, 19, 66
Siemens-Schuckert company 19, 57
Skerries, County Dublin 28
Skorzeny, Otto 199–200
Smyllie, Robert Maire (Bertie) 12, 64, 65, 66, 90
Solomons, Bethel and Estelle 45
Soviet Union 98, 116
Spender, Stephen 166
Spider (*die Spinne*) 200
Spiegelfeld, Grete 28, 203
SS 96–99, 117, 135, 174, 197–98
    and the Spider 200
Stadlen, Erich 82
Staffe, A. 190
Stalingrad 131–32
Stalin, Josef 103
Starkie, Walter 32, 33, 45
State Labour Service, German 15
Steiner, Rudolf 216
Stephan, Enno 116
Stieber, Helmut and Erika 210
Strasburger, Gerhard 179, 180, 183–84, 209
    recovery from TB 215
Streicher, Julius 12, 59
Stuart, Francis 113, 115, 128–29, 136, 139, 220
Stumpf, Guenther 62, 64
Stumpf, Robert 56–57, 86, 101
Sudetenland 47–48, 78–79, 97, 156
Sutton Hoo 211
Sydnow, C.W.V. 190

Tanne, Ulrich 128
Tanne, Wilhelm 28, 63

Theresienstadt concentration camp 83, 126
Thomsen, Henning 87
Trankner, Max Civtor Francis 87
Trankner, Oskar Paul 87
treaties of 1919 47, 73, 75
Trinity College Dublin 32, 200
Trotsky, Leon 103
Truman, Harry 209
Tschumi, O. 190
Tullamaine school 21, 23
Turf Development Board, Irish 23, 57, 78, 87, 88
Tyrol, South 47

Unemployment Relief schemes 40

van Bemmelen, Jaap 125
van Bemmelen, Johan Frans 8, 19
van Bemmelen, Jozien 124–25, 167
Vatican 196, 197, 199
Veesenmayer, Edmund 110, 142, 143–44
Versailles, Treaty of 47, 65, 66, 67, 73
Vienna 51, 53, 73
Viking artefacts 39
von Dehn-Schmidt, Georg 59, 194
von Kuhlmann, Wilhelm 59
von Ribbentrop, Joachim 60, 108, 113, 115, 142, 167
von Thadden, Eberhard 145
von Weinertsgruen, Friedrich Maier 96–97, 98, 156, 222

Waffen SS, *see* SS
Wagler, Bruno 61, 62
Wallace, Pat 36, 38, 40, 44, 196, 219
  on Mahr's research 73
Walshe, Joe 72, 77, 87, 88

Wannsee Conference 121, 126, 220
Warburg Institute 82
Warnock, William 129, 139
Waterloo Place, Dublin 19, 24, 55, 63
Weckler, Friedrich 66
Wensel, R. 64
Wesley College 21, 22, 23
Westropp, M.S. Dudley 189
Wiesenthal Centre, Simon 220, 221
Wilde, Sir William 37
Winkelmann, Franz 56, 101
Winkelmann, Nadja 107
World War II **68–104**

Yeats, Jack B. 45
Yeats, William Butler 45

Zionist Federation 51
Zurich 26
Zweig, Stefan 73–74